Leading and managing youth work and services for young people

Kevin Ford, Rob Hunter, Bryan Merton and Deirdre Waller

The National Youth Agency

Acknowledgments

This book was written by:
Kevin Ford, Rob Hunter, Bryan Merton and Deirdre Waller
Kevin Ford edited the book.

Their right to be identified as the authors of this work is hereby asserted in accordance with the Copyright, Designs and Patents Act 1988.

It has been developed from the Transforming Youth Work Management Reader (ISBN 0-9532230-1-9). We gratefully acknowledge the comments and contributions to the development of the reader from:
John Thurlbeck, Anthony Lawton, Mary Marken and Chris Whiley,
and from the members of the Transforming Youth Work Management Development Group:
Mary Atkinson, Training Manager, YWCA
Paddy Hall, Consultant, FPM
Sarah Hargreaves, Director of Programmes, FPM
Martyn Livermore, Director Life Long Learning, Norfolk County Council
Viv McKee, Director of Policy and Development, The National Youth Agency
Kenny Paton, Chief Executive, Nottinghamshire CYP
Susie Roberts, Head of Youth and Community, Bracknell
Colin Shearer, Operations Director, The Duke of Edinburgh's Award
John Thurlbeck, Head of Youth and Community, Sunderland
Eric Watts, Chief Executive, Association of Principal Youth and Community Officers

The Transforming Youth Work Management Programme was developed by a consortium of The National Youth Agency, the Association of Principal Youth and Community Officers, the Department for Education and Skills and the University of Leicester Management Centre and FPM.

Published by

The National Youth Agency

Eastgate House
19–23 Humberstone Road
Leicester LE5 3GJ
Tel: 0116 242 7350
Fax: 0116 242 7444
E-mail: nya@nya.org.uk
Website: www.nya.org.uk

ISBN 0 86155 319 5
Price: £24.95

Printed by The Nuffield Press Ltd., Oxford.

Contents

Foreword

    Tom Wylie, Chief Executive, The National Youth Agency   v

Introduction   1

Chapter One

    The context: youth work and services for young people   7

Chapter Two

    You as a manager: some principles for thinking and learning   23

Chapter Three

    Understanding the modern service-providing organisation   37

Chapter Four

    Strategic thinking, planning and managing change   57

Chapter Five

    Modern management   75

Chapter Six

    The impact of the external environment   105

Chapter Seven

    Managing your resources strategically   121

Chapter Eight

    Managing for high performance   155

Chapter Nine

    Managing innovation   179

Chapter Ten

    Managing your stakeholders   187

Chapter Eleven

    Managing youth work: a look to the future   209

Chapter Twelve

    Making it happen   223

Chapter Thirteen

    Further reading   231

Index   239

The authors and publishers are grateful to the following sources for permission to reproduce material in this book: the Audit Commission, Nicholas Brealey Publishing, Harvard Business School Publishing Corporation, John Kotter, Henry Mintzberg, Simon & Shuster UK and John Wiley & Sons.

Every effort has been made to give the correct attribution and references for material used. Please inform the publisher of any errors or omissions.

The National Youth Agency is grateful to the Department for Education and Skills for its support of and assistance with this publication.

department for
education and skills
creating opportunity, releasing potential, achieving excellence

Foreword

Tom Wylie, Chief Executive,
The National Youth Agency

Managers of youth services have a complex and challenging task. But they also have the power to make changes for the better – to shape the way in which work is delivered and improve its relevance, quality and impact. As funders call for greater responsiveness and more outcome for less inputs, it can be all too easy to turn the gaze inwards and focus too heavily on ticking off the targets without taking a broader view of the work.

This book will help to broaden the focus by providing managers – across all organisations that provide services used by or targeted at young people – with the opportunity to catch their breath, pause in what they do, take stock, think, analyse and reflect on their practice. They emerge all the stronger, better and more enthusiastic for it. By helping to build their capacity to manage and adding to their fund of knowledge and ideas, we hope it will help them steer successfully through turbulent waters and motivate them to provide even better services for young people.

Introduction

We shall not cease from exploration
And the end of all our exploring
Will be to arrive where we started
And know the place for the first time.

Poet T S Eliot in 'Little Gidding', one of the Four Quartets, written in 1942

This book is aimed at leaders and managers of youth work and services which provide opportunities for personal and social development to young people. It is written at a time when concern about young people's education, health, welfare and place in society is central to much policy making, is the focus of increasingly strident media attention and is at risk of escalating into moral panic (for example about crime and disorder). It is a time when young people have better prospects than ever before, whilst at the same time facing new risks and challenges that make the transition to adult life particularly hazardous for many.

Youth work can play a vital role in this turbulent environment, by providing opportunities for young people to establish a relationship with an adult (the youth worker) through which they can participate in personal and social development activities which are likely to improve their lives.

The leaders and champions of youth work and youth organisations have a superb opportunity to promote the value and impact of their work with young people to an audience that is eager to hear about it. Success will help to secure the resources which are vital to developing and sustaining the work. Without it the opportunities for young people will remain restricted. If the leaders and managers are to be successful they will need to be very effective in performing their roles. The field needs to have good leadership and skilled management at all levels. This book is a contribution to achieving this.

It has been developed from a reader produced to accompany a management development programme for youth work managers in England [1]. It focuses on the practice of leadership and management in the context of services that work with young people. It provides a framework to explore leadership and management, so that managers are better able to lead, sustain and develop services which enhance the lives of young people.

The focus of the book is on local authority youth services and voluntary sector youth organisations. These services are concerned primarily with providing opportunities for informal social education and development rather than formal education, health, social services or the criminal justice system. However, as we will discuss in Chapter One, informal learning and development can be supported in any service for young people. The book will therefore be relevant to managers in other services which provide some youth work or similar opportunities for young people.

We live in a world in which those in work feel themselves to be under constant pressure to do more and to be seen to be doing more. We can easily become trapped in a spiral of ceaseless activity and lose sight of what the activity is for. This is particularly true of public service managers who are caught in the twin beams of demands from government paymasters for improved performance (usually translated into 'do more for less') and the demands of service users for better, more responsive services ('do more things, more flexibly, where I want them, when I want them at no or low cost to me'). There is a risk that

---

1   The Transforming Youth Work Management Programme, funded by the Department for Education and Skills from 2002–04. Details from: www.fpmonline.f9.co.uk

leaders and managers will neglect the role that they are paid extra to carry out – thinking, reflecting and learning so as to steer the service towards its purpose. Even the busiest managers must find time to think and reflect, otherwise they will become increasingly ineffective.

A hiker came upon a lumberjack hacking away at a tree trunk with a blunt axe. 'Why don't you stop and sharpen your axe?', she enquired.

'Don't be ridiculous! I don't have time to do that – I have a target to reach and I am already behind schedule.'

The aim of this book is to help leaders and managers of services for young people to pause and to sharpen their axes.

Managers of organisations that provide services to young people are facing new challenges which resemble many of those faced by managers in other service-providing organisations over the past twenty years. The task is not just to recognise the challenges, or to develop skills to respond in the short term, but to build the capacity to lead and manage in a world where change and complexity are and will be a permanent feature of the landscape.

There is a huge literature on management. Most of it is still unduly focused on manufacturing industries and most is heavily influenced by American research on American corporations. There is a smaller, but growing literature looking at service providing organisations generally. There has been much recent writing on public service management, along with the development in Britain of new centres to focus on leadership in key public services – the National Centre for School Leadership, the Centre for Excellence in Leadership (post 16 education) and the University of the National Health Service. There is no current national focus on the leadership and management of youth work or more widely on informal education.

This book seeks to equip managers with knowledge and ideas that will free them to navigate a route for their organisations through constant change, in ways which embody their values, and make a real and lasting difference to the young people they serve. We believe that modern managers at all levels, must be able to lead (inspire and motivate people towards delivering really good services to young people) as well as manage the actions, information, finance etc that make up working life. For organisations to deal well with complexity and change requires them to have managers who can think, make decisions and take risks in the pursuit of clear aims. These managers will empower their staff to do the same.

This book provides ideas and models which will help to develop managers' capacity to lead effectively. There are many approaches to leadership – we do not favour any single one. The overwhelming conclusion from both research and observation is that what makes an effective leader depends on the context[2]. What works in one setting may not in another; what works for one person one day may not work for the same person some days later. We hope that the ideas will help you to build your confidence in your capacity to deploy your skills, experience and humanity as a leader. This may be using what Joseph Badaracco[3] describes as quiet leadership: 'The most effective leaders are rarely public heroes ... They move patiently, carefully and incrementally. They do what is right – for their organisations, for the people around them and for themselves – inconspicuously and without casualties.'

---

2   See Peter Drucker's foreword to Hesselbein, F., Goldsmith, M., and Beckhard, R., (1996), *The Leader of the Future.* San Francisco: Jossey Bass.
3   Badaracco, Joseph (2002) *Leading Quietly*, Boston: HBR Press.

It could equally be through louder styles of leading, using the styles described as pace-setting or commanding by Daniel Goleman[4].

Finding your way through the material

We have set out to gather what we see as most useful from the literature on general management, service management and public service management and to apply it to the specific challenges faced by managers of youth work and services working with young people.

The material is organised into 12 Chapters:

Chapter 1: The context: youth work and services for young people
Chapter 2: You as a manager: some principles for thinking and learning
Chapter 3: Understanding the modern service-providing organisation
Chapter 4: Strategic thinking, planning and managing change
Chapter 5: Managing a modern service for young people
Chapter 6: The impact of the external environment
Chapter 7: Managing resources strategically
Chapter 8: Managing for high performance
Chapter 9: Managing innovation
Chapter 10: Managing your stakeholders and partnerships
Chapter 11: Managing youth work organisations: a look to the future
Chapter 12: Making it happen
Chapter 13: Resources

The main content is structured using a process model of management that combines the experiential learning cycle (we learn by reflecting on our actions) taken from Kolb[5], with some of Bob Garrett's ideas on strategic management[6] and ideas of double loop learning drawn from Pedlar, Burgoyne and Boydell[7].

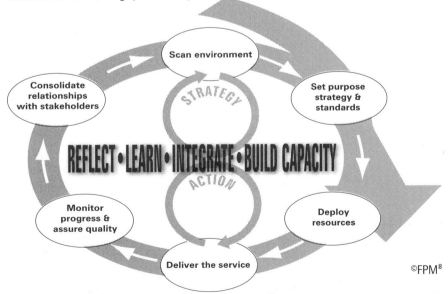

©FPM[8]

4   Daniel Goleman, Richard Boyatis and Annie McKee (2002) *Primal Leadership – realizing the power of Emotional Intelligence*, Boston Mass: Harvard Business School Press pp71–80.
5   Kolb, David (1974), 'On Management and Learning Process' in Kolb, Rubin and McIntyre (eds) *Organisational Psychology: a Book of Readings*, 2nd edition.
6   Garrett, Bob (1997) *The Fish Rots from the Head*, London: Harper-Collins.
7   Mike Pedlar, John Burgoyne and Tom Boydell (1991) *The Learning Company – A Strategy for Sustainable Development*. London: McGraw Hill.
8   Kevin Ford (2002) *Managing Better*, Leicester: National Institute for Adult and Continuing Education

The model provides a framework for thinking about management and leadership. It is premised on the idea that if managers are to deliver action effectively they need to work through a cycle of scanning, planning, deploying resources, delivering the service, monitoring progress, reporting to stakeholders and building the relationship with stakeholders.

This overall cycle (as represented by the outer circle) consists of two complementary cycles – at the top is a strategy cycle which drives and is in turn driven by the action cycle at the bottom of the figure.

The two cycles are held together by the process of reflecting, learning, integrating and building capacity in both the manager and the organisation. We work through each of the elements of the model in more detail below:

Scan the environment: is the process of looking for and gathering information about the organisation's external and internal environments. It involves lifting the mind out of the day to day business and looking very clearly at what is going on around and inside the organisation. Effective scanning will give early warning of change and enable the manager to respond.

Set purpose, strategy and standards: involves the manager in making certain that there is a suitable and clear statement of the purpose of the organisation. Many public sector bodies struggle with this as their aims are to provide a universal service, usually without sufficient resources ever to fully achieve this. Once the purpose is clear then the manager is in a position to set the strategy for the organisation or the part of the organisation that she or he is responsible for. This in turn leads to planning and setting standards for performance.

Deploy resources: In this part of the role the manager is responsible for making sure that all available resources are used to best effect in delivering the strategy, to achieve the purpose. The resources include finance, the people (staff and volunteers) who deliver the service, information and knowledge, premises, equipment and so on. Inspiring and motivating the workforce is a fundamental challenge for the managers of youth work organisations and is a test of their leadership.

Deliver the service: This is the point at which everything must come together so that young people are provided with a really good service. Most youth work is delivered by youth workers (typically part-time) working in dispersed settings often with little or no direct supervision. The preparation for the work and the follow up through 'off the job' supervision are essential in order to deliver consistent, high quality services.

Monitor progress and assure quality: You cannot monitor progress if your purpose, aims and objectives are not clear. Similarly it is not possible to judge quality if the organisation has not established standards for doing so. This part of the manager's role involves using information about what has been done to make judgments about progress, adjust plans and celebrate successes. Historically youth services have not been particularly good at monitoring their performance or providing evidence of its impact. This is changing and the effective leader will find ways to win the support of staff for delivering measurably high levels of performance in their work with young people.

Consolidate relationships with stakeholders (including partners): In the last part of the role the manager seeks to ensure that the organisation has effective relationships with key stakeholders. This includes accounting for the work that has been done (for example to councillors, young people and funders); positioning the organisation in the minds of potential and actual partners; sustaining and developing existing partnerships.

The model is dynamic and non-linear – there are connections between all the main elements. It is designed to provide a map on which you can locate your management and leadership activity. We use the model throughout the book to inform you about where you are. Management is not a linear process – managers move in and out of each of the various roles described but keep returning to the central box to reflect, think and learn.

The contents of the book are structured throughout to enable you to think about and explore leadership and management at three main levels:

1. Principles and ideas about organisations, leadership and management in general.
2. How these apply to organisations that work with young people (service providing organisations).
3. How this relates to the particular demands being made as a result of policy changes in England.

As you read we ask you to think at each of these levels. Some chapters focus on concepts, others on context or on capacities. Each chapter has a number of 'Reflection' questions, which ask you to pause, reflect on the reading and apply it to your own situation and practice as a manager. This follows the principles of reflective learning.

We also draw your attention to the sources of the models and ideas in footnotes. A resources list is provided at the end of the book to aid further reading, study and self-development.

The materials make the assumption that the reader has some prior knowledge of management basics and reasonable practical experience of management. In places we provide a reminder of key principles and theories, but our focus is on ideas that will extend and develop managers who already have some experience. For these reasons we do not cover management basics such as health and safety, child protection, employment regulations, work planning, time management etc.

We hope you will enjoy reading this book and find things within it that will help you to provide better services to young people.

Managers have the power to alter situations – for their services and for the young people who use them. This power can be used in ways that enhance the lives of young people and the people who work with them. Management is not dull science but an art; not a burden but a privilege; not a set of constraints but a liberating framework of ideas and techniques. As a manager you will need to call upon your capacity to lead if you want to bring your organisation, department or unit to life, to try out new ways of doing things and to get the best from those who work for and with you. Above all you will need to keep a clear and unwavering sense of the purpose of the work and the courage to pursue it – to enable young people to learn, develop, build relationships and make the transition to a fulfilled adulthood.

Chapter One:
The context: youth work and services for young people

This book is about leading and managing youth work and services for young people. In this chapter we set out what we mean by youth work and services for young people and why they are important. We outline the particular challenges faced by leaders and managers of these services. This provides a first step towards a description of the characteristics of the leadership and management role in youth work organisations and services. It provides the beginnings of an answer to the questions: what is particular about the role? How does this differ from the role of other service providers and managers in other sectors?

What is youth work?

The National Youth Agency describes youth work as a process which 'helps young people learn about themselves, others and society, through informal educational activities which combine enjoyment, challenge and learning'[1]. The young people involved in youth work are aged between 11 and 25, but there is a focus on the 13 to 19 age group. Youth work promotes personal and social development and enables young people to have a voice, influence and place in their communities and society as a whole.

At the heart of youth work is the relationship that develops between the young person and the youth worker. It is through this relationship that the youth worker enables and encourages the young person to learn and develop. The relationship is voluntary – chosen by the young person, starting with where the young person 'is at' and agreeing action through a process of negotiation. This makes the youth work relationship significantly different from the relationship between a young person and a teacher, social worker, health worker, or most other professionals.

Youth work provides opportunities outside the formal education system, for young people to learn and develop. It seeks to integrate young people into society as it is (to socialise them) at the same time as enabling young people to question the very norms and institutions of the society into which they are being integrated. Hence the long tradition of youth work in challenging negative racial, gender and physical stereotypes and working with young people to get their voices heard so as to reduce exclusion and disadvantage. Youth work is therefore both conservative (in seeking to socialise and integrate) and radical (in seeking to expand young people's capacity to make sense of their world, so as to be better able to challenge prejudice and injustice as it affects them and others). It is, in its own small way, as agent of social change.

We argue in Chapter 10 (see pages 187–207) that youth work managers and leaders have not paid enough attention to recording the impact of the relationships built through youth work. Youth work helps to build relationships between adults and young people, between young people themselves and between young people and their communities. It is a producer of 'social capital' – the glue that holds societies together. It is unusual among all the services which work with young people in having this as one of its primary purposes.

1   From *The NYA Guide to Youth Work and Youth Services* (2003) Leicester, The National Youth Agency. www.nya.org.uk

Youth work has moved out of the policy shadows and into the limelight in the UK in recent years. David Blunkett, then Secretary of State for Education and Employment, described it in a speech in 2001 as:

'Youth work changes lives. It provides opportunities for young people in a wide range of settings including sport, the arts and the community. It helps them develop the personal skills they need to make a success of their lives. It allows them to influence and shape their lives and the services available to them. And it allows them to put something back into their communities. There are few more important investments than in the future of young people, and few better ways of delivering change than through good youth work.'

The UK Government set out a vision for the future of youth work in England in *Transforming Youth Work* and the subsequent paper *Resourcing Excellent Youth Services* . It is worth noting that while youth work is a consistent process across the UK, the policies and structures which support it are different in Scotland, Wales, Northern Ireland and England. This book focuses on England but makes some reference to approaches being adopted elsewhere in the UK.

Transforming Youth Work sets out the government's view of the components of good youth work. It:

- Offers quality support to young people which helps them achieve and progress
- Enables young people to have their voice heard and influence decision making at various levels
- Provides a diverse range of personal and social development opportunities
- Helps prevent disaffection and social exclusion

Further development of policy towards children and young people has led to a statement of 'five outcomes' to which all services (including youth work), in England should contribute:

- Be healthy – enjoying good physical and mental health and living a healthy lifestyle
- Stay safe – being protected from harm and neglect and growing up able to look after themselves
- Enjoy and achieve: getting the most out of life and developing broad skills for adulthood
- Make a positive contribution: to the community and to society and not engaging in anti-social or offending behaviour
- Achieve economic wellbeing.

Managers of youth work organisations which receive money from government will need to be able to show that their work leads to measurable results in one or more of these five outcomes. Good youth work is capable of contributing significantly to all five outcomes but has often lacked reliable evidence to make its case.

The nature of youth work makes it somewhat abstract and difficult to explain. It is a process of supporting and enabling young people's learning and development through a voluntary relationship between the youth worker and the young person. (Although the voluntary relationship can be negotiated within the context of an involuntary means of contact such as when a young people is in a pupil referral unit). Youth work takes place outside formal learning (although it may be linked to it, for example a youth centre in a school, which works with some young people during school hours). Youth work involves

---

2 Transforming Youth Work – developing youth work for young people. (2001) London, DfES and Connexions. Available at: www.connexions.gov.uk/publi.htm
3 *Resourcing Excellent Youth Services* (2002) London, DfES and Connexions.
   Available from: www.connexions.gov.uk/publi.htm
4 See *Every Child Matters – the next steps* (2004) London, DfES.

both informal and non-formal learning. Informal learning takes place through everyday activities. It is typically not structured and not intended to lead to a pre-planned result or certification. Non-formal learning also takes place outside school but is structured, based on learning objectives, learning time and specific learning support and is intentional. It often leads to certification.

Youth work managers must manage a service which integrates informal learning with interventions which lead to non-formal learning. They manage a purpose which integrates socialisation of young people with questioning the status quo and giving voice towards social change. The management of such a service is a complex, delicate and subtle process. If it veers too far towards the informal, it is little different from recreation, social and leisure activities; if it veers too far towards the non-formal it may start to look and feel like school. If it swings too much towards the radical it may be seen as campaigning and preaching, too far towards socialising and the service looks like an agent for the indoctrination of the young.

One of the central challenges for managers is to manage a service of subtlety and complexity in an environment in which government funders demand clear, concrete, planned outcomes. The two things are not incompatible, but considerable skill is needed to manage the tensions between them effectively.

What is the youth service?

The 'youth service' was defined by the UK government in 2002 as 'a complex network of providers, community groups, voluntary organisations and local authorities, which has as its primary purpose the personal and social development of young people[5]. The youth service originated in clubs and projects run by voluntary organisations in the 19th century. Bernard Davies in his rich history of the youth service in England describes how many of the early initiatives echoed with the Victorian equivalent of today's concerns about young people: fears over safety, worries about lewd behaviour, health, diet and panic about poor young people not learning suitable trades so that they could find gainful employment[6]. State recognition for the youth service dates from the outbreak of the Second World War in 1939, when government enlisted the major voluntary organisation which had developed informal approaches to working with young people, to establish a 'service for youth'. This was to be administered through local youth committees in each local authority.

Since then the youth service in England has continued to reflect its voluntary sector origins, and has remained a service with a relatively weak basis in statute (ie the 1944 Education Act which requires local authorities to secure 'adequate facilities for further education' including 'adequate facilities for recreation and social and physical training'). Despite recent policy initiatives in England, access to youth work for young people remains hugely inconsistent and dependent to a large extent on the way in which local government interprets its duties and priorities. Spend per head of the local population of young people varies to a considerable degree (from £260 per head per year at the highest to just £29 at the lowest[7]).

The last major review of the youth service by Alan Thompson in 1982[8] highlighted its primary function as meeting the developmental needs of young people. Thompson

5   See *Resourcing Excellent Youth Services* Ibid.
6   See Davies, Bernard (1999) *From Voluntaryism to Welfare State – A History of the Youth Service in England*, Volume 1: 1939–1979. Leicester: Youth Work Press. Pages 7–12.
7   From Transforming Youth Work, Ibid.
8   Thompson, Alan (1982) *Experience and Participation: Report of the Review Group on the Youth Service in England*.

suggested that there were four characteristic contributions made by youth services to young people's development. These are worth repeating here as they remain influential:

1. **Experiential learning** – learning by doing and reflecting (not by being taught)
2. **Participation in decision-making** – taking and following through shared decisions
3. **Voluntary involvement** – choosing to take part
4. **Non-directive relationships** – between young people and youth workers based on mutual respect.

Thompson stressed the importance of the universality of the youth service but recognised its role as a 'rescue service' for some young people. This role of targeting and rescuing young people has been increasingly emphasised in subsequent policy and funding of youth work. Services for young people are being directed at those most in need. There is an inherent risk that the nature of the services may change if they are perceived to be only 'rescue'.

This is a serious dilemma for managers of publicly funded youth work services. It may be increasingly difficult to defend the value of generic youth work for all young people, when most of the spending is on work directed at young people in the greatest need. Most young people find the transition to adulthood troubling at some time and may get huge benefit from participation in youth work. Preserving opportunities for generic youth work which such young people remains a challenge.

Reflection

Do you accept the definitions of youth work and youth services above? If not, how does it differ from your own definitions?

How do the definitions affect the way in which youth work and youth services are understood by others? How easy is it for leaders of youth services and youth work to be effective when the definitions remain intangible and somewhat abstract?

What approaches do you use to explain youth work to people who have no previous knowledge of it (including young people who may want to get involved)? What works best?

Most youth services are based in local authority education departments. Figures gathered from local authorities by The National Youth Agency[9] suggest that:

- about 60 per cent of young people come into contact with the youth service at some point between the ages of 11 and 25;
- around 3,000 full-time youth workers and over 21,000 part-time youth workers are employed in England; and
- there may be as many as half a million people working as volunteers in the youth service in England.

In addition a huge amount of youth work is provided by voluntary youth work organisations, for example, a recent estimate for the workforce of the church's youth organisations is estimated at over 6,000 full-time equivalent youth workers.

Whilst local authority youth services are thus distinctive they are not the only place in which youth work is carried out. For example, youth work may be used as a process by a wide range of other agencies which work with young people, even through youth work is not their primary purpose. A sports club might involve youth workers to engage young people in youth work through sport; a professional soccer club may lead a project involving youth work to address racism; a library might involve the youth service to help it to engage young people in reading.

Leading and managing a complex web of services

Managers of services which seek to provide youth work have a complex task as a direct

---

9   Survey of Youth Services (2003) Leicester, The National Youth Agency.

result of the type of service they offer. Youth work is by its nature diverse and complex, it involves a wide range of different activity and it can take place in a huge number of locations. In this section we explore some aspects of this complexity in more depth.

Figure 1.1 shows where youth work takes place in the wider picture of services provided to young people.

Figure 1.1: Location of youth work

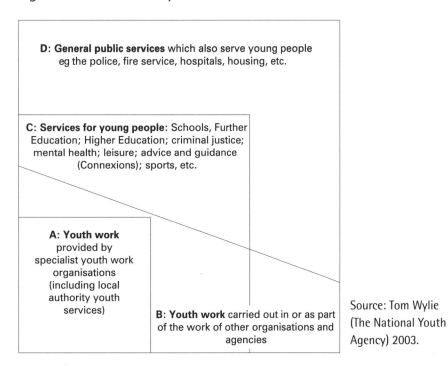

D: General public services which also serve young people
eg the police, fire service, hospitals, housing, etc.

C: Services for young people: Schools, Further Education; Higher Education; criminal justice; mental health; leisure; advice and guidance (Connexions); sports, etc.

A: Youth work provided by specialist youth work organisations (including local authority youth services)

B: Youth work carried out in or as part of the work of other organisations and agencies

Source: Tom Wylie (The National Youth Agency) 2003.

The model gives a map and may be useful to managers in clarifying the expectations that they and their agencies have of their work and how it relates to other services. Youth services do not have a monopoly on youth work. Indeed, as the model suggests, there may be more youth work taking place outside youth services than within them. In domain A we find organisations which specialise in youth work: local authority youth services, clubs for young people, youth work projects etc. In domain B we find youth work sections or units which are part of other non-youth work organisations (eg youth projects in Groundwork – a large environmental charity, youth work in Connexions) and youth work which occurs alongside other more general work (eg the employment of a youth worker to work in a multi-agency drugs project or a Youth Offending Team, the development of youth work as part of the offering of a housing agency). The diagonal line marks the boundary between youth work and the wide range of other services which young people may receive. In domain C we find general services specifically for children and young people and in domain D are found all the other services which young people use from time to time. The model can assist managers to look at the entirety of services which impact on young people and locate where their particular service fits in. It may also help to counter any tendency for youth services to see themselves as the sole providers and arbiters on all things to do with youth work. The local authority youth service does have a critical role in providing strategic leadership to youth work in their area. Specialist youth work agencies will be looked to for leadership on practice. But others have a very significant contribution to make. This is discussed more in Chapter 11.

The second important point to take from the model is that youth work cannot be defined by its location, only by the nature of the work itself (as discussed in the preceding section). Youth work is a process and as such can take place in a huge variety of locations. One of the challenges to youth service managers will be to support the provision of good quality youth work in agencies which have no real history of providing it. This links to partnership working which is discussed in greater depth in Chapter 10. As an example much youth work takes place in schools and further education colleges – contributing both to formal education programmes (such as personal, social and health education, and citizenship education) and informal education (such as lunchtime and after-school provision open to all young people, programmes with young people who are having difficulties at school; anti-racism work and so on).

There is some evidence that the amount of youth work taking place outside specialist youth work agencies has grown in England over the last decade. This is good if it means more young people benefit but presents challenges about quality and consistency of provision. The English inspection body for youth work – Ofsted – focuses its efforts on local authority services (each of which can expect to be inspected once every four years). It does not yet effectively cover the considerable volume of youth work outside these services.

The model can be used to explore the relationship between Connexions (the national service providing information, advice and guidance to young people through the work of personal advisers) and Youth Services. The work of Connexions is in domain C, that of the youth service in domain A. Partnership working may lead to some Connexions personal adviser work taking place in youth service settings, and some youth work taking place in Connexions service settings (such as in schools). This will be aided by both agencies and their professional staff understanding and respecting each others' roles and ways of working. It is damaged by any sense that either profession or service is seeking to extend its domain to 'take over' the other.

The model highlights the complexity of managing youth work as part of wider services for young people. This complexity is made greater by the complexity of managing youth work itself (as discussed before) and the fact that youth work takes place in a variety of different physical settings, as shown below. Again the process is consistent whilst the location of the work varies enormously.

Physical settings in which youth work may take place:

- Buildings – youth clubs and centres operated directly by local authorities or by voluntary organisations. They range from well equipped purpose built youth centres catering solely for young people to clubs based in premises shared with other organisations such as community centres and village halls. Larger youth centres will offer a mix of provision open to all young people and sessions which target specific groups of young people or cater for particular interests.
- Detached work – making contact with young people who cannot, or choose not to, use youth centres. Detached youth workers meet young people in their own spaces, for instance parks, bus shelters, shopping centres or on the street. Through developing non-judgmental relationships they work with individuals and groups to help them address the needs they identify and engage with other relevant agencies.
- Outreach work – encouraging young people to make more use of existing provision or to develop new provision.

- Mobiles – converted buses or other vehicles taken to particular localities, offering young people opportunities to meet together, take part in structured programmes and gain access to resources, information and advice.

Within these different physical settings the youth work may be generic or may have a particular focus such as:
- Information, advice and counselling projects.
- Specialist projects, targeting particular groups of young people, for instance Asian young women or young people in or leaving care.
- Specialist projects focusing on specific activities, for instance young volunteer projects, motor projects or magazine projects.
- Cross-community and international work, in Britain or abroad, which brings together young people from different cultures and countries on joint projects, through which they find common ground while recognising and valuing differences.

The youth work manager must be skilled at managing this wide range of activities, in a wide variety of settings and with a wide variety of young people. In addition youth work stresses the importance of young people participating in decisions that affect them. This could be in decisions about the services themselves or participation in wider decision making in the local council, elections and so on. This again has implications for management. The effective manager in a youth work organisation will be skilled at involving young people and will ensure the existence of good systems and procedures to support this. Above all the manager will demonstrate in her or his deeds the principle of really listening to young people and responding to the issues they raise.

All of the above takes place in a context in which government, as the main funder of youth services, requires that services demonstrate their contribution to the achievement of prescribed targets in relation to young people (eg achievement of accredited learning outcomes, reduction in teenage pregnancy rates, reduction in levels of crime and disorder).

Thus, the youth work manager must be skilled at managing a complex and subtle service due to the nature of youth work itself; must be able to manage the tensions between this work and the expectations of government around delivery of outcomes; must be able to oversee the delivery of the complex service in and through a wide variety of locations using a wide range of activities. All of which takes place against a history of a Cinderella service, lacking recognition and frequently short of resources.

How is youth work different from other services that work with young people

The previous paragraphs make clear that youth work is a process of personal and social education through the relationships that develop between the youth worker, the young person and others. The relationships are voluntary in nature and the process starts where young people are – with their own view of their lives, the world and their interests. In this way it differs completely or in degree from most other services that work with young people. Youth work is about more than open ended convivial relationships. As The National Youth Agency describes it:

'it encourages young people to think critically about their lives and values, offers new experiences and challenges, aims to raise young people's aspirations and to draw out their abilities. Through the professional relationship youth workers encourage and challenge young people to think about their behaviour and its consequences, and to question their prejudices and assumptions. They support young people to work with others and to respect and value difference. They encourage young people to take on greater responsibility for themselves and others and to work effectively as a team, judging when to stand back and when to intervene. They allow young people the freedom to make mistakes – but ensuring that they then learn from them.

Even when activities appear to be purely recreational or social, the best youth workers will convert the activity into learning and draw out educational elements. A passing comment may be the starting point for discussion of serious issues. The worker's task, therefore, is to plan and provide appropriate experiences, to take advantage of those which arise spontaneously, and to foster learning by employing a range of interpersonal skills such as counselling, advocacy, group work and community development.

Youth work aims to help young people gain control over their own lives, while respecting the lives of others. Youth workers need detailed knowledge of the local community and the circumstances of young people, together with an understanding of the ways in which legislation and wider policy developments affect young people and youth work. Based on this, they seek to ensure that young people can gain the information that they need, in ways that they understand, to make informed choices about their lives. Youth workers are not expected to be an expert on everything affecting young people. But they are expected to be aware of other local agencies and what they can offer young people, and to recognise when they need to involve people with specialist skills and knowledge, while continuing to support the young person concerned.[10]

Reflection

We argue that youth work management is made complex by the nature of youth work itself. Do you agree?

How does managing youth work compare with other services that work with young people such as; schools, social work, Connexions personal advising?

In summary, youth work leaders and managers preside over a professional service which is about the informal development and learning of young people. It is in the nature of development that it is unpredictable, messy and complex. Local authority youth services in England are funded largely from the public purse, through mechanisms which are increasingly led by prescribed targets. This creates some tensions and dilemmas for managers which are explored further in the next section.

Towards an understanding of youth work management

A colleague with long years of experience as the Head of a Youth Service asked us whether there were any characteristics of managing youth services and youth work organisations which were different from those in general management. This section explores our response which was to categorise the characteristics at three levels:

1. in some respects youth work management is the same as all management – and general management thinking is relevant
2. in some respects youth work management has characteristics which are the same as other public service management – here thinking about the management of public services is more relevant
3. in some respects youth work management has characteristics which are unique to managing youth work – here there is a general absence of literature and thought: there is a need to understand the particular characteristics of managing youth work

We now look in more detail at levels two and three.

---

10   From *The NYA Guide to Youth Work and Youth Services*, ibid.

Managers of public services in the United Kingdom have been through a period of enormous change over the last quarter century. As discussed throughout this book, public services have been through (and are still going through) a revolution which parallels that in the commercial world, towards flexible, responsive, consumer driven services. The days of Henry Ford's 'you can have any colour car you want as long as it is black' are long gone.

The public sector has followed the commercial world in identifying leadership as an essential ingredient in transforming organisations. The argument goes that if we are going to do things differently we need good leadership at every level to win people over to the new ways of doing things, to inspire belief that it will work and be better, and to urge higher quality and levels of performance. It is no coincidence that the New Labour government has created four new public sector leadership 'colleges' – for school, health, post-16 education and local government. The source for the work that led to this book is another such initiative – the Transforming Youth Work Management programme which provided senior youth work managers with an opportunity to develop their skills as leaders and managers of modern youth services and organisations.

The voluntary sector in the UK has taken a similar stance, lobbying for resources to be devoted to building leadership capacity in the sector as a pre-condition to the sector playing a more active role in the delivery of public services for government[11].

There is nothing unique about the need for effective leadership – it is a constant across all spheres of endeavour. However, leaders in public service organisations have been shown to have particular characteristics[12]. In particular the approach to, and delivery of strategy in the public service sector is different to that found in the commercial world[13]. The central difference is the way in which the services are resourced and the relationships between the users, governors and the main stakeholders in the process of resource allocation.

In commercial organisations there is a relatively easy cycle of resourcing. At its most basic, money is invested to start the enterprise. If the products or service delight the customer they produce sales income and create demand for more. The sales income gives a return to the investors and provides the basis for more investment to make more products or provide more services. The business strategy involves focusing on how to secure the market, create demand, satisfy the demand, beat any competition and grow in the future. The strategy is based on the principle of building profits.

In the public service sector this simple set of operating rules does not apply. Users do not usually pay the full (or in some cases, any) of the cost of the services they receive. Many crucial services are still popularly regarded as 'free' – schools, healthcare. A problem with such universal provision is that it can weaken the relationship between service users and providers. Users rely on voice and influence to secure responses from the services – they can rarely take their custom elsewhere. The service providers, on the other hand, have very close relationships with funders (government and its agencies, both national and local). Services are shaped and delivered in response to budgets which are allocated by political decision makers in central and/or local government. The services are supposed to reflect need, but often reflect the historical relationship between service providers and government funders (both local and national). The provider interest is limited by the setting of standards by Government and the operation of inspection and compliance regimes. It has also been under siege by successive measures to increase the power of the user's voice in service planning and delivery.

11   *Leadership, Leadership, Leadership* (2003) London, Association of Chief Executives in Voluntary Organisations.
12   Beverley Alimo-Metcalfe (2003).
13   See for example Wilkinson, David and Pedlar, Mike (1995) Strategic Thinking in Public Service in Garratt, Bob (Ed) (1995) *Developing Strategic Thought.* London, Harper Collins.

Service providers do not necessarily see a relationship between the effectiveness of their services and the resources that are allocated to them. Creating demand through excellence may be counter productive as there will often not be new resources to enable the demand to be met. Public services operate in an ethos of rationing – limited resources that can be stretched by greater efficiency, but which can frequently only meet part of the political demand. How do we ration such services? The great shadow of Victorian workhouse philosophy still hangs over many public services: the state should provide for those who cannot provide for themselves, but we must not make the provision too comfortable, attractive or easily accessed. To do so would be an incentive for people not to look after themselves and makes it harder to get the support and money from others, who do look after themselves, to pay for the public services in future. If you do not accept the comparison try applying it to council housing, prisons, or even aspects of the health service.

The public service sector is the major mechanism for the implementation of government policy. It is by nature political. Public services provide a means to redistribute wealth – the better off pay for services for those who cannot afford to pay otherwise.

The New Labour Government in the UK has made public service reform a priority since its election in 1997. The Prime Minister set out four principles of public service in 2001[14] which attempt to move them away from the ethos of the workhouse:

1. 'It is Government's job to set national **standards** that really matter to the public, within a framework of clear **accountability**, designed to ensure that citizens have the right to high quality services wherever they live.
2. These standards can only be delivered by **devolution** and delegation to the front line, giving local leaders responsibility and accountability for delivery, and the opportunity to design and develop services around the needs of local people.
3. More **flexibility** is required for public service organisations and their staff to achieve the diversity of service provision needed to respond to the wide range of customer aspirations. This means challenging restrictive practices and reducing red tape; greater and more flexible incentives and rewards for good performance; strong leadership and management; and high quality training and development.
4. Public services need to offer an expanding **choice** for the customer. Giving people a choice about the service they can have and who provides it helps to ensure that services are designed around their customers. An element of contestability between alternative suppliers can also drive up standards and empower customers locked into a poor service from their traditional supplier.'

Youth service managers and managers of youth work organisations which receive funds from government are expected to address the principles set out by the Prime Minister. The principles reflect much of the thinking about service provision to be found in the commercial world: flexibility and closeness to the customer; emphasis on quality; empowerment of staff at the front line to take decisions about the service so as to respond to customer needs; emphasis on good leadership and management. The principles also include some differences to commercial thinking: the private sector is based on customer choice and has been in retreat from centrally determined and imposed standards for some years (see for example the collapse of the once invulnerable Big Mac, to be replaced by local variations!) on the basis that they are often inappropriate and do not secure real commitment at a local level. The emphasis on accountability is less of a feature in the commercial world (although it has been receiving more attention as a result of boardroom excesses and corporate misbehaviour).

14   Speech given by Tony Blair on 16 October 2001.

Example of modernisation: Choice-based letting

A district council developed a policy of choice-based letting for its council housing. This was based on the idea that tenants should have access to choice in housing, just like the commercial housing world. There was concerted opposition to the idea from some housing professionals, whose job was to decide what housing was appropriate for which tenants and to allocate it on a strictly rationed basis. 'If we give them choice, they won't want to live in most of our housing stock' they argued. 'Precisely' came the reply. The council has implemented the policy which has led to some unpopular stock being demolished. Tenants value the opportunity to choose their housing (within limits of what is available).

The challenge for youth work managers is to offer young people services which are responsive and flexible so as to meet their needs; give them a choice; are well led and managed; delegate decision making to the front line; are open and accountable; conform to national standards (as enshrined in the Ofsted inspection framework[15] and in Resourcing Excellent Youth Services[16]). The managers are expected to make this offer to all young people. Youth services are expected to be universal, but at any one time only reach about an eighth of the 13 to 19 population. To increase the reach would appear to require more resources and greater efficiency. Government has set out benchmarks for increased reach but these fall far short of universal provision.

Consequently, leaders and managers of youth work organisations need to be highly skilled at understanding the basis on which decisions about resources are made. It is above all a political process. The approach that leaders take to developing strategy must reflect an understanding of how the different levels of the political process affect the resources that are and will be put at their disposal.

Managers who lead youth services and youth work organisations operate in an environment of complex inter-acting domains, each of which requires particular skills and approaches.

Figure 1.2: Zones of interest in work with young people

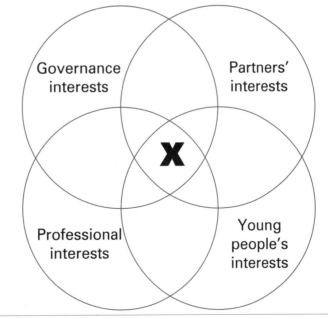

15   Framework for Inspection of Youth Services. Ofsted from website: www.ofsted.gov.uk
16   *Resourcing Excellent Youth Services*, ibid.

Four main domains affect the task of delivering the youth work service and achieving its outcomes. These are show in Figure 1.2 and comprise: governance interests, young people's interests; partners' interests and professional interests. The model is adapted from one developed in relation to young people's active involvement by The National Youth Agency[17].

Figure 1.2 shows the service provision taking place where the four circles interlock, in area X. We argue that it is the nature and combination of these zones which give youth work management its unique characteristics. It is worth noting that the same four zones apply to any public service if service user is substituted for young people.

Delivering the service and its outcomes

To explain the model a little more we begin in the centre, with the delivery and outcomes of the service. Here the influence of all the other zones is felt, but the task of the manager is to lead and manage the delivery of the service. In this part of the diagram the role of the manager is much the same as for any other service (to plan, organise, coordinate, direct and control). These tasks are covered in the main chapters of this book. However, in delivering youth services the manager faces particular challenges such as: how to manage services that are based on open ended relationships, how to involve young people in service design and delivery, and how to demonstrate outcomes and impact on young people. Developmental activities may not easily lend themselves to a simple instrumental approach to measurement, yet the manager cannot simply retreat on to professional high ground, in which he or she objects to being made accountable on any terms other than those of a professional youth worker. Young people, the wider public, public funders are all entitled to a reasonable assessment of what difference investing money in youth work makes, to the young people involved.

Critical questions for managers here are:

● Do we have clear purpose, objectives and strategies to deliver them?
● Do we know which young people we are providing the service to and why? (Do we have good information on their needs? Does our spending and activity reflect priority needs?)
● Do we have sufficient resources (finance, people, premises, equipment, etc.) to deliver the quality and quantity of services that will meet our objectives?
● Is our approach to leadership and management appropriate for a small service working through a dispersed staff, in a wide variety of settings and ways?
● Do we have adequate systems in place to record and measure the outcomes and impact of the service?

Taking account of young people's interests

In recent years there have been concerted efforts to increase the influence of the service user in service planning. In some cases this has involved using the market to provide direct choice eg giving money to buy support services directly to disabled people through the Direct Payments scheme. In most it has involved strengthening the user voice through consultation about plans. Government has put particular emphasis on increasing young people's voice, for example the ground breaking framework for the involvement of young people at all levels of the Connexions service. The UK Government pledged, in Every Child

---

17   See Bill Badham (2003) *Hear By Right*. Leicester. The National Youth Agency.

Matters (2003) to put children and young people at the heart of services that support them. The effective manager of a youth work organisation or service must build in the involvement of young people to every aspect of the service. This may mean transforming its culture.

The way in which young people access youth services and organisations is affected by their perception of the impact the service has on them and their peers, what it has to offer, who is offering it (the image of the youth work professionals). The demand for youth services may, however, have a weak impact on decisions about resourcing them. As the model shows, the biggest influence on overall resourcing decisions is the pressure brought to bear on elected politicians and public servants.

Most young people aged 13 to 19 do not have a vote, so their influence is very limited. Politicians are more likely to be swayed by the voices of adults in the community, who may be responding to a very different view of what young people need. The skilled manager is required to understand both sides of this dilemma and to work with both young people, adults and elected politicians to negotiate a path that meets all their different needs. This is some distance from the relative simplicity of offering a service to those who will pay for it.

Figure 1.3: Managerial domains of public services working with young people

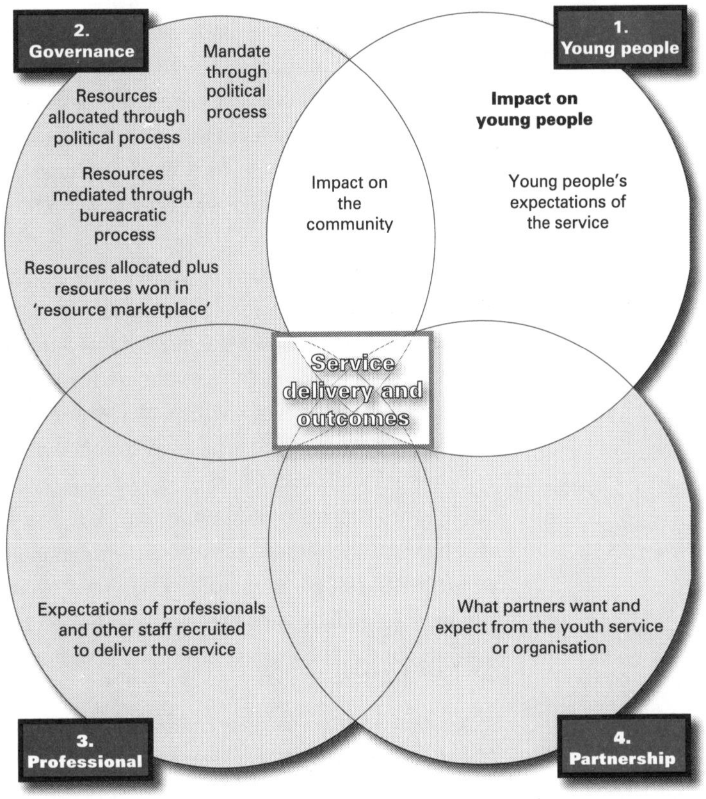

Source: Kevin Ford (2004) Strategic Leadership in Youth Services, Leicester, FPM.

Similarly, public servants are mostly in contact with professional youth workers and managers, rather than young people themselves. Part of the offering of the youth service and many youth organisations is their skill in involving young people in decisions about the services they receive. The challenge is to find valid and effective ways to enable the voice of young people to be heard by decision makers. This is explored exhaustively in *Hear By Right*[18] which sets out standards and easy to use approaches for organisations to meet them.

Questions for managers in relation to this domain are:

● What relationship does the service or organisation have with the young people it serves? How do you know?
● How do young people influence what the service does?
● How do we ensure that young people's views about the service influence political decision makers and public officials when it comes to resource allocation?
● How does the service or organisation enable young people to make their voices heard?
● Do you use effective approaches to leadership and management when engaging with the young people who use the service?
● How do young people contribute to judgments about the value and effectiveness of the organisation or service?

Taking account of the professional domain

The work of professional youth work staff is affected by the norms and expectations of the profession itself. The 'professional domain' is where the interests and culture of the profession itself interacts with the process of service delivery. For example, the health service has been criticised for failing to really focus on health. Its focus has always been on illness. This reflects the focus of the medical profession which is the dominant professional group in the health service. This domain includes the impact professional cultures, practices, pay, status, conditions of service, etc. have on the delivery of the service.

Youth work as a profession is relatively young and relatively weak. Its practitioners have been criticised at times for not being able to explain youth work in simple terms, and for not being able to promise clear, predictable outcomes from their work. When in discussions about resources for youth work the profession may find itself described as acting in its own (producer) interests. A critical challenge for managers is to avoid being seen as a self-interested professional and to speak for and with the young people they serve.

Youth work has no professional body, but has built up a strong tradition of practice. This includes its methods of working with young people (the overlap between the young people's interests and the professional interest) and its methods of supporting staff to do the work (especially the practice of professional supervision). The service manager must take account of these traditions in the planning and delivery of the service.

In addition, youth work grew from the activities of volunteers and voluntary organisations. Much of the work is still delivered by part-time workers and volunteers. The management of a service in which professionals work alongside volunteers, poses some significant challenges. There has been a trend in local authority youth service towards employing fewer part-time staff, but with each working on more substantial contracts. This makes it more realistic to invest in part-time youth worker training and the provision of proper professional support. Case work from the Community and Youth Workers' Union suggests

18   Badham, Bill (2003) *Hear By Right – standards for the active involvement of young people in local democracy.* Leicester. The National Youth Agency.

that many part-time youth workers do not receive high quality management, sometimes not even getting basic support and guidance on matters of health and safety or child protection. Again, it is vital that the youth work manager ensures that the greatest level of managerial support is directed to the staff and volunteers who actually deliver the service. The less romantic aspects of ensuring a high level of professional practice, like health and safety, are essential.

Critical questions for managers are:

● Are the professionals who deliver the service appropriately trained? If not what additional training does the organisation need to provide to remedy this? What arrangements are there for continuous professional development?
● Is the service organised in ways which are compatible with the professional culture? If not how should it be changed?
● How are the professionals held to account for their work and activities, particularly by non-professionals?
● Are there any tensions between the professional interests and the interests of the young people? (Such as: the times where, and locations at which young people want services may not fit with preferred working practices).
● Is the organisation up to date with professional thinking and practices?
● Are the challenges of delivering a service through paid staff working alongside volunteers being met effectively?

Taking account of governance interests

Resources for public service, including youth services and youth work organisations, flow as a result of political decisions made by elected politicians. The decisions are made in a political culture and may be the result of ideology, opportunism, pragmatism, reforming zeal, genuine knowledge and passion or plan panic. One certainty is that many decisions will not have an entirely rational basis. How else did we get the Millennium Dome, the (never used) advanced tilting passenger train, or the Euro Fighter?

It is the task of the leaders of youth work agencies to build a real understanding among politicians of what youth work is and what it can achieve. As a small service, often without much glamour attached to it (will championing youth work advance my political career?), youth work has not generally been in the forefront of political debate. Managers must understand that politics is a highly competitive marketplace of competing interests and create the time to position their service or organisation with politicians. Some of this will be done through direct contact with politicians: presenting them with the case for youth work, set in political terms (how the work with young people is helping to advance their policies and is winning the support of the community). Every youth service needs to have champions among the locally elected politicians. Direct contact between politicians and young people themselves is probably the most powerful way to make the case. However, much influence in this domain is achieved via the civil servants and other public officials who implement policy and advise the politicians on progress.

To influence this domain effectively managers must be able to deal well with professional civil servants and public officials, who work in a classic professional bureaucracy. The officials must be presented with a well argued, evidenced and rational case for the impact of youth work. It must speak to their concerns, which is the achievement of targets and

Reflection

Consider your own role as a senior manager of a service that delivers youth work. Analyse where you spend your time, the main challenges and dilemmas etc using the model in Figure 1.2 Where do the main conflicts in your role come from? Are there areas of your work which you tend to neglect or which require you to develop new skills? What action is prompted by reflecting on the model?

outcomes set by politicians. Youth services, along with many other public services, have not been in the forefront of implementing performance management and have often been criticised by governors for not having sufficient evidence to support their claims of impact. The youth work manager needs to be able to operate effectively with politicians and public servants who are highly instrumental (wanting concrete evidence of impact) in their culture – the way people think, see the world and act. This is discussed in more detail in Chapter 11 when we look at ideas for assessing the impact of youth work in the future.

Questions for managers about this domain are:

- Do we have an effective relationship with politicians who make decision about our resources?
- Do we communicate a persuasive case for youth work to both politicians and key officials outside of the youth service?
- How well do we involve young people as champions of youth work and its impact?
- How well do we marshal support in the local community for our work, so as to influence decisions about resources?
- Do we have evidence of the impact of the work we do with young people which is expressed in terms that are meaningful to politicians and public officials?

Taking account of partners' interests

Youth work organisations and services work with a wide variety of partners. This is discussed in detail in Chapter 10. The rise of interest in youth work as a process which can reach and engage with some of the most excluded and disaffected young people, has led to considerable interest from partners. The development of children's services under one roof, in local authorities, will likely accelerate this trend. As with all the previous domains, the effective manager must be clear about what the service can offer and on what terms. Otherwise the partners may draw the service away from its primary purpose, draw resources away to suit their interests and so on. Managed effectively partnerships bring the opportunity to widen the reach and impact of youth work on young people and to build greater understanding of what it is and what it can offer among partners.

In summary the four zone model suggests that the really effective manager of a youth work service or organisation must have highly developed skills to be able to operate effectively in all four zones as well as being able to manage the delivery of the service. What is unique about managing youth work is the way in which the four domains combine to have impact on the delivery of a complex and subtle service as discussed earlier in this chapter. Managing youth work presents a potentially rewarding challenge, but is far from straightforward.

Chapter Two:
You as a manager: some principles for thinking and learning

Introduction

As a prelude to embarking on this programme about management, this section sets out some essential principles for thinking and learning and looks at some immediate issues facing you as a manager. Although some of the principles and ideas may be familiar, it is worth taking a little time to remind yourself about them. This chapter provides brief coverage of the following areas:

- Culture and values
- Thinking
- Being creative
- Making sense
- Reasoning
- Learning
- Developing as a manager

Culture and values

Our values inform all that we do. They constitute the core of our view of the world – the things to which we accord value, for which we will work, promote, lead our lives by and, if necessary, fight. Each of us holds our own unique set of values. All are affected and informed by the environment within which we live, our upbringing, life experience, the prevailing culture around us and other influences.

Culture can be understood as having three layers,[1] as shown in figure 2.1 The outer layer represents what a person will experience immediately. For example, in a youth centre this is the appearance of the building, the equipment, the way the staff act and behave. We are finely tuned as human beings to draw a huge number of conclusions about the way things work from very limited, immediate information. The artefacts and products of the organisation can be managed relatively easily to reflect your values.

The middle layer involves the norms (what is considered to be right/wrong, normal and acceptable) and values. These may be seen in artefacts, objects, behaviours, and so on. However, this layer is deeper and may be less obvious. Norms develop in all groups and are expressed as how things should (or must) be. Values relate to what is considered to be good or bad, and are more aspirational – they are how we would like things to be. The norms and values of an organisation can be managed, although changing them is generally a slow process that requires commitment from all involved.

---

1   Trompenaars, Fons and Hampden Turner, Charles (1997) *Riding the Waves of Culture – Understanding Cultural Diversity in Business*, London: Nicholas Brealey Publishing.

Figure 2.1: A model of culture

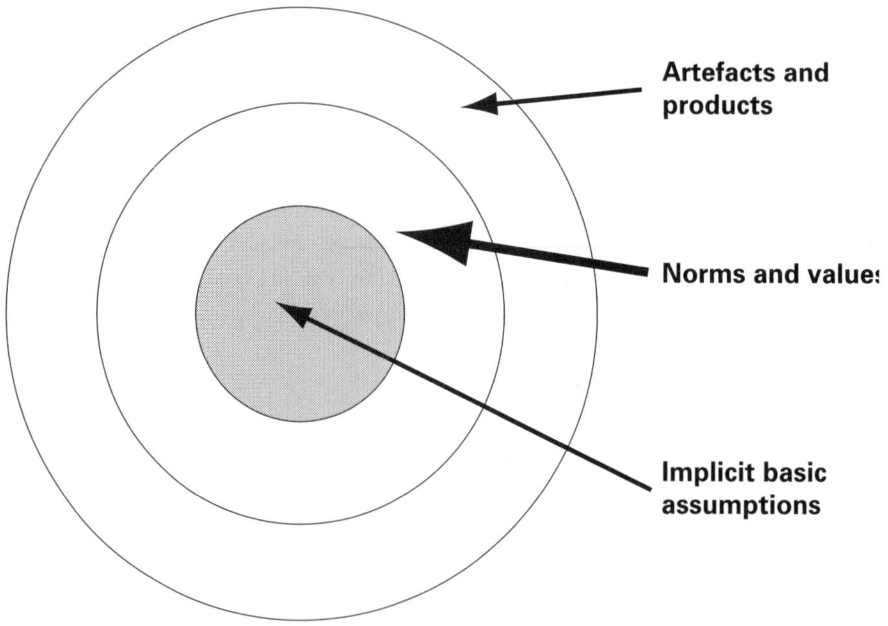

Trompenaars and Hampden Turner, 1997

At the heart of a culture are underlying, implicit basic assumptions about the way the world is and works. These assumptions are absorbed from the person's surrounding culture and form the lens through which everything is seen and understood. Trompenaars and Hampden Turner argue that these underlying assumptions are hard to get at and are not easily open to change, but also argue that they can be understood, and the differences that are uncovered, respected and reconciled.

Culture provides the context within which a manager works: the culture of the project, programme or service; the culture of the local authority or organisation; the culture of the region or nation, and so on. Understanding culture is crucial for managers as they seek to influence the behaviour of staff and volunteers in order to provide effective services to young people. For example, consider a youth organisation operating in an inner city area in which local black and Asian young people have grown up in a youth culture which distrusts and perceives the police to be discriminating against them. Before any real progress can be made, the staff in the organisation must gain an understanding both of this culture, and that of the police. This may raise challenging questions for the staff involved, and for their managers.

We can only understand other cultures through the filter of our own. This may at times result in discomfort or inner conflict, when we meet cultural norms or values that are sharply different from our own. An illustration is the value attached to time. In Northern Europe and the USA there is a tendency to place considerable importance on punctuality, getting things done on time and so on. This is not a universal value. In many other cultures time is seen as flexible, things will be done eventually – why the big rush? This is not superficial – it is an expression of a different way of seeing the world. It can cause huge frustrations and misunderstandings.

Reflection

How do you enable your staff to recognise and understand different cultures among the people with whom you work? How do you respond to different cultural norms and values when they directly impact on providing your service (for example attitudes to time)?

It also leaves managers with a dilemma. How far can or should a manager accept different standards of behaviour (such as time-keeping) when there appear to be different cultural norms among the workforce? Can the organisation legitimately set out its own standards and culture and ask all its staff to conform to them?

Values are a large part of what motivates people to work in an organisation. If people feel in tune with the values of the organisation and are likely to be rewarded for working in ways that accord with the values, then they are more likely to feel motivated, work harder and create a purposeful workplace. We can categorise values in a variety of ways. These usually range from the high level of principle and belief to the more practical level of behaviour and action. It is helpful for a manager to be aware of her or his values and how they inform the work. Managers of youth work organisations are usually expected to hold a number of key values, including:

- integrity
- respect for people in general, and for young people
- justice and a commitment to challenge unfair discrimination
- tolerance and celebration of differences
- honesty
- passion for learning and development

If a youth work organisation is to be true to its values of respect for every individual, it must have conscious and visible processes to support the values. The challenge for managers is to develop a culture in which people are respected, differences valued and where action or behaviour that people perceive to be out of line is open to challenge. It is not a case of accepting all differences of value and culture without criticism. Managers have to find a way to unite people to deliver the services for which the organisation exists. As one writer described it, the trick is to be able 'to disagree without being disagreeable'.

The UK Government set out a clear set of values to underpin youth work in England in its document *Resourcing Excellent Youth Services* (2003)[2]:

- Young people choose to be involved, not least because they want to relax, meet friends and have fun.
- The work starts where young people are – with their view of the world and their interests.
- It seeks to go beyond where young people start, in particular, by encouraging them to be critical and creative in their responses to their experience and the world around them and supporting their exploration of new ideas, interests and creative ability.
- It takes place because young people are young people, not because they have been labelled or categorised as deviant.
- It recognises, respects and is actively responsive to the wider network of peers, communities and cultures which are important to young people.
- Through these networks, it seeks to help young people achieve stronger relationships and collective identities – for example, as black people, women, men, disabled people, gay men or lesbians – and through promotion of inclusivity, particularly for minority ethnic communities.

2   *Resourcing Excellent Youth Services*, ibid.

- It is concerned with how young people feel and not just with what they know and can do.
- It is concerned with facilitating and empowering the voice of young people.
- It is concerned with ensuring that young people can influence the environment within which they live.
- It respects and values individual differences by supporting and strengthening young people's belief in themselves and their capacity to grow and change.
- It works with other agencies which contribute to young people's social and personal development.
- It complements and supports school and college based education by encouraging and providing other opportunities for young people to achieve and fulfil their potential.

A critical question for young work managers is how far their work lives up to the values above. Would a visitor to a voluntary youth organisation or a youth service see and feel these values being put into practice? What would it look like? Have managers spent time identifying norms of practice and behaviour which would accompany these statements of value.

Charles Hampden Turner (a management writer and former youth worker) offers another view of the values and behaviours of effective managers.[3] He suggests that managers are not separated from their work and their people. They push the sum total of their own morality, values, creativity and humanity into the world. What he regards as 'radical' managers:

1. Hang on to their perceptions of poverty and injustice without giving up their determination to try to do something about both.
2. Periodically take the risk of changing the way they think and act. They are not complacent or rigid.
3. Continually seek new and greater levels of skill and knowledge.
4. Are genuinely committed to others.
5. Are willing to risk suspending their own assumptions and be vulnerable to new ideas, concepts and so on. They are able to admit to changing their minds!
6. Make a real and conscious effort to contact and understand other cultures, minority groups and other organisations.
7. Form cooperative relationships for the benefit of their organisations but only after a rigorous process to explore and understand the value of the relationships.
8. Integrate their experiences with learning from debate, discovering new ideas and concepts and debate with others.

To see yourself as others see you ...

You will have a sense of your own values and how you do things. Others may not see you in the same way and the difference between the two perceptions may be a cause of misunderstandings or even conflict. The different areas of awareness can be mapped using the figure below: The Johari Window.[4]

---

3 Hampden-Turner, C. (1994) *Corporate Culture*, Great Britain, Hutchinson Books Ltd.
4 Developed by two psychologists, Joseph Luft and Harry Ingham; see Luft, J. (1969) *Of Human Interaction*, Palo Alto, CA: National Press.

The four-paned 'window', as illustrated below, divides personal awareness into four different types: open, hidden, blind, and unknown.

Figure 2.2: The Johari Window

	Known to self	Not known to self
Known to others	Open	Blind
Not known to others	Hidden	Unknown

Reflection

Use the Johari Window to reflect on how far you have shared your own values with your work colleagues. Are you working together within a large open area, or are your interactions held back by lack of knowledge, both ways? What might you do to build a larger open area?

1. The 'open' quadrant represents things that I know about myself, and that you know about me; information and perceptions are checked both ways. This includes factual information, feelings, values, motives, behaviours, wants, needs and desires. In the early stages of any interaction this pane is small; with good communication it grows. The larger this part of the window, the more effective interactions are likely to be.

2. The 'blind' quadrant represents things that you know about me, but of which I am unaware. An obvious example would be if I unknowingly have some food stuck in my teeth. I rely on feedback to become aware of the fact, and to be able to take action in response. Others may perceive that my actions are based on values they do not accept. Unless they give me feedback I have no way of knowing, and misunderstandings can result.

3. The 'hidden' quadrant represents things that I know about myself, that you do not know. I have a choice as to whether I share this information with you. The more of myself that I am willing to share, the greater the size of the open area of the window, and the less room there is for misunderstandings.

4. The 'unknown' quadrant represents things that neither I know about myself, nor you know about me. This is the area of the subconscious and unconscious mind.

Understanding your own values, those of your organisation, those of your staff and those of the young people with whom you work is an important management skill. All human activity is influenced by values. The process of understanding calls upon the second topic in this section: thinking.

Thinking

One of the most important activities a senior manager must be able to find time for, is to think. As Edward de Bono put it: 'Thinking is the ultimate human resource. The quality of our future will depend entirely on the quality of our thinking.'[5]

5   de Bono, Edward (1982) *de Bono's Thinking Course*, London: BBC Books.

We all think most of the time as we carry out everyday work. However, this thinking is usually in reaction to immediate events and stimuli. Effective managers need to create time and tools to step back from the everyday to reflect and to think. The really innovative and inspirational manager:

Reflection

When do you do your best thinking?

How do you secure time for thinking?

What tools or techniques do you use to enable you to think?

Have you ever said to someone: 'I can't do that as I will be doing some serious thinking ...' (compared with – 'sorry I shall be in a meeting')?

● makes the time to think; and
● has developed tools to help her or him think well.

This sort of reflective thought requires time without interruption. This might be short or long, but should allow the mind to gather itself and think, rather than just react to events. Some people use journeys for thinking. Others think in the bath. Some think over a cup of tea or a cigarette; during a walk, swim or bike ride. However you do it, your schedule as a manager must provide you with space to think reflectively.

There are many tools to help us think. Nearly all force us to pause and do things in a different way from normal. We explore some examples later in this section.

In a world of constant change and increasing complexity, managers not only need to be able to think, but also need ways to unlock their capacity to develop new solutions to difficult problems. This is the skill of being creative.

Being creative

Joyce Wycoff describes creativity as: 'Bringing new meaning or purpose to a task, finding new uses, solving existing problems or adding beauty or value.'[6]

Being creative often entails that 'A-ha' moment; not necessarily one of recognition but one of curiosity. It implies seeing something as if for the first time, and wanting to explore it deeper or follow wherever it appears to be leading. It means not necessarily being satisfied with what you see or are told, but being willing to look for different meanings or interpretations because those available are unconvincing. Creativity can also involve taking an existing idea or model and adapting it for a new circumstance. The invention of *Post-It* stickers (was this a good idea?) involved finding a new purpose for a glue 'that did not stick', which had been discovered by accident.

Creativity is sometimes described as 'divergent thinking', involving a search for options in respect of a problem for which there appears to be no single solution. The idea is to generate alternatives, combining different elements in different ways to see what solutions you might arrive at.

Divergent thinking, as opposed to convergent thinking, is an approach to problem-solving much favoured by the renowned writer on thinking, Edward de Bono. He believes we spend too little time on defining a problem because we have been led to believe that the problem is obvious. Instead, we spend our time using techniques to solve what may be the wrong problem. While convergent thinking applies a narrow focus and has a tendency to probe deeply, lateral thinking is forever considering alternatives, not least looking at something from different angles.

---

6   Wycoff, J. (1991) *Mindmapping*, Berkley Books: New York.

Tools for creative thinking

The PMI

In his popular Thinking Course,[7] De Bono proposes a number of tools (usually cast in the form of mnemonics to help people recall and therefore use them). One of his best known is PMI, which is a powerful yet simple tool to help people quickly evaluate things (ideas, suggestions, activities etc.). The PMI is a scanning tool that ensures we use three perspectives when coming to a judgment (rather than just one). P = Plus, M = Minus and I = Interesting. So, in response to the suggestion that all cars should be painted yellow. De Bono offers the following:

P (plus)

- easier to see on the roads
- easier to see at night
- no problem in deciding what coloured car you want
- no waiting to get the colour you want
- easier for the manufacturer
- the dealer would need less stock
- it would take the 'macho' element out of car ownership
- cars would tend to become just transport items
- in minor collisions, the paint rubbed off on to your car is the same.

M (minus)

- boring
- difficult to recognise your car
- very difficult to find your car in a car park
- easier to steal cars
- the abundance of yellow could tire the eyes
- car chases would be difficult for the police
- witnesses to accidents would have a harder time.

I (interesting)

- will different shades of yellow emerge?
- will people appreciate the safety factor of better visibility?
- will attitudes towards cars change?
- will the trim acquire a different colour?
- will it be enforceable?
- who might support the suggestion?

APC

The mind tends to like certainty and the consequent security. It likes to see patterns. The alternative – chaos – can be unnerving. This is one reason that the consideration of alternatives is often avoided. It also suggests that people cannot make up their minds, so they tend to make a decision and then justify it rather than listing and weighing the options. To help us do what our minds instinctively recoil from de Bono suggests another

---

7   See footnote 5.

tool, APC.[8] This stands for Alternatives, Possibilities, Choices.

Looking for alternatives can be fun. For example, think of the alternative ways of emptying a glass of water without damaging or tilting it.

Doing an APC means stating the alternatives and listing the possibilities or choices. It may relate to defining or finding the solution(s) to a problem. The point is that there are always more ways of seeing or thinking about things than we originally thought. As Mike Liebling, director of Trainset puts it, 'If you have one idea, it's a compulsion. If you have two ideas, it's a dilemma. If you have three or more ideas, then you have a choice'.

Six thinking hats

De Bono also provides the idea of 'six thinking hats' to use in collective decision making.[9] We have seen it used very effectively to unblock partnership meetings. It uses the principle that people think and behave differently for different types of problem. If a group is using the wrong sort of thinking, it will be ineffective. Similarly, if different members of the group are thinking in completely different ways, it may get in the way of discussion and decision making. By agreeing all to put on the same type of hat, the method enable groups to think clearly and freely together.

The six thinking hats are:

White Hat	Neutral, data and information. People put aside proposals and arguments and focus on information.
Red Hat	Emotion, warmth, feelings, intuition, hunches. Permission to put forward feelings.
Black Hat	Stern, judgmental. Critical judgment, evaluation, identifying problems and flaws. Allows careful consideration so as to avoid mistakes.
Yellow Hat	Optimistic, logical, positive. Looks for opportunities and benefits based on reason and logic.
Green Hat	Creative thinking hat. Growth, organic. Seeks new ideas, alternatives, creative effort.
Blue Hat	Blue sky, overview. Looks at the process being used, reflects back what is happening in the meeting. Calls in other hats.

Using the hats requires the convenor of the meeting to focus the group members on examining the problem using one of the hats at a time. The convenor keeps returning people to the appropriate style. The result is that everyone works in a similar way and dissonance is reduced. The six hats' method also provides the group with a vocabulary to describe the way they are interacting. It may also help group members to become aware of preferred or dominant styles of thinking. Referring back to the Johari Window (page 27) helps to build a bigger open area for the group to work in.

Fuzzy state thinking

Another aspect of creativity worth considering is 'fuzzy-state thinking'. If we have a problem or challenge in our service or organisation, the tendency is to concentrate on it until we find a solution. Sometimes when we do this it can feel like we are either going round in circles or running up against a wall.

---

8   De Bono, Edward (1992) *Serious Creativity*, London: Harper Collins, pp77–85.
9   Ibid.

The alternative is to allow the mind to wander off into a 'fuzzy state'. There is considerable research evidence that suggests that a fuzzy state can be quite a fertile one in which to generate new ideas. 'Sleeping on it' or doing something completely different provides ways to allow the brain to wander into this fuzzy state. The technique is to find ways to prevent yourself from pushing too hard for an immediate solution.

Mind mapping

Tony Buzan[10] has developed the idea of mind maps to aid thinking. The problem or issue at hand is written in the centre of the page, and the main thoughts are drawn as branches as shown (figure 2.3). Buzan recommends that you draw the maps large and in colour. The method enables many aspects of a problem to be laid out in relation to each other. It helps you to make connections, and new ideas or solutions often emerge.

Figure 1.3: Mind Mapping

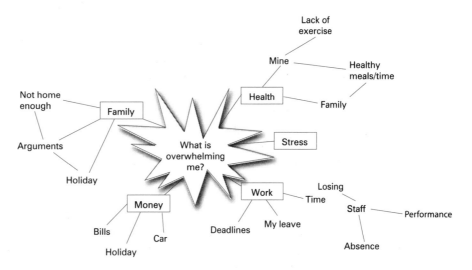

Making sense

We integrate our values, our thinking skills and our creativity when making sense of the world around us.

Every individual learns from birth how to make sense of things. Each person does this in their own way – it is a function of many factors, including personality, upbringing and learned behaviours.

The way we do things, including managing, is made up of a mix of perceptions, thoughts and feelings, which we process (through our personality and disposition) leading to action. Some action is reflex, involving little thought. Other action may be thoughtful. Some action is without much feeling. Some may be an emotional response.

As an effective manager you need to be aware of how you learn best, how you see the world, your main personality traits, how you think, how you react to particular stimuli, and so on. The awareness means that you are better able to deploy your own skills and talents

---

10   Buzan, Tony (1982) *Use Your Head*, London: Ariel/BBC Books.

to good effect, rather than bobbing about like a cork on the currents of circumstance, making decisions based on partial information and little thought.

We will not go into any depth here, but will provide a brief introduction to two useful tools: the Myers Briggs personality test and Peter Honey's Learning Styles analysis.

Myers Briggs

Myers Briggs provides information on underlying personality types that influence behaviour. The test has been widely used for many years. Jung identified three basic criteria by which personality could be classified:

Introversion vs Extroversion (I – E)

The source and direction of energy expression for a person. The extrovert has a source and direction of energy expression mainly in the external world, while the introvert has a source of energy mainly in the internal world.

Sensing vs Intuition (S – N)

The method of information perception by a person. Sensing means that a person believes mainly information he receives directly from the external world. Intuition means that a person believes mainly information he receives from the internal or imaginative world.

Thinking vs Feeling (T – F)

How the person processes information. Thinking means that a person makes a decision mainly through logic. Feeling means that, as a rule, he makes a decision based on emotion.

Isabel Myers-Briggs added a fourth criterion:

Judgment vs Perception (J – P)

How a person implements the information he has processed. Judging means that a person organises all his life events and acts strictly according to his plans. Perceiving means that he is inclined to improvise and seek alternatives.

The result of the test is a score on each scale, leading to 16 main personality types. The value of the information from Myers Briggs' tests (or similar) is to provide an insight into some of the ways we process information and see the world at a deep level. For example, a manager who knows that he or she is strongly intuitive and feeling may need to adapt his or her natural approach when communicating with someone who is sensing/thinking, otherwise neither may hear or understand what the other is seeking to communicate.

There are several interesting websites giving information on Myers Briggs, some of which allow you to carry out quick self analysis using a version of the test (eg www. teamtechnology.co.uk)

Peter Honey has developed an approach to analysing learning styles to which we refer later in this section (page 35). You can also find information at www.peterhoney.com

Reasoning

As a senior manager you are expected to produce a wide range of reports. In most cases you may be asked to develop a sound and reasoned argument. This may be second nature, but it is worth checking that the principles are clear. Also, senior managers spend significant time reading other people's papers, reports etc. and need to have strong skills to analyse their arguments.

Quinn[11] emphasises that arguments have three elements:

- **the claim** or conclusion: what point is being made
- **grounds** or evidence that support the claim
- **the warrant** or link between the grounds and the claim: are you justified in making the claim you have made from the evidence you have mustered?

As an example, the director of a local youth employment project might make the claim that staff sickness is affecting the number of young people the project can help. He cites as evidence the information that since the staff numbers fell due to sickness, the numbers of young people seen have fallen. The warrant he is using is that staff numbers directly affect the number of young people who can be seen.

This warrant may be justified, but you would need to see more of the evidence being used before you would know.

Deductive argument uses the same three elements identified by Quinn, and makes its claim (or conclusion) based on the truth of the evidence presented. So, for example: all living people breathe (evidence); I am breathing (evidence); therefore I am alive (warrant and conclusion). Deductive argument hinges on whether it is valid to draw the conclusion from the evidence.

This may seem both basic and obvious, but policy-makers persist in using invalid arguments to guide their policies towards young people. As a champion of work with young people you must have well-developed tools to question such arguments.

For example:

- we put up CCTV in the shopping area
- crime rates fell
- therefore CCTV reduces crime (and we should install it all over the place).

The claim cannot be deduced from the evidence (for example, what else may have led to a fall in crime rates?).

However, it may be reasonable to make the claim, on the grounds of probability. This is known as **inductive argument** when the evidence does not prove the conclusion, but gives

Reflection

Next time you have to read a report in which someone is making a claim, try using Quinn's three concepts – claim, grounds and warrant – to analyse the strength of the argument. Try it as a test on your own arguments, in your plans and reports.

11   Quinn, Robert E., Faerman, Sue R., Thompson, Michael P. and McGrath, Michael R. (1996), *Becoming a Master Manager – A Competency Framework* (2nd edn), New York: John Wiley.

reasonable grounds for drawing it. Continuing with CCTV, the argument might develop:

● There were no other measurable changes related to crime in the area over the period in which the CCTV was installed.
● Professor Ulysses J. Bogus of Little Rock University has demonstrated that CCTV reduces crime rates in 87 per cent of locations around the world.

This further data strengthens the case for the conclusion being valid. It is worth noting when people introduce authorities to support their arguments. We do so throughout these materials, but the authority should not necessarily be accepted without question. Authorities differ in their interpretation of data; they may come from different fields or they may simply disagree with one another.

In mounting an argument it is important that you are able to make a distinction between:

● description – simply describing how things are; and
● analysis – exploring and seeking to understand and explain why the things observed are as they are.

Many reports are weak in that they describe, but do not attempt to make any sense of what has been described. The reason for bombarding you with models, theories and tools through this programme is to give you more ways to make sense of your observations – to enhance your capacity for analysis.

Example

● Description: team meetings struggle to make decisions and frequently end in disharmony. Members do not seem to listen to each other.
● Analysis: using the six thinking hats model (see page 30) you identify that certain team members always seem to use a particular hat. One member tends to go green and creative, which infuriates another, who tend to use the white hat and wants facts and data.

Reflection

Look at the arguments you have made for a new development or allocation of resources. How well did you use observation and analysis? Were your conclusions empirical or prescriptive?

Once the analysis has been done it is possible to draw conclusions or try to suggest solutions to problems. There are two main types of conclusions:

● empirical – based on how things actually are (ie research or observation)
● theoretical/prescriptive – based on a theory or idea of how things ought to be.

The development of Connexions provides an interesting case study in producing an argument. It uses empirical evidence to draw the conclusion that not all young people get the best start in life. It concluded that the existing services for young people were in need of transformation. It then moved to a prescriptive conclusion, setting out a new service, based on a set of principles and ideas.

Learning

Our approach to management learning is based on the experiential learning cycle developed by David Kolb[12] (see next page). Kolb argues that we all learn most by doing, pausing to reflect on what we have done, analysing and extending from our reflections to consider others' thinking and ideas, then using what we have learned to plan our next actions. The cycle leads to a spiral, with continuous learning and improvement in the quality of the actions.

Figure 2.4: The experiential cycle

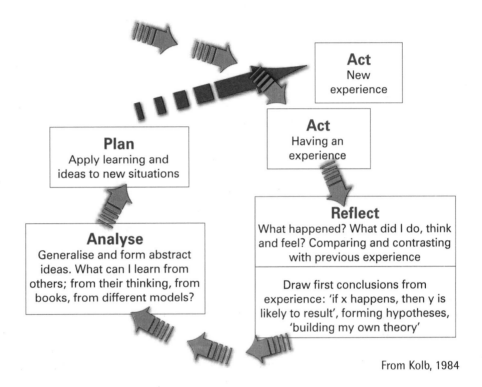

From Kolb, 1984

Honey and Mumford[13] suggest that individuals tend to learn using a preferred or dominant learning style based on the cycle. They identify four main styles: activists, reflectors, theorists and pragmatists.

To illustrate the styles, we have applied each one to a simple problem: how to get a large table out of a room.

Activists Throw themselves into new experiences and learn from so doing. Get bored easily if no action. *Pick up the table and start moving towards the door, possibly before checking anything about the request to move it.*

Reflectors Stand back and consider problems from many angles before taking action. Collect data and seek rational planned approach. *Sit round the table to explore what has been requested, the dimensions of the table, door, etc. and the mechanics of moving it.*

---

12 Kolb, D. (1984) *Experiential Learning: Experience as the Source of Learning and Development*, Engelwood Cliffs NJ: Prentice Hall.
13 Honey, P. and Mumford, A. (1992) *Manual of Learning Styles*, Maidenhead: Honey.

Reflection

Think about the way you approach learning. In what circumstances do you learn best? Can you recognise any of the four learning styles in yourself? What are the implications of your learning style for your development as a manager?

Theorists Will want to locate any action into a sound framework of theory or principle. Put a premium on rational thinking and analysis. *Will sit round the table and discuss why it is that there has been a request to move it, principles underpinning its movement and so on.*

Pragmatists Like to put ideas into practice. They enjoy analysis and synthesis only where it can be applied to a problem or situation. *This group would introduce a theory on table moving and rapidly organise to move the table using the theory as a guide.*

Awareness of your learning style and that of your colleagues helps to enlarge the open area of the Johari Window (see page 27) and so improves the effectiveness of your interactions. It also helps you to identify what you need to learn best. This is vital information for your own continuing professional development as a manager.

Developing yourself as a manager

Every manager should have a conscious plan for his or her self-development. This is part of learning from experience, and building your skills and knowledge so as to continue to be effective. Youth work organisations promote the value of learning and development for young people. It is vital that the same values are applied to all their staff.

Reflection

What steps do you take to ensure your own continuing professional development? How do you decide where your development priorities lie? How is your professional development linked to the organisation's strategu and priorities?

It is extremely useful to build up a profile of yourself as a manager so that you can plan and track your development. The profile helps to identify the key areas in which you may need to take action, such as reading, developing skills or trying out ideas.

A useful source for developing yourself as a manager is the excellent book *A Manager's Guide to Self-Development*.[14] It contains numerous exercises as well as a structured approach to building your profile.

As a professional manager you should expect to devote a sensible amount of time to your own continuing professional development. In many professions there is an expectation that this will involve at least ten days a year.

---

14   Pedlar Mike, Burgoyne John & Boydell, Tom (2001 4th edition) *A Manager's Guide to Self-Development*, London: McGraw Hill.

Chapter Three:
Understanding the modern service-providing organisation

Introduction

Local authority youth services, voluntary organisations providing services to young people, and partnerships of organisations working with young people are all service-providing organisations. Most of the literature on management has focused on manufacturing industry. There is a growing literature on general service provision with a smaller literature on public service provision.

Public service agencies and organisations provide services for public benefit (rather than profit). A youth work manager needs to have a clear understanding of the purpose and nature of his or her organisation, what is affecting it and how it is changing. This chapter establishes some key concepts and tools for understanding your organisation, whether it is in the public or voluntary sector. It focuses on the centre of our management model as shown below. The chapter covers:

● Organisation
● Seeing the organisation
● A systems approach to analysing the organisation
● Service-providing organisations
● Public services

Figure 3.1: The experiential cycle

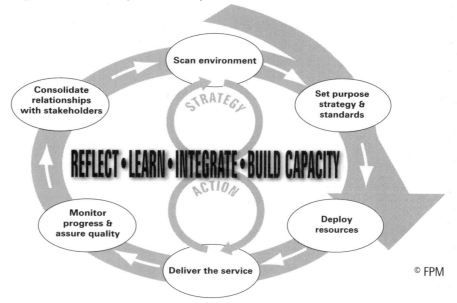

© FPM

Organisations

All managers work in some form of organisation. It is essential to have some tools for thinking about organisations. This is particularly true of public sector organisations where there is a historic tendency for managers to become preoccupied with structures. The way in which an organisation is structured is only part of the process of organising. The whole of the process of organising should be in order to deliver the purpose of the organisation.

Buchanan and Huczynski[1] offer a simple definition of organisations as social arrangements for achieving controlled performance in pursuit of collective goals. In essence organisations are made of people who work together to pursue a common aim. The arrangements within the organisation determine where power and influence lie and how resources are directed.

Organisational configurations

All organisations are made up of a number of building blocks which are coordinated in different ways. Mintzberg[2] identified six basic building blocks of organisational design:

- The operating core where the basic work is carried out – the youth centre, the Connexions premises, the street corner, the school. This covers all those involved in face-to-face work with young people.
- The strategic apex is the senior management of the organisation.
- The middle line refers to all managers between the strategic apex and the operating core.
- The technostructure which designs systems and processes. This could include quality assurance managers who write procedures, curriculum/accreditation managers or coordinators who devise recording mechanisms or finance teams who design financial recording processes.
- The support staff including admin staff, caretakers, cleaners, IT technicians etc.
- The ideology or culture of the organisation including values, beliefs and underlying assumptions.

The relative size and importance of these building blocks will vary with the circumstances. For example, ideology is likely to be more important in an organisation working with young people than in a factory making widgets, while the reverse may be true for the technostructure. The ways in which the activities are coordinated will also vary. The main coordinating mechanisms are:

- **Mutual adjustment** through informal contact between people, particularly in the operating core. This works well where people work closely and informally together and is particularly appropriate for teams working on a new project.
- **Direct supervision** through the hierarchy where instructions are passed from the strategic apex through the middle line to the operating core. This implies that senior management involves itself in the detail of how work with young people takes place and that middle managers' role is to ensure that these detailed instructions are carried out. This mechanism is likely to have limited relevance for those involved in youth work.
- **Standardisation of work processes** through systems which specify how work should be undertaken. The systems are usually designed by those in the technostructure. While some standardisation is occurring as a result of meeting external demands (REYS, Ofsted, project funders etc), responding to the differing needs of young people limits the effectiveness of standardised processes.
- **Standardisation of outputs** is increasingly used in work with young people. Many of the REYS targets are output measures (percentage of young people reached, percentage achieving accredited outcomes etc.) as are many of the cross-cutting targets.

1   Buchanan, D. and Huczynski, A. (1973, third edition), *Organizational Behaviour*, London: Prentice Hall.
2   Mintzberg, H. (1979), *The Structure of Organisations*, New York: Prentice Hall.

- **Standardisation of skills** is one of the key coordinating mechanisms for youth work and other professional service organisations. Professional training is a key mechanism for ensuring that the operating core has the skills necessary to function effectively.
- Equally powerful for organisations involved with young people is standardisation of norms where it is expected that those in the operating core will share the same values and beliefs.

Combining the building blocks with coordinating mechanisms led Mintzberg[3] to come up with six organisational configurations which are summarised in the table on the next page. These are:

1. **Simple structure**
   This is usually found in small informal organisations dominated by a leader who provides vision and direction. The organisation is small enough to allow direct supervision of activities and everybody is expected to 'muck in' and do what is necessary. These organisations are very flexible in response to changing circumstances. Small voluntary organisations may have elements of this configuration.

2. **Machine bureaucracy**
   In machine bureaucracies, standardisation of work processes is very important so the technostructure will be large. These are usually large, mature organisations operating in relatively stable environments. Efficiency and cost reduction are paramount and the work is often routine.

3. **Professional bureaucracy**
   Here the professional work is standardised through ensuring that staff have the skills needed to perform. The emphasis is on training and sharing of good practice. Large youth work organisations are likely to have significant elements of this configuration.

4. **Divisionalised structures**
   Divisionalised structures are found in large complex organisations such as local authorities or large voluntary organisations working with a variety of target groups or across a wide geographical area. Here control is operated by specifying outputs required and in some cases financial performance. Elements of this structure are found where work with young people is delivered through contracting arrangements with other organisations.

5. **Adhocracy**
   In these organisations the emphasis is on innovation and change. Success depends on mutual adjustment within the operating core and a supportive management style. Project teams form, are disbanded and new ones are created. Opportunities are seized and projects are designed by the operating core as one-offs in response to demand. Organisations working with the hardest to reach young people can operate in this way.

6. **Missionary organisations**
   Missionary organisations have a dominant ideology which attracts individuals who share the missionary vision. It is this commitment that drives the organisation and there is little reliance on systems and structures. Missionary organisations are often found in the voluntary sector.

In reality very few organisations fit these stereotypes exactly and different parts of the organisation may operate in different ways. What is important is whether the way the organisation is structured helps it to achieve its purpose.

---

3 Ibid.

Table 3.2: Summary of organisation types

Structure	Age and size of organisation	Key part of organisation	Key coordinating mechanism
Simple	Young/small	Strategic apex	Direct supervision
Machine bureaucracy	Mature/large	Technostructure	Standardisation of work
Professional bureaucracy	Varies	Operating core	Standardisation of skills
Divisionalised	Mature/very large	Middle line	Standardisation of outputs
Adhocracy	Young/variable size	Operating core + support staff	Mutual adjustment
Missionary	Middle aged/small or large with small enclaves	Ideology	Standardisation of norms

Stage of development

The way an organisation is configured is often a reflection of its developmental stage. Young small organisations may have little in common with large mature ones. A recently formed small local voluntary organisation needs a different structure to an established local authority youth service. Connexions partnerships, while young, are relatively large and bring together existing organisations in what might be termed a loose divisionalised structure.

Greiner[4] described organisations as going through five phases of growth, with a crisis phase needed to move from one phase to the next. During the first phase, new small organisations grow through the creativity of the founders backed by a committed workforce. This works until the organisation grows too large to operate in this way and experiences a crisis of leadership when the founders find themselves lumbered with unwanted management responsibilities. To move the organisation on, competent managers are employed and phase 2 is characterised by a directive management style which works until lower level managers and employees begin to feel restricted which brings on a crisis of autonomy. In phase 3, authority is delegated to lower level managers to enable them to respond more flexibly to user needs. The distance between top management and those delivering the service grows and lower level managers begin to develop their own approaches to the work which naturally leads to inconsistencies. The result is a crisis in control which leads to strong attempts at coordination in phase 4. Much of this coordination is achieved through systems, processes and recording mechanisms which eventually leads to a crisis of red tape. This is overcome by strong interpersonal collaboration in phase 5 where teams and task groups proliferate. Meetings, conferences and training programmes are used to provide coordinating mechanisms.

Greiner's original work was carried out when few organisations were in phase 5 and he predicted that the likely crisis would be emotional and physical exhaustion brought on by the intensity of team work and the constant pressure for new solutions. Revisiting

Reflection

Think about your organisation or agency in relation to:
• the Mintzberg model
• Greiner's model.
What stage of development are you at? Does the model reflect your perception of the main issues and challenges facing the organisation?

What particular insights do the models give you in planning action to resolve some of the issues?

---

4   Greiner, L. (1972), 'Evolution and Revolution as Organisations Grow', *Harvard Business Review*, July/August, 1972.

his earlier work in 1998[5], Greiner's view was the phase 5 crisis was in fact the realisation that problems could not be solved internally and he proposed a new phase 6 – network organisations – where problems were solved through partnerships and alliances.

Whether organisations actually go through all these phases sequentially is a matter for debate. Many youth work organisations demonstrate elements of phases 4, 5 and 6 which may explain why the role of leader/manager is a complex one.

Figure 3.3: Greiner's original 5 phases

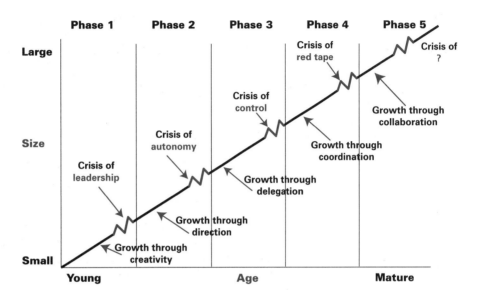

Seeing the organisation

Often we assume we see when we do not. I decided to return to drawing a few years ago, after a gap of nearly twenty years. The art tutor began by making the point that drawing was not about the technical task of manipulating a pencil, piece of charcoal or brush. 'Drawing is about learning to look and to really see', she said. The course then proceeded to enable its students to strip the scales of preconception from their eyes. The result was to see the ordinary and familiar with new eyes.

Management is not unlike drawing – it has its technical side, but at the heart of effective management is the process of looking and seeing your organisation with tremendous clarity. This chapter explores ways to do this.

It is worth taking a few minutes to consider the nature of the 'organisation' within which you are a senior manager. Use the following questions to reflect before reading on:

1. It is assumed that you know what an organisation is. Do you? How would you describe your organisation or service to a visitor from Mars, who had absolutely no idea about earthly things?
2. Think about the part of the organisation you manage – the whole service or organisation, part of it, a particular function, etc. How would you describe this? Is it any different to your description in 1?

5   Greiner, L. (1998), 'Evolution and Revolution as Organisations Grow', *Harvard Business Review*, May/June, 1998.

3. How would you describe the culture ('the way we do things around here') of what you manage?
4. What image would you use to capture the type of organisation in which you manage (ie a mental picture of the organisation)?
5. Think of other organisations – do you use different mental pictures to think about them? If so what are they?

The way we perceive organisations affects the way we approach managing in them and how we respond to organisational issues. Since late Victorian times organisations have commonly been regarded as being like machines, seen as closed systems, in isolation from the wider environment and other influences. This led to an absolute approach to management, which looked for rigid rules, regulations and processes that would deliver the required results in all circumstances.

This style of management is very evident in Weber's concept of bureaucracy.[6] Weber emphasised rational systems of management with clear, transparent rules and procedures. Bureaucratic approaches dominated local government until the 1980s and are still very apparent.

Recent writers, such as Gareth Morgan, have stressed how the way we see organisations affects our understanding of them.[7] Our understanding is framed by the mental image we use to describe organisations. Morgan suggests that most people use one of a small number of metaphors to see, think about and describe organisations, including:

● **Organisations as machines:** designed to achieve pre-determined goals, ordered, rational. We talk of things 'running like clockwork', 'breakdowns', 'repair'. People are components in the machine and tend to be viewed mechanistically or as an impediment to the smooth operation of the machine (as in 'running this project would be easy if it wasn't for the people').

● **Organisations as organisms:** the organisation is like an organism, with a life cycle and a complex relationship with its environment. Its parts are interconnected, and the whole is much greater than the sum of the parts. The organism learns by doing and is able to do more, better. It is continually replenishing itself, so does not break down (except under extreme duress!). The environment is dynamic and constantly changing.

● **Organisations as brains:** the organisation acts as a brain, receiving, processing and learning from information. The brain is self-organised rather than pre-programmed. In this metaphor the organisation can be seen as a network of connections through which information flows and ideas emerge. The internet is an example of how this might operate. Ideas, opportunities and 'values' emerge spontaneously as a result of joining things. An organisation of this sort cannot be controlled from above – the manager's task is to keep making the connections and ensuring that information flows through the system.

● **Organisations as cultures:** the organisation is seen as a collection of ideas, values, behaviours, norms, rituals and beliefs. Many aspects of culture are implicit – the new member of the organisation has to work out what is important by interpreting the cultural norms and symbols. The behaviour of 'heroes', what is celebrated and how, what is rewarded and what is punished, all act as powerful communicators of the culture. Organisations working as cultures are held together by a shared set of values and beliefs, which may be implicit or may be made very explicit as in mission statements (see almost any youth service or voluntary organisation), statements of

6   Weber, Max (translated by A. M. Henderson and Talcott Parsons) (1947), *The Theory of Social and Economic Organisations*, New York: Free Press.
7   See Morgan, G. (1986), *Images of Organization*, London, Sage Publications.

principles (see the Connexions service[8]), and statements of values or practice (see, for example, the Nolan principles of public life[9]).

● Organisations as political systems: the organisation is a complex mix of groups and individuals with conflicting interests seeking to win and use power. This metaphor assumes that there is conflict and struggle between the various interests. It is in marked contrast to the unitary (all share same overriding interests) view that characterises the machine, organism, brain and culture metaphors.

The implications of each of the five metaphors are set out in table 3.4.

Table 3.4: Five ways to see an organisation

Metaphor for the organisation	Roots	Implications for youth workers	
		Regarding management	Regarding Organisation
Machine	Scientific management and rational approaches to management – bureaucracy, management by objectives, etc.[10] Stresses rational planning, order and control.	Priority is performance. Concern with targets and delivering pre-set outputs efficiently. Transactional leadership used.	Concern for order and control. If all the pieces fit properly and are in order, the organisation will work well. A unitarist view.
Organism	Draws from cybernetics, biology and ecology. Emphasises continual change and adaptation to the environment. Solutions emerge from complex interactions. Stresses the inter-relationship between all parts of the system.	Stresses the importance of seeing the system as a whole. Keeps clear outcome in mind but uses a flexible range of styles to achieve it. Delegates and empowers. Transformation and transactional.	Emphasises the links between different parts of the system. Lots of communication. Information technology very important. Fluid, flexible and dynamic. Holistic view.
Brain	Draws on computing, information technology, neuroscience. The organisation is seen as an information processing system. The parts organise themselves (in the way that a brain develops). The brain learns – inquiry and self-criticism are vital.	Managers ensure information flows and connections are made. Emphasis is on limits and constraints (rather than ends and targets). Solutions emerge like thoughts. Emphasis is on leadership.	The organisation is seen as self-organising. Connections enable it to process information. Action emerges (rather than being planned). The network is unitary – all in it share a common purpose.
Culture	Human relations school of management;[11] sociology. Emphasises shared commitment to common values, vision and beliefs. Has a unitary view – 'we're all in this together'.	The role of the manager is to establish and sustain the culture. Strong emphasis on people in the organisation. Transformational leadership with clear statement of overall purpose.	Organisation is seen as unitary – everyone shares an interest in its health and wellbeing. Seeks commitment and belief in the organisation. People work in teams. Sense of sharing and joint enterprise.
Political system	Political science and theory. Emphasises the existence of many different interest groups, each seeking power and influence and in a continual struggle for supremacy.	Negotiates deals with different interest groups in order to secure power and resources. Emphasises the interests of stakeholders. Transformational and transactional.	Composed of different interest groups seeking power and influence. A plural view.

8   DfEE (2000) Eight principles of Connexions in *Connexions: The Best Start In Life for Every Young Person*, London: DfEE.

9   Available from www.archive.official-documents.co.uk/document/parlment/nolan/nolan.htm (1996).

10 Taylor, Frederick (1911), *The Principles of Scientific Management*, New York: Harper and Brothers. Taylor proposed that it is possible to analyse all jobs scientifically, break them down into component parts and manage people to deliver each part. This led to production lines eg. in the Ford Motor Company.

11 For example Mayo, Elton (1933) *The Human Problems of an Industrial Civilisation*, New York: Macmillan. The human relations school recognised that people were motivated by social concerns: belonging, commitment, cohesion, etc. Other key writers include MacGregor (1960), Maslow (1954) and Hertzberg (1959).

Morgan suggested several other metaphors. One of particular interest to managers involved in education and seeking change is the idea of **organisations as psychic prisons**. This rather alarming description sees the organisation as a psychic phenomenon – it exists in the minds of people as much as in day-to-day concrete reality. In this metaphor people can become trapped in the prison of their imagined idea of the organisation. This can be limiting and destructive. When managers seek to change an organisation they frequently run into the limitations of the psychic prison – people are unable to see how things could be different.

Morgan quotes Plato's Cave[12] as an example of a psychic prison. It is described below as it seems very relevant to educational work with young people.

Reflection

Do you see any psychic prisons among the staff in your organisation?

Some starters you might explore:
- Management is by its nature oppressive.
- All young people are free to choose whether to enter into a relationship with youth workers.
- Commerce and industry is automatically bad.
- The idea of equality of outcome.
- Social control is a bad thing.

Plato's Cave

The Greek philosopher Plato gives us an allegory of a cave to allow an exploration of reality, appearance, knowledge and understanding.

Picture an underground cave with its entrance, a long one, open to the light across the whole width of the cave. People (prisoners) live in the cave from childhood with their legs and necks in bonds so that they can only see in front of them and are unable to turn their heads around. They are facing the back wall of the cave, away from the entrance.

The only light comes from a fire burning outside the entrance to the cave. Between the fire and the prisoners there is a wall behind which people are moving, carrying all sorts of objects. The light from the fire projects an image of the people and the objects they carry on to the back of the cave where the prisoners can see it. The prisoners also hear sounds from the people outside. The prisoners equate reality with the strange shadowy images they see, and they connect the sounds to the images as best they can. Reality and truth for the prisoners are limited to the images they see and the sounds they hear. The prisoners are able to construct a reality from this, through talking with each other, naming the things they see and trying to make sense of it.

Imagine that one prisoner is released and leaves the cave. The prisoner is confronted with a different reality. It is possible that the prisoner would find the brightness of the light and the strangeness of the new reality too much, and simply return to his cave. Suppose he does venture out and explore the new reality. If he returns to the cave, he can never again see the images on the wall as the truth. But if he tries to explain to the other prisoners that what they see is false he will likely be ridiculed. The cave dwellers' reality is the cave with its dark shadows, not the 'real' world outside.

For Plato the cave stands for the world of appearances and ignorance, with the journey outside representing learning and knowledge.

We often assume that people want to pursue knowledge and wisdom. Many are trapped in their psychic prisons and will actively resist attempts to draw them outside to witness a different reality. Managers may find it helpful to reflect on Plato's Cave when seeking to change their organisations.

---

12 Plato (1941) *The Republic*, Oxford, Clarendon.

A systems approach to analysing the organisation

Having looked at the nature of organisations in general and how we see them, we now consider in more detail an organic systems model for thinking about the elements that make up an organisation.

The US consulting firm McKinsey developed a systems approach to analysing the organisations with which it was working. It viewed the organisation as a system of interrelated and interdependent parts and argued that an effective manager should be aware of the impact of change in any of the seven main areas of the organisation. The McKinsey 7S Framework provides seven headings (the seven Ss) as a way of exploring each aspect of the organisation and seeing how they interrelate.

Figure 3.5: The 7S Framework

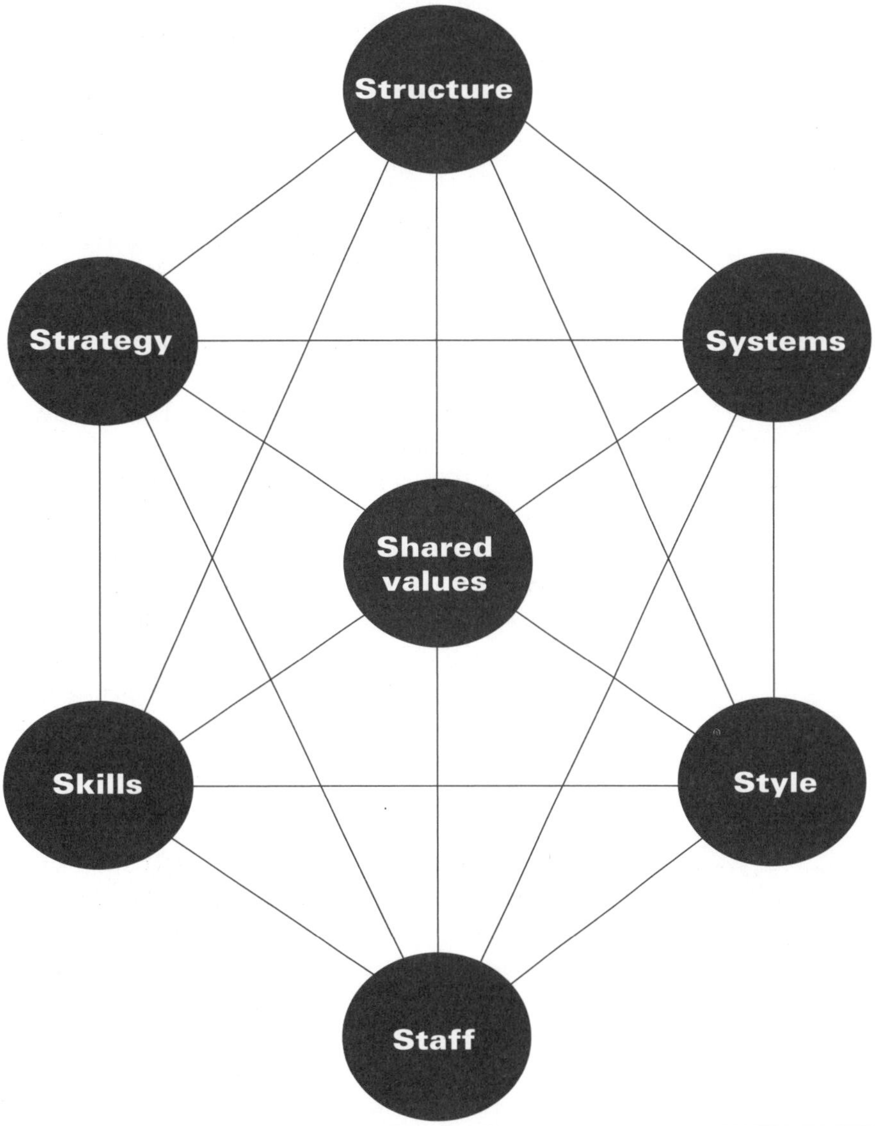

Each of the seven Ss is explored below.

1. **Shared values**

    An effective organisation has a clear, shared set of values that guide the way it works. These should be visible in everything the organisation does. The values are closely related to the organisation's purpose, which also needs to be clear to all concerned.

    What are the values of the organisation (eg what is important, what matters to it, what are the underlying views of the world)? To what extent are they shared by all those involved? How do you know? What are the outward signs of the shared values being put into practice?

2. **Strategy**

    There should be a clear strategy to achieve the organisation's purpose.

    Is there a clear strategy? Does everyone know what it is? Does it lead to clear goals at all levels of the organisation? Can the progress towards the goals (and the strategy) be easily measured and understood?

3. **Structure**

    The structure of the organisation should help it to deliver its purpose. Each part should add to the organisation's capacity to do its job well.

    Is the structure of the organisation fit for purpose? Is it clear and understandable? Do the parts of the structure fit together so that they all add value to it?

4. **Systems**

    Every organisation needs to have efficient and effective systems in place, for example for managing staff, creating a safe and healthy environment, communicating between people in and outside the organisation, involving young people in decisions, and gathering and using information.

    Does the organisation have systems and agreed procedures that cover its main activities? Do the systems work? Is everyone in the organisation clear about them? Are they reviewed regularly and improved as a result?

5. **Staff**

    The organisation needs to have the range of staff that will enable it to be effective. This includes staff at different levels, in different roles, covering different functions, bringing different experience and perspectives and so on.

    Does the organisation have the right jobs (ie are all the jobs helping to achieve its purpose)? Do the current staff roles cover all that needs to be done? Are there any gaps? Are the staff deployed so as to make best use of their roles (eg do professional staff spend too much time doing administrative roles? Do staff roles fit the times and locations that best suit the service users?).

6. **Style**

    Every organisation develops a distinctive style or culture – the way we do things around here. It is vital that the culture fits the values and the purpose of the organisation. For example, if the organisation believes in involving young people in decisions that affect them it would be expected to show this in all aspects of its work. This would not fit well with an organisation that excluded young people from its decision making.

7. **Skills**

An organisation needs to have the skills – both in its staff and as a whole – to be good at what it does.

Do the staff possess the skills individually to be effective in their work? What does the organisation do to develop these skills? Does the sum of the staff's skills give the organisation all that it needs to be effective?

Managers frequently make the mistake of trying to change one part of the organisation without considering its impact on the other six Ss. Perhaps the most common example is the imposition of structural change. In our work with youth services, over three quarters had been through significant structural change in the last two years. Few had coupled this to a systematic process of organisational change that would have dealt with issues arising in the other six Ss.

The model has wide applicability in the public and voluntary sectors. For example it has been used as a basis for guidance on building successful urban partnerships[13] and is used in the guidance *Hear by Right*, on involving young people in decision making.[14]

The importance of organisational values

The shared values of the organisation lie at the heart of the 7S model. In an increasingly fragmented world the values of the organisation bind its people together. When someone agrees to join the organisation they agree to accept and abide by its values.

An organisation's values are those things, behaviours, people, principles, beliefs and so on which are accorded value in the organisation. They are a vital part of the organisation's culture and cannot be separated from the values held by the individuals in the organisation or from the prevailing values in the society outside the organisation. Different things are valued differently in different societies and organisations. We explored the nature of values and their relationship with culture in Chapter Two (see page 23).

Youth work organisations are value, rather than profit, driven. They exist to achieve value based results in the world. One of the key roles of the modern leader in a value driven service or organisation is to manage the organisation's values. We explore the central task of managing values in Chapter Five.

The importance of organisational culture

The other aspect of the 7S model we want to draw out in more detail is that of style or culture. Rather than accepting the culture as a given, an effective manager will take steps to build and develop the culture that best fits the organisation's purpose and values.

Organisational culture has been described as 'the way we do things around here':

> *... the deeper level of basic assumptions and beliefs that are shared by the members*

---

13 Russell, Hilary (2001) *Local Strategic Partnerships: Lessons from New Commitment to Regeneration*, Bristol: The Policy Press.
14 Wade, Harry; Lawton, Anthony and Stephenson, Mark (2001) *Hear by Right, Setting Standards for the Active Involvement of Young People in Democracy*, Leicester: The National Youth Agency.

of an organisation, that operate unconsciously, and define in a basic 'taken for granted' fashion an organisation's view of itself and of its environment. It's the way organisational members behave and the values that are important to them.[15]

Knowing your organisation, which includes being clear about how others – both internal and external – see it, is a crucial base from which to manage the culture and change it where necessary.

More recent work in schools by the Hay Group[16] carried out for the National Centre for School Leadership has used a different and more powerful definition of organisational culture: those things that are held to be true, and those things that are held to be right. This work has identified a number of cultural norms which are found in higher performing schools

The relationship between culture and performance

The Hay Group research identified 15 components of organisational culture and explored whether there were differences between the components seen by staff as most characteristic of their school, in schools which had been found to be performing at different levels. The research found that there were significant differences in the perceived cultures between successful and less successful schools.

The results show that all schools are defined by cultures which focus on measurement which reflects the external environment. They also all value working together and learning from each other. Successful schools are however distinctive in that they:

● have a hunger for improvement and are ambitious for all students. They expect staff to be prepared to make personal sacrifices to put pupils first;
● do not believe in making allowances for good effort without results and are significantly less tolerant of mistakes. While they are not without warmth and humour, staff comfort is not a defining feature of their ethos; and
● are more likely to take value-added seriously.

They have disciplined, goal-oriented cultures with a strong sense of mission and a strong sense of who the school is for. Being a 'nice place to work' is not their raison d'être. Above all they are ambitious, believing they can equal the best in the world. They are ambitious for every pupil, not just those with the greatest potential.

This 'hard' culture is tempered by a collaborative approach to work which stresses support for, and learning from, each other. There is not a narrow focus on targets. They also believe in building learning capability in the pupils and adding value to every individual.

Whilst Hay only looked at schools we consider that there are lessons for all leaders of public services in their findings. Youth work managers who are leading their services should look at the culture and ask themselves whether it corresponds to the features of high performance.

Johnson and Scholes' developed a different model of organisational culture[17]. This has at its core values, beliefs and attitudes, which we have explored earlier. Influenced by and stemming from your organisation's values, beliefs and attitudes are:

15 Johnson, G. and Scholes, K. (1993) *Exploring Corporate Strategy*, London: Prentice Hall.
16 Hay Group
17 Ibid.

- **Stories** – What are the stories in your organisation and what core beliefs do they reflect? How pervasive are these beliefs through the levels and departments of the service or organisation? Do the stories relate to strengths or weaknesses; to successes or failures; to conformity or mavericks? Who are the heroes and villains? What norms do the mavericks deviate from?
- **Routines and rituals** – Which routines in the service are emphasised and what behaviour do they encourage? What are the key rituals and what core beliefs do they reflect? What do training programmes emphasise? Is it easy to change routines and rituals?
- **Symbols** – What language and jargon is used and how accessible is it? What aspects of strategy are highlighted in publicity? What status symbols are there in the organisation? To what extent do symbols emphasise conformity? Are there particular symbols that denote the organisation?
- **Power** – How is power in the organisation distributed and on what is it based – legitimate authority? expertise? coercion? control of resources? charisma? personal networks and connections? How does 'who holds what power' influence the beliefs of the service?
- **Control systems** – What is most closely monitored or controlled? What is rewarded in the organisation and what is 'punished'? Are controls related to history or to current strategy? Are there many or few controls?
- **Organisational structures** – Are these flat or hierarchical? mechanistic or organic? formal or informal? Do they encourage collaboration or competition?

Reflection

Use the models of organisational culture described opposite to think about the culture of your service, organisation, unit, etc. How far does the culture fit the values and purpose? Are there any elements that jar?

Charles Handy uses a different way to describe and analyse organisational culture, which focuses on the nature of the relationships and power in the organisation.[18] He identifies four main organisational cultures:

- **Power culture** (the web) in which there is a central dominant person or group. All the organisation's activities are controlled from the centre with connections radiating out from the centre much like a spider's web.
- **Role culture** (Greek temple) in which roles and rules rather than individuals in the organisation are given primacy. This is similar to the idea of bureaucracy described by Max Weber at the end of the 19th century.[19]
- **Task culture** (matrix) in which the organisation is focused on the achievement of explicitly specified tasks (goals). People and roles are organised to achieve the tasks in a matrix of connections which are flat – they cut across the organisation.
- **Person culture (cluster or constellation)** in which the individual is all important. The organisation is there to support and serve the interests of the individuals within it. This form of organisation is common for groups of professionals.

Handy argues that you will find elements of all the above cultures in most organisations but that one type of culture is usually dominant. Each has strengths and weaknesses.

Organisational culture and youth work organisations

The elements of culture highlighted so far apply to all organisations. There may be particular aspects that refer to statutory or voluntary organisations that work with young people. For example:

- Many youth workers are in the work because they identify strongly with young people

18 Handy, Charles (1985), *Understanding Organisations*, London: Pelican Books.
19 See footnote 6.

who are having a tough time with authority. This and the fact some are only interested in 'the real work with young people' (and may themselves have weaknesses in the underpinning administrative tasks) can easily create an 'us and them' climate with management.

- Youth workers are 'on the front line', a long way – physically and psychologically – from headquarters. They often like it that way, although berate management for neglecting them when it suits! Managing at a distance has particular challenges.
- The organisation's 'prime technology' is a strong influence on its culture.[20] If empowerment of young people is your prime technology, then a culture in which not only young people, but also staff, develop an expectation of empowerment, can be a roller coaster to ride.
- The external environment also influences organisational culture. Until recently youth workers have derived some of their identity from a collective sense of battling bravely, but in isolation, on behalf of young people against adult society. There are signs of this cracking, of other services engaging in similar processes with young people, so this 'lone against the world' stance will need re-negotiation.

Reflection

What would you see as the ideal (or necessary) elements of an appropriate culture for a youth work organisation?

Service-providing organisations

Youth work organisations are service providers. We explore here some of the important features of any organisation that provides a service.

What is a service?

A service can be defined as 'Any activity or benefit that one party can offer to another that is essentially intangible and does not result in the ownership of anything.'[21] So offering youth work is a service!

Services have two essential features:

- They are **intangible** – a service is a process or act – no ownership is transferred. This intangibility makes it harder to measure the effectiveness of a service than account for the production of widgets.
- They involve the **simultaneous involvement** of the service provider and the customer. Services therefore combine production and consumption and consist of an interaction between the service provider and the service user or customer. The complex interaction is the service.

Services cannot be stored (they are short lived). Because they rely on an interaction between people, they have built-in variety (they are 'heterogeneous').

All service providers must choose where to focus their efforts. Without doing this it is impossible to make the most strategic use of your resources. Robert Johnston from Warwick Business School has developed a number of useful tools for thinking about services.[22] He describes a service as having a customer and an operational perspective, which overlap to give the 'service experience', as shown in figure 3.6.

Managers must retain an overview of the whole service, but they will spend little of their time in the shared square of the service experience. There is a therefore a risk for all services that managers will become operations focused rather than customer focused. Recent classic examples of this include the huge fall in profits of Marks and Spencer when

---

20 Bartol, K. and Martin, D. (2000), *Management*. London: McGraw Hill.
21 Kotler, P. (1997), *Marketing: Analysis, Planning, Implementation and Control*, Englewood Cliffs, NJ: Prentice Hall.
22 Johnston, Robert and Clark, Graham (2001), *Service Operations Management*, London, Prentice Hall.

it stopped providing the service its customers wanted, or British Airways when it failed to notice some customers wanted cheap, no frills travel.

For a senior youth service manager, the operational pressure may take the form of demands from politicians for strategic planning or fighting the corner of the service, or fire-fighting crises such as poor staff performance or disciplinary procedures. This creates the danger that the manager takes her or his eye off the quality of the 'service experience'.

Figure 3.6: Components of a service

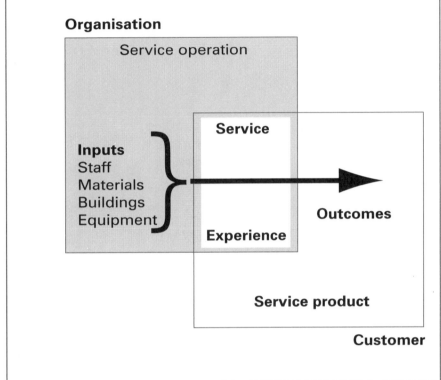

from Johnston and Clark, 2001[23]

This is an adaptation of the Inputs – Process – Outputs – Outcomes model that forms the basis of most of the current systems employed by central and local government and the voluntary sector for performance management (eg Best Value and the Excellence Model which we will look at in Chapter Seven.)

In developing a service the manager must be clear about four critical questions, all underpinned by clarity of the principles and values that lie behind the service:[24]

1. Who is the service for?
2. What is the 'offering'? This is the sum of the 'customer experience' and the outcomes for the customer.
3. What is the service delivery system (the people, premises, materials, processes, equipment used etc.)?
4. What is the desired 'image ' of the service – the position it holds in the minds of the people who may want to use it?

---

23 Ibid.
24 Normann, Richard (2000), *Service Management*, Chichester: Wiley.

These four elements of service provision are mutually reinforcing as shown in figure 3.7.

Figure 3.7: The elements of any service

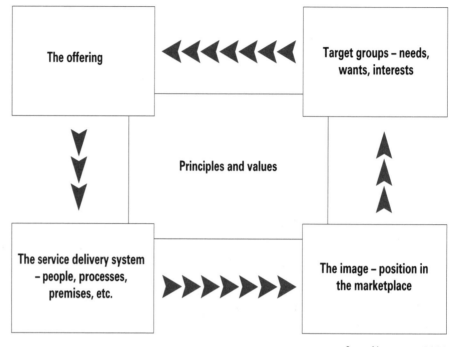

from Normann, 2000

Dilemmas for youth work managers

The statutory youth service has always claimed to be universal. It is open to all young people and premised on a free choice to participate. However, not all young people use the statutory youth service (typically it reaches about 14 per cent of young people).

For many years youth services have been urged to focus on those with greatest need, as a way to make best use of a scarce resource. This focusing has become sharper with the advent of the social inclusion policies of the New Labour government.

Youth services are therefore both **universal** and **targeted**.

This presents a problem when applying the model above, as it is not clear exactly who the service is aimed at. Is it all or some young people? Is the service about mass use or about discrete, varied interactions between professional youth workers and particular young people?

Silvestro et al[25] provide a useful tool for analysing this dilemma, which explores the volume of a service (the number of users) set against the variety of the service offered (see figure 3.8). A highly varied service is one in which the offering to each customer is nearly unique, and is reliant on the skills of a professional (for example, seeing a therapist). A mass service offers a tightly defined service that is the same each time it is used (such as the speaking clock, or a meal at McDonald's). Here the staff are less skilled and are expected to deliver tightly specified action.

---

25 From Silvestro, R., Fitzgerald, L, Johnston, R. and Voss, C. (1992), 'Towards a Classification of Service Processes', *International Journal of Service Industry Management*, vol. 3, pp62–75, quoted in Johnston and Clark.

Between the extremes of professional service and mass service lies the idea of the 'service shop'. This offers the users a more standard formula with some unique elements. An example would be a health club that offers a range of services in a standard package, but with a degree of customisation possible to meet individual needs. In a service shop some of the tasks usually carried out by highly qualified professionals are delegated to 'semi-professionals' at lower cost.

Another example might be a health centre, in which a range of professionals provide services that are shared out across professional demarcation lines so as to meet patient needs most effectively. Nurses and paramedics may take some of the tasks from the doctors.

Figure 3.8: The Volume–Variety Matrix

Reflection

Look at figure 3.8 and consider where your youth organisation or service lie on the continuum.
How far are you a professional service, a service shop or a mass service?
It is interesting to map the Connexions service onto the same continuum.
If you work in a voluntary organisation, do you face a similar set of dilemmas in deciding whether you provide a mass (universal) service or a low volume, varied and professional one? If you aim to provide both, how in practice do you manage effectively?

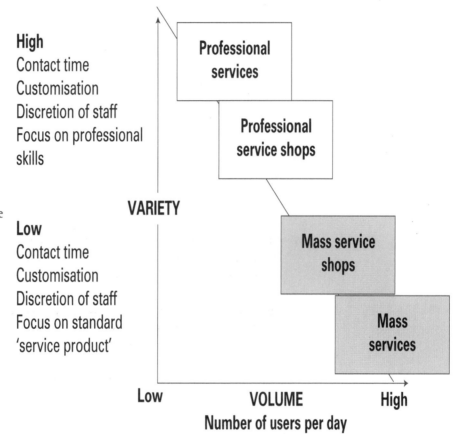

Silvestro et al, 1992

Focusing the service

How does a service focus its activities to best effect? This is a key issue for youth work organisations, which are generally poorly resourced and aim to meet the needs of, potentially, a mass audience.

Johnston again provides a useful framework. He sets the range and variety of services against the number of markets served (see figure 3.9). The 'number of markets' can be translated as the number of target groups of young people served.

Figure 3.9: Four service concepts

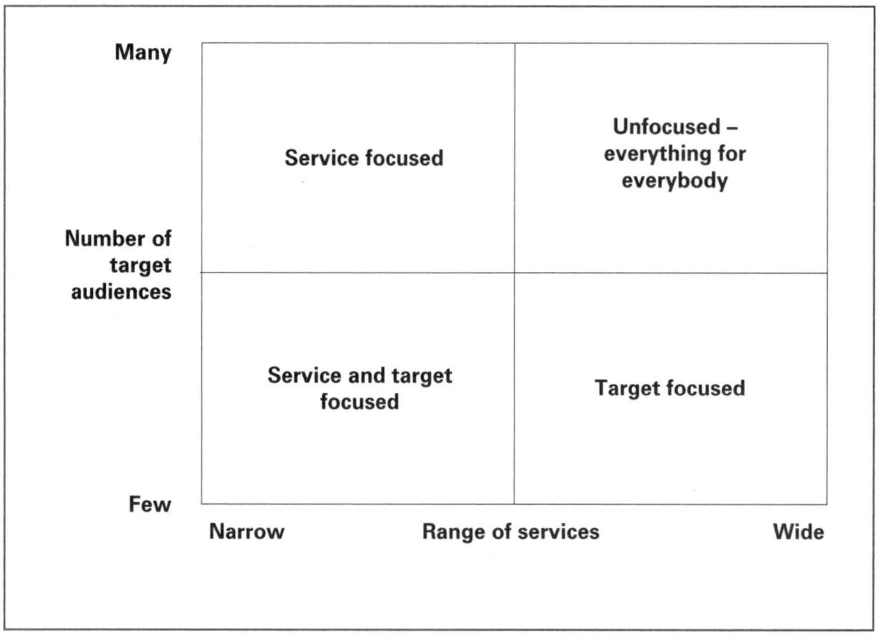

After Johnston and Clark, 2001[26]

- The service focused organisation provides a tightly focused service to a wide range of target audiences. An example would be the Duke of Edinburgh's Award.
- The target focused organisation offers a wide range of services to a narrow audience. Many youth centres fall into this category, by virtue of geography. A youth project aimed at Muslim girls would also fall in this box.
- The service and target focused organisation has a narrow, tightly defined service offered to a particular target group. An example might be an initiative to develop cricket for a group of inner city children, or the provision of an after school homework club for children at risk of exclusion.
- The final category appears to be the mindlessly optimistic organisation – all things to everybody. However, many of the most successful service organisations can be put into this box, for example Disney, Tesco and Virgin. On closer examination these organisations succeed by focusing the component parts tightly on one of the three other service concepts. The added value is brought by the scale of the whole organisation, giving it power to bulk buy, provide high quality centralised support etc., and its management expertise. A large and well-resourced youth service might fit into this category.

The other way an organisation can operate successfully in the 'all things to everybody' square is for the staff to be skilled at providing a variety of services, which can meet the needs of the varying target audiences. A small youth service with well-developed staff might fit into this category.

Public services

In a marketplace individuals and organisations develop goods and services in response to people's wants and needs and their ability to pay. It has been recognised even by the most radical free marketeers that the free market does not in itself meet the needs of all citizens

---

26 See footnote 22.

(particularly those with the most limited resources) and requires some level of regulation (including some by UK Government).

Public services have grown up as a result of a collective desire to make sure that certain needs are met by gathering money centrally (usually through taxation levied by central and/or local government) and using this money to provide services for the general public good. This has broadly divided into universal services (such as roads, healthcare, education and police) and services targeted on those most in need (such as council housing, social security and disability benefits).

Most public services have traditionally mainly been provided through public agencies, which applied bureaucratic approaches to service delivery. As people in developed countries grew used to greater choice and responsiveness in the marketplace many public services began to appear inflexible, unresponsive and expensive. There was consequent pressure for change. The New Labour government was voted to power in 1997 and again in 2001 to a large extent on its pledges to improve public services.

Professor John Stewart, of Birmingham University's Institute for Local Government (INLOGOV) has argued that the private sector is driven by the need to create demand, whereas the public sector is driven by the need to ration use. This division summarises a key strategic dilemma facing policy-makers and managers in public services – how to offer a flexible, responsive, user centred and high quality service, without creating demand that cannot be met. The great danger with any process that emphasises rationing is that the focus shifts away from meeting need (or demand) and towards the process of rationing itself.

If neither markets alone nor public bureaucracies are seen to be effective at delivering public services, then what approach should services be taking? A new way of working somewhere between traditional bureaucracies or hierarchies and the marketplace is emerging. As we will see later, much of the UK Government's thinking and policy on partnership relates to the development of this new way of working.

John Bryson, a professor of public sector leadership, is quoted by Osbourne and Gaebler:

'In the past, we let markets work until they failed; then we responded with public bureaucracies. We're struggling to figure out a new way, somewhere between markets and public bureaucracy. So far, there's no theory guiding it. People don't have a real clear idea of why past practices aren't working, or what a new model might be. So they can't learn from success or failure: there is no theoretical framework people can use to integrate their experiences.[27]

Choice and voice

In a free market, the key relationship is between the purchaser and the supplier or provider of goods or services. The purchaser has the power to go elsewhere if unsatisfied (**choice**) or to complain to seek an improved service or redress (**voice**).

In a public service, this direct relationship is broken as the user or receiver of a service seldom pays for it directly. This is also true for most voluntary organisations. Consequently, users of public services tend to be reliant on voice (complaint and influencing). This is

27 Osbourne, D. and Gaebler, T. (1992) *Reinventing Government: How the Entrepreneurial Spirit is Transforming the Public Sector*, Reading, MA: Addison-Wesley.

Reflection

What is your view of the nature of public services? Where does it come from? Is the change described in public service provision a real one, or a temporary fashion?

Do you accept the separation between public control and accountability, on the one hand, and delivery by any agency that delivers well on the other? If public services are about rationing demand, how can they also be responsive to changing need?

How can you, as a manager, balance the need for accountability with the provision of services for young people which are free to take reasonable risks?

reflected in, for example, the current emphasis on consultation with and participation by young people in decisions about the Connexions service. This emphasis on users is a public service version of the shift in the commercial world towards emphasising the importance of the customer.

There has been a consistent process over the last quarter of a century that has questioned whether public services should necessarily be provided by the public sector. What matters is the quality and value of the service provided (particularly as judged by its users), not who delivers it. The requirement of Best Value follows the principle that services should be provided by whoever is best able to provide them and should be competitive in terms of both price and quality. Best Value brings a consumerist approach to the heart of public service management.

Delivering a modern youth service in England

The UK Government set out in 2002 a clear specification of what a local authority youth service should look like in Enlgand.[28] This was described as a 'once in a generation' leap forward and establishes benchmarks for the performance of youth services.

The youth service is described as a 'complex network of providers, community groups, voluntary organisations and local authorities'. This is a much broader description of the youth service than has typically been used in the past and sets managers the challenge of gathering sufficient information about the vast range of voluntary youth work which takes place in any given area.

Whilst representing a significant change in the position and acceptance of youth services, *Resourcing Excellent Youth Services* continues to present managers with the dilemma of delivering universal and targeted services on very restricted budgets. Youth service managers are expected somehow to provide youth work opportunities for all young people. This has never been achieved (approximately 14 per cent of young people appear to use local authority youth services in England). A consequence has always been for youth work managers to pay lip service to the idea of universality whilst focusing their attention on a number of targeted projects or activities. As we have seen in this chapter, effective service management requires absolute clarity about where to put the best efforts of the service.

---

28 *Resourcing Excellent Youth Services.* Ibid.

Chapter Four:
Strategic thinking, planning and managing change

Introduction

Services which work with young people in the UK and in many other parts of the world are in a state of rapid change and development in order to meet young people's needs most effectively. More than ever before, managers of organisations working with young people need to be strategic and be able to manage the changes necessary to convert their strategy into action.

This chapter explores the concept of strategy, introduces strategic thinking tools and applies them to some of the key strategic dilemmas currently facing senior youth work managers.

This chapter focuses on the centre of the management model – building your understanding of the concept of strategy. This is linked to the top right hand quadrant of the model (Set purpose, strategy and standards), with some consideration of scanning the environment.

The chapter covers:

● Being strategic
● Strategic thinking
● Applying strategic management to youth work organisations
● Converting strategy into action
● Managing change to deliver your strategy

Finally we explore the manager's role in the active management of the organisation's values and its culture.

Figure 4.1: The experiential cycle

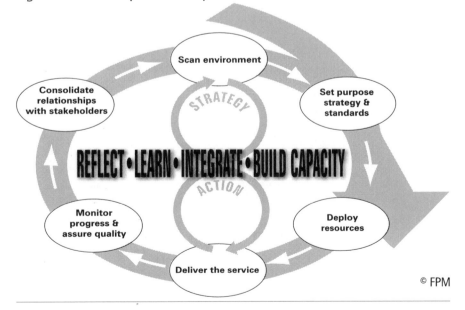

© FPM

Being strategic

What is strategy?

Tim Brighouse, Director of Education for the City of Birmingham, has described strategic thinking as 'seeing the other side of the mountain'.

Strategy is a simple concept: you see the other side of the mountain, then takes steps to get there. Figure 4.2 illustrates this.

Figure 4.2: Seeing the other side of the mountain

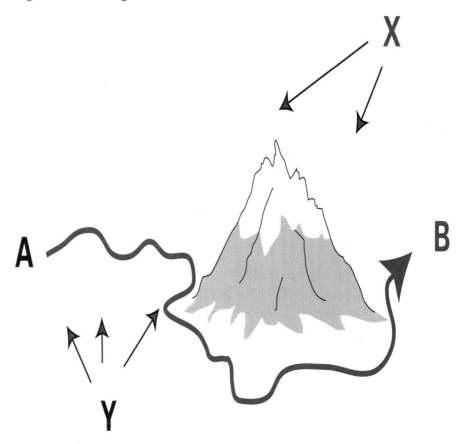

Strategy involves being clear about where you start from (A), being clear about where you want to get to (B) – in line with your purpose – and plotting a course to get from A to B whilst being aware of the forces in the external and internal environments that might throw you off course, (X and Y – the equivalent of wind and terrain). The strategic manager is able to adjust the course to keep pursuing the strategy, sometimes even abandoning the original course to take an entirely new one (such as going over the mountain rather than round it).

Strategic management is concerned with the formulation and implementation of strategy within organisations. Strategy combines:

- awareness of the external environment
- clear purpose
- capacity to deliver (core competencies ie is competent and effective in all areas of the 7S Framework – see page 45)
- flexibility of action (effective plans to implement the strategy and the capacity to respond quickly to changes in the environment).

Many private corporations devoted a great deal of time during the 70s and 80s to complex forecasting and constructing detailed long-term plans. The success of this approach was mixed – humans are not good at making predictions, things seldom work out how we planned. Many strategic plans were out of date before they were printed. Since then there has been a marked shift to a more flexible way of creating strategy. The new approach appears to focus strongly on values and purpose at the top of the organisation. There is a shift away from seeing the organisation as a machine and towards the other metaphors such as culture, organism or brain (see page 42).

The more recent approaches to strategy have moved away from the idea that the organisation should seek to determine its long-term actions and mould the world to suit, towards the idea of emergent strategy. This concept derives from advances in the science and technology of complexity, which suggest that order and progress arise spontaneously out of chaotic systems. Rather than seek to control the chaos, the modern leader engages with it, embraces it and develops an organisational capacity from which strategies can emerge.

Max Boisot[1] describes emergent strategy as:

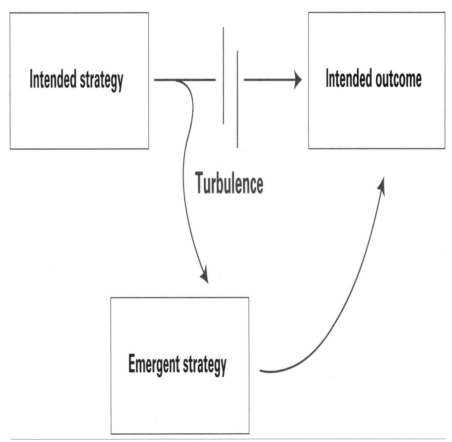

_____

1   Boisot, Max 'Preparing for Turbulence' in Bob Garrett (1996), *Developing Strategic Thought*, London: Harper Collins.

The new strategy emerges as a result of turbulence, which was not predicted. Note that parts of the intended strategy also continue. In cases of extreme turbulence the whole intended strategy may be lost.

Example: The Connexions Strategy

There are some signs that the UK Government is willing to move away from the confines of traditional top-down determined strategy and experiment with emergent strategies. For example, the development of Connexions is a mix of the determined and emergent, with local Connexions partnerships being given some freedom to develop strategies as they emerge within the overall Connexions framework. However, there are considerable tensions in this. More than one Connexions partnership has found that the approaches it developed (emergent) were overtaken by new requirements from the centre. Other services have been frustrated by the lack of central advice about what was required.

Strategic thinking is a deep process that affects every action a manager takes. It is a state of mind. Once a leader or manager acquires the capacity to be strategic, it pervades her or his life. In chess, a great game of strategy, a good player never stops thinking and planning. There is no such thing as an idle move. Every move is directed towards a single clear purpose. All combine to build (one hopes) an irresistible force.

Charles Hampden Turner uses a different analogy – steering a ship – to explore the behaviour of a strategic leader.[2] He suggests an elegant way to combine the elements of determined strategy and emergent strategy.

- The leader is leading so that he can learn and learning so he can lead.
- The ship is erring (going off course) so it must be corrected.
- Steering the ship involves maintaining continuity in the midst of change.
- By keeping the ship on course the leader is the cause of the ship's position, yet is also affected by it.
- Every element of the system (wind, sails, rudder, tides) is independent of the other, yet dependent on it.
- Every element of the system can be analysed as a separate part but combines together as a whole.

Strategic thinking involves, and therefore embraces opposites, conflicts and a degree of chaos. The strategist is resilient in the face of uncertainty. Hampden Turner suggests managers learn to chart the dilemmas on two axes indicating each polarity, for example between cost effectiveness and value added. The chart is used to explore the dilemma. The whole process avoids getting stuck in 'either/or' mode, which is rigid and works against strategic thinking.

Strategic thinking needs to be distinguished from planning. Planning is the means for putting into effect the actions that emerge from the strategy, and occurs after strategic thinking has taken place.

The absence of a clear long-term vision effectively prevents both strategic thinking and subsequent planning.

2   Hampden Turner, Charles (1960) *Charting the Corporate Mind*, Oxford: Blackwell.

Strategic thinking

Strategic thinking is almost impossible if managers do not make time to reflect and think. It is not the same as day-to-day problem solving. If you are enmeshed in operational detail it will be hard for you to think strategically.

Strategic thinking requires that the thinker pays attention to the wider world as well as the world within the organisation. Henry Mintzberg's views on strategic thinking are beautifully summarised in a short article 'Strategic Thinking as Seeing'.[3] He puts forward the idea that strategic thinkers must be able to see things in seven different ways (and more or less at the same time).

1. **Seeing ahead** – a clear vision of the future, what is likely to happen next, based on ...
2. **Seeing behind** – a clear understanding of the past linked to intuition and creativity.
3. **Seeing above** – the capacity to lift the mind above the detail and see the bigger picture, linked to ...
4. **Seeing below** – the ability to see the bits of detail that really matter (Mintzberg talks of finding the diamond in the rough). The playwright Alan Bleasedale captured this part of strategic thinking with the line 'on such small things the world turns'.
5. **Seeing beside** – the capacity to see new ways to do things, make new connections between things, to think laterally and creatively.
6. **Seeing beyond** – having and holding a vision of the future as it might be, inventing a world that would not otherwise be. This relates closely to the capacity to play with ideas, play being characterised by the reorganisation of reality to fit the game, rather than the other way around.
7. **Seeing it through** – all the thinking in the world will be of little use if it does not lead to some action or change.

The capacity to think strategically is something that managers at all levels need to develop. Youth work managers need to have clear strategic thought to be able to make sense of the complex environment in which they work and to fashion their work to achieve the greatest impact.

Levels of strategy

Strategy can be considered at different levels. One metaphor for thinking about the levels is the sea. The strategic thinker is seeking to get to a distant place across the ocean. First there must be a clear vision of the place (even if it is founded more on faith than rationality, as in the case of the early European explorers who set out without maps in the belief that there was 'something out there'). Once the voyage is underway the ship is affected by three main types of current, which Mintzberg has likened to three levels of strategy:

1. **Surface currents** – which are easily detected, can be mapped and taken into account so as not to be pushed off course. These currents may change quite quickly.
2. **Underwater currents** – harder to detect, usually slower moving, but very powerful. Not subject to rapid change.
3. **Deep ocean currents** – very hard to detect, very slow to change but change in them can create a huge impact (eg El Nino, or the cataclysmic predictions of what would happen if the Gulf Stream was reversed).

---

3   Pure Gold: Garratt, Bob (ed.) (1996) *Developing Strategic Thought*, London: Harper Collins.

Strategy may be decided explicitly, and may be written down in some kind of document. However, even if an organisation does not articulate a strategy, this does not mean that it does not possess one. An organisation's strategy is revealed by its decisions and its actions. For many organisations the revealed strategy may diverge from intended strategy.

Example: Strategies affecting youth work

- At a **surface level** managers must think about their organisation's goals, or the particular strategy for youth work in an area or neighbourhood.
- At the level of **underwater current** the manager must consider deeper changes such as the impact of the Transforming Youth Work agenda, Connexions or the National Strategy for Neighbourhood Renewal.
- At the level of **deep ocean currents** the manager must consider the general shifts in the way public services are being organised, the wider global changes to the economy, the position in society, etc.

Ofsted inspectors look at the leadership and strategic management of services that work with young people. Effective strategic managers will need to be able to demonstrate the clarity of their strategy as well as show that their staff understand it and know how to put it into action. We look at the link between strategy and operational plans and targets later in this chapter, on page 67.

The capacity to detect changes in the currents that will affect our strategies has been likened to radar. Good strategic managers will pick up early signals, often intuitively, of the significance of a change for the strategy.

Applying strategic management to youth work organisations

Senior managers in organisations that work with young people must answer the strategic management questions posed earlier:

- Is there a clear, unambiguous purpose in the organisation's work?
- Do you have acute awareness of the external environment and how it is affecting young people and the organisation?
- Are you clear about the organisation's capacities: the things it does really well (its core competences)?
- Is your organisation able to deliver flexible, responsive action?

Clarity of purpose

So what is the business of a youth work organisation or service? Over the years they have suffered from a perception that they are woolly, well-meaning creatures, with a tendency to retreat to the moral and ethical high ground when faced with criticism. In many places statutory youth services have worked to very limited budgets, with limited interest and support from either the public or elected members. In some areas the opposite has happened (as described in Mary Marken's study *High Performing Youth Services*[4]) and work with young people has flourished.

---

4   Marken, Mary (2000) *Higher Performing Youth Services*, Leicester: The National Youth Agency.

Here we explore the clarity of purpose of youth services and youth work organisations.

The purpose of youth work has been described in various ways. The Association of Principal Youth and Community Officers suggested:

Effective youth work creates and utilises educational opportunities for young people so that they can:

● reflect upon issues important to them;
● be challenged and think for themselves;
● learn to articulate their own views;
● be sensitive to the feelings and opinions of others;
● extend or develop, skills, attitudes and values; and
● make informed choices in their daily lives.[5]

The National Youth Agency has described four ways in which youth work helps young people:

1. Assists with their personal and social development through informal education.
2. Supports other agencies to develop styles of work which are effective with young people.
3. Enables young people to have a voice and influence.
4. Operates at the interface between the private worlds of young people and the aspirations of public policy.[6]

A local authority youth service describes its purpose as 'to provide and facilitate informal educational opportunities, which enable young people within its target age range (13-19), to maximise their potential, to respond critically and creatively to their everyday experiences, and to contribute to the cultural and political life of the city.'

Three related but different descriptions; each of which may leave the reader still wondering 'so what exactly is the business of the youth service or youth work organisation? How would I tell if it was any good?'

Mark Smith,[7] writing in 1988 – well before Connexions appeared – pointed out that there is 'a range of ideas about what the proper purpose of youth work might be. Such divergence is inevitable given the various interests involved. Again, there are debates as to the actual functions of youth work. Does it promote the welfare of individuals, serve to secure existing power relations, promote community or what?' He then goes on to describe youth work as educational, expresses concern about its likely demise, and suggests that the concept of youth work is dynamic and constantly reinventing itself.

The examples give a sense of what youth work is about. One would expect to find clarification as to:

● Which young people (all, some, few)?
● Where?
● Which are the highest priority and why?
● What sort of education? Is any sort of personal development allowed? Are all perspectives valued equally? How is the success of the education measured – by input

5   Standing Conference of Principal Youth and Community Officers (1999) *Youth Work Works*, Leicester: The National Youth Agency.
6   The National Youth Agency (1999) *Modern Services for Young People*, Leicester: The National Youth Agency.
7   Smith, Mark (1988) *Developing Youth Work, Informal Education, Mutual Aid and Popular Practice*, Milton Keynes: Open University Press.

or by results? If by results what sort of results are wanted?

There continues to be a real challenge to youth work managers who are being urged to proceed down a managerial route, in describing youth work organisations in ways that fit a managerial perspective. Many appear to retreat – implicitly or explicitly – into professional educator mode and describe a service based on inputs, with results hinted at rather than clearly stated. The voluntary relationship with young people is frequently cited as a defence of this position.

Transforming Youth Work[8] suggests that youth services should:

● Offer quality support to young people, with a clear focus on those aged 13–19 which helps young people achieve and progress.
● Enable the voice of young people to be heard, including helping them to influence decision making at all levels.
● Provide a rich diversity of personal and social development opportunities and choices to young people to include voluntary action, peer support and mentoring.
● Promote 'intervention and prevention' to address the individual, institutional and policy causes of disaffection and exclusion.
● Be well planned with clear aims and objectives and focused on achieving outcomes that reflect the needs and priorities of young people at the local level.

This policy has been extended by a further document, *Resourcing Excellent Youth Services*[9], that introduced, for the first time, a set of national standards for youth work provision for the youth service. These standards were drawn from work undertaken by The National Youth Agency, initially described in the Agency's publication *Quality Develops – Towards Excellence in Youth Services*[10] and youth services were encouraged by the Department to work towards these standards in the context of their total resource allocation.

Work continues to further develop specific youth service performance measures and, in December 2003, the Secretary of State, Margaret Hodge, identified in the Department's Planning Guidance to Local Authority Youth Services for 2004–2005 the following four benchmarks for youth services to work towards:

● The level of reach into the resident 13–19 population (against a benchmark of 25 per cent)
● The level of participation of the 13–19 population in youth work (against a benchmark of 15 per cent)
● The proportion of participants in youth work who gain recorded outcomes (against a benchmark of 60 per cent)
● The proportion of participants in youth work who gain accredited outcomes (against a benchmark of 30 per cent)

The success of the youth service will ultimately be measured against Connexions Performance Indicators and a range of other cross-cutting targets. This means that the youth service strategy will need to be able to deliver results against the **Connexions Partnership Performance Indicators**:

● The proportion of 16 to 19-year-olds in employment, education and training.
● Attendance rates in compulsory education.

---

8 DfES (2001) *Transforming Youth Work*, London: DfES.
9 DfES (2002) *Transforming Youth Work: Resourcing Excellent Youth Services*, London, DfES.
10 The National Youth Agency (2001), *Quality Develops*, Leicester: The National Youth Agency.

- The proportion of the cohort taking part in personal development opportunities.
- The proportion of the cohort who have been helped by a Connexions intervention.

as well as cross-cutting targets:

- Numbers of 16-year-olds obtaining five or more GCSEs.
- Numbers of 19-year-olds achieving NVQ Level 2s.
- Reduction of school truancies by 10 per cent.
- Reduction in number of under-18 conceptions.
- Ninety per cent of those supervised by Youth Offending Teams in education, training or employment.
- Proportion of young people with a drug related problem who are referred to specialist support.
- Local targets (agreed with UK Government Offices) to improve participation amongst a local priority group (for example, minority ethnic community, travellers).

The nature of this ongoing debate on youth work outcomes has been further complemented by The National Youth Agency's publication *Managing for better outcomes in youth work*[11], published in January 2004. This document distils the essence of a national seminar held in November 2003 and some further research on the subject of youth work outcomes and seeks to contribute to the debate about the effectiveness of youth work and, in particular, to move beyond a simplistic consideration of its costs in an attempt to ascertain its value. With greater clarity about the benefits to young people and their communities can come a closer relationship with strategy and with performance management towards ends that are both clear and helpful.

At the same time, The National Youth Agency is also developing 'Kitemarking' as a means to enable youth services to show how they are 'fit for purpose'. This work runs parallel with much of the emerging debate on standards, benchmarks, funding levels and the nature of the involvement of young people that will further require managers to focus strategically on the positioning of their youth service or youth work organisation for the future.

Reflection

How clearly does your organisation or service state its purpose in working with young people?
Is the 'business' clear?
Does anything remain woolly or unclear?
How might it be improved?

For voluntary youth organisations, the strategy will need to include the level of engagement with the statutory sector and, if engaged, how to deliver on similar targets. This will draw on your local voluntary sector compact, relationships with key partnerships (such as the Local Strategic Partnership and Connexions) and so on. The level of engagement may be very high – in one area the whole Connexions service is being delivered by a voluntary organisation. In one London borough the voluntary sector is being commissioned to deliver the bulk of the youth work in the area.

Impact of UK Government strategy

A good strategist develops tools for scanning the external and internal environments to detect changes that will affect the strategy. Examples of these tools are readily available in the publications on strategy in the further reading chapter.

Three significant external developments inform the present and future of work with young people in England:

---

11 The National Youth Agency (2004), *Managing for better outcomes in youth work*, Leicester: The National Youth Agency.

- The Connexions Strategy and Service.
- Transforming Youth Work – an agenda to strengthen and enhance work with young people.
- The Children Bill and Every Child Matters: The Next Steps – an agenda to transform children's services to maximise opportunity and minimise risk for every child and young person.

Connexions was initially seen by many as a threat to traditional youth work, although these fears appear to have diminished. Transforming Youth Work represents an enormous opportunity to extend and develop traditional youth work, integrated and connected to the development of Connexions. The Children Bill is seen as the most far-reaching reform of children's services for 30 years, placing children and their families at the heart of services provided by UK Government. It is closely aligned with proposals for further changes to the standards agenda for health and social services, as well as reform proposals for the Youth Justice system. Their collective impact, both strategically and operationally, on youth services is yet to be clearly identified but there is no doubt that these legislative and associated developments present youth services with an opportunity to position themselves much more visibly in the delivery of effective services to and on behalf of young people.

Whilst using the book you will have the opportunity to focus on strategic dilemmas raised by these three developments. In addition, managers need to be aware of a number of other developments in the world around them. Some are outlined in Chapter 6.

The Transforming Youth Work agenda calls for a number of key changes. Each may have implications for your work as a manager. The main changes include:

- Improving the quality of all services available to young people.
- Improving the clarity of purpose of work with young people so that it produces clear outcomes.
- Improving methodologies for delivering youth work and sharpening recording of achievement.
- Improving staff recruitment, training, development and deployment.
- Ensuring we hear as wide a range of voices in our client group as possible, both in our own organisations and in external agencies and communities affecting their lives.
- Implementing the Youth Service Pledge – which has implications not only for youth work provision but also for your role in interagency activity.

Further to this, the Children Bill sets out the legislative and other changes that the UK Government is proposing with regard to the children and families' agenda, which will encourage partnership working and sharpen accountability by:

- a new duty on agencies to cooperate among themselves and with other local partners to improve the wellbeing of children and young people so that all work to common outcomes;
- a tighter focus on child protection through a duty on key agencies to safeguard children and promote their welfare through new Local Safeguarding Children Boards and a power to set up a new database containing basic information about children;
- clear overall accountability- through a Director of Children's Services who will be accountable for local authority education and children's social services and lead local

change, and a Lead Council Member for Children's Services;

● enabling and encouraging local authorities, Primary Care Trusts, and others to pool budgets into a Children's Trust, and share information better to support more joining up on the ground with health, education, and social care professionals working together based in the same location such as in schools and children's centres;

● creating an integrated inspection framework to assess how well services work together to improve outcomes for children; and

● new powers to intervene in children's social services where an area is falling below minimum standards and intervention is absolutely necessary.

The Bill will also create a Children's Commissioner, a historic first for England, to be a voice for all children and young people, especially those who are most vulnerable. The Commissioner will:

● draw on children's views and make sure they are fed into policy making and service delivery, both locally and nationally;

● advise UK Government and engage with others, such as the media and business, whose decisions and actions affect children's lives;

● work with relevant ombudsmen and statutory bodies to ensure complaints systems are in place and are effective and child friendly;

● at the Direction of the Secretary of State, investigate individual cases that have wider relevance for children; and

● be independent of UK Government and report annually to Parliament via the Secretary of State.

Some of these changes may be delivered through specific initiatives but others will need to be embedded in the organisation's culture. This will lead managers into a process of significant culture change.

Converting strategy into action

The final skill the strategic manager needs is that of converting strategic thought (usually developed by a small group of senior managers) into practical action by all of your staff. This forms the vital task of connecting your strategy to your operational management. One model for understanding this task is the double loop process.[12] This is a central feature of learning organisations – those that 'facilitate the learning of all their members and continuously transform themselves'.[13]

The double loop process is shown in figure 4.3. It enables the manager to visualise and deliver her or his role in connecting the higher level strategy cycle with the actual work on the ground. Many organisations and managers fail to do this and the results are a separation of the strategic from the day to day, such as:

Lots of activity on the ground but without focus or clear priorities. Busy, busy – like a hamster in a wheel.

Staff doing the work do not see how it fits in to the bigger picture (or may not even know there is a bigger picture). This leads to fragmentation and lack of consistent quality. It may affect morale and motivation.

12 See Argyris, Chris (1999) *On Organisational Learning* (2nd edn), Oxford, Blackwell.
13 Pedlar, Mike, Burgoyne, John and Boydell, Tom (1991) *The Learning Company – A Strategy for Sustainable Development*, London: McGraw Hill.

● Senior managers spend their time discussing and refining strategy, producing plans and so on without this connecting to the day-to-day work. Planning becomes divorced from reality and may become unrealistic or be seen as a marketing exercise to secure funding rather than a fundamental process to hold the organisation together.

● The focus of the organisation moves away from action as senior managers attention gets too abstract – they get lost in the stratosphere and suffer from 'paralysis by analysis'.

● The organisation does not learn from successes and failures in a way that really influences its strategy and future direction. It keeps going over the same old ground.

Figure 4.3: The double loop process

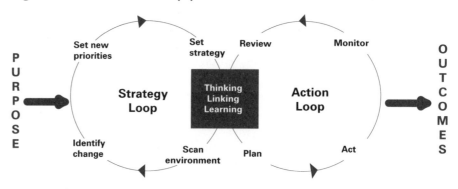

You can use a number of methods in your work as a manager to avoid the pitfalls described above and to build a learning organisation:

1. Keep a clear mental map that includes both loops.
2. Make sure your organisation is effective in both loops.
3. Set clear priorities with unambiguous success criteria (or standards). This makes it easier to set clear objectives and targets at the operational planning level. Staff need to have clear, measurable and deliverable targets, with support to enable them to deliver. Staff also need to know what discretion they have to focus on particular priorities in response to the young people using the service.
4. Communicate the strategy to all your staff in an appropriate way. Don't overload people with pages of high level gobbledegook. but make sure all your staff are clear how their actions contribute to the achievement of the strategy. Do not rely on paper to achieve this. In practice you have three main tools:
   ● Team meetings to cascade the strategy through the organisation; every team meeting should refer to the strategy.
   ● An annual conference for the whole organisation or service to enable everyone involved to hear about the strategy, review what has been learned from action and feed this into the strategy loop, and look at how the strategy will translate into action.
   ● Managing by walking about: getting out and about to talk to staff, get a sense of what is being done, pick up issues and problems and ensure that staff know about the strategy and their role in it. This is not breezing in, saying a few words and breezing out again, but involves spending time with staff, really listening to them and letting them know they are valued members of the organisation.
5. Use the strategy and plans to inform supervision sessions with staff.
6. Make sure that your system for gathering management information (monitoring

progress towards plans) is linked to the strategy – not to some historic convention for information gathering, or to the requirements of outside bodies without reference to your own strategy.

Putting the strategy into action demands good delegation. By providing all staff with a sense of the overall purpose and where they fit into the strategy, it should be easier to delegate authority for delivering action. Effective delegation involves:

● Agreeing clear and deliverable outcomes (linked to the strategy).
● Making sure the people you delegate to have the skills, experience and motivation to deliver. Setting up relevant support and learning to ensure this.
● Agreeing standards for delivery.
● Agreeing the manager's authority and level of discretion to act.
● Agreeing the budget, authority to spend within it and discretion to vary elements whilst keeping within it.
● Setting up a regular reporting process, which looks rigorously at progress to plans.

Your approach will vary depending on the manager to whom you are delegating. We look at different management styles in Chapter 5.

Reflection

Explore the management of your organisation or service using the double loop process. How well does the organisation connect strategy to action? Reflect on the approaches you use to connect strategy to action by your staff. What works and what could be improved? Think specfically about how you delegate. What problems arise? Are there patterns to these problems? How might the problems be overcome – by changing what you do or by enabling your staff to change the way they work?

Once a matter has been delegated, it is up to the person to get on with the work in her or his own way. This may involve mistakes, and the process of delegation should ensure that the risks are reasonable. Too many managers do not let go and delegate with elastic, continuously bouncing back to meddle. Many organisations that provide services to young people face a strategic dilemma. Senior managers need to delegate to the next layer of managers but cannot do so effectively because the managers lack experience and/or skills. This is a consequence of years of restricted funding to support youth work, and appears to be a system-wide issue. It may also reflect an ambivalence to management by managers who feel uncomfortable with taking an active role as a leader, or with working in an organisation committed to empowering its staff. This can result in senior managers getting dragged down into operational matters or inexperienced managers being thrown in at the deep end with consequent risk of failure.

The double loop process constantly draws out things that need to be changed so as to improve your organisation's services. The final part of this chapter explores your role in managing change in order to deliver your organisation's strategy.

Managing change to deliver your strategy

Change is constant. The management task in relation to change is therefore to empower people to embrace change, not to get people to cope with it.

Changes look different to people, depending where they sit: in an under-performing youth service or a high performing voluntary agency or vice versa; in a strategic management role, an operational management role, or as a part-time face-to-face worker; as someone who throughout his or her life has relished novelty and change, or as someone for whom change, whether personal or professional, has made them fearful.

Honest management theorists suggest that for all the studies over the past two decades, there is limited clarity about what works when managing change. It is easier to identify where mistakes have been made. The following model borrows heavily from the work of Kotter,[14] Fullan[15] and Egan[16] and may provide some pointers for those leading and managing change in youth work organisations. It does not form a rigid sequence of steps and in any change initiative managers would need to address several steps, both in parallel and by revisiting them.

1. **Understand where the pressure for change is coming from**
   - This helps you to decide on your response. The pressure may be external or internal. Some change is required – you have no choice – such as responding to Connexions, or Ofsted requirements, or responding to a directive from above. Some change is a matter of choice. Separate the change into 'have to', 'want to' and 'might do'.
   - If the change is under your control (part of your own strategy) are you clear why you want to change and can you explain this to others?
   - It is also worth looking at the Rosemary Stewart model in Chapter 5 (page 79), which describes demands, choices and constraints. Look at the pressure for change and locate it in the relevant area.

2. **Who are the stakeholders?**
   - Who has an interest in, or will be directly or indirectly affected by the change? How might they be affected? Local residents, elected members and staff of other services may be affected, depending on the change, as well as young people and delivery or administrative staff, colleague managers and yourself.
   - Given the greater joining up of services in partnerships and collaborations, you will need to develop considerable skill in managing the various stakeholders affected by particular changes.

3. **Make clear why you need to change and establish a sense of urgency**
   - Frame the need for change as a problem, and then focus on the problem as seen from different angles. This helps to hold off rushing to premature solutions. Saul Alinsky, the US community activist, suggested in his *Rules for Radicals*[17] that if you really examined the problem hard and creatively enough, you would find in it the seeds of a solution. Examining it in this way may clarify whether action would be timely. If so, how do you pose it in a way that focuses people's attention and gets it higher up competing agendas?
   - Involving stakeholders in the early stages of framing the need for change and exploring ideas is a tried and tested way to secure their commitment. Managers often face a dilemma in that they are not given time to do this – change must be delivered quickly, in line with someone else's agenda.

4. **Emphasise the benefits of the change**
   - There is sometimes cynicism in organisations about why management is proposing change. Who will benefit? Is it needed?

5. **Form a powerful guiding coalition**
   - Who will steer this change through the organisation? All the literature suggests that change needs to be a mixture of top down and bottom up. A strategy needs to

14 Kotter, J. (1994) *Why Transformation Efforts Fail*, Boston: Harvard Business Review.
15 Fullan, M. (1993) *Change Forces*, Lewes: Falmer.
16 Egan, G. (1994) *Working the Shadow Side*, San Francisco: Jossey Bass, pp220–223.
17 Alinksy, Saul (1971) *Rules for Radicals*, New York: Vintage Books.

involve in some way – not only through a core group – a mixture of those people who hold different forms of power and influence, staff for whom the experience would be realistically developmental, and key stakeholders.

6. Create a vision for what things will be like and communicate the vision
   - What will the service look like when this change has been brought about? John Kotter,[18] the management guru, suggests that the leader who does nothing else but act as guardian of the vision and values and spends time networking, both internally and externally to promote them, will be doing his or her job.

7. Remember that change is a journey, not a blueprint
   - Change is not easy or linear. You need to develop a problem-solving mentality, a resilience and a fascination with organisational dynamics that sees setbacks as challenges, and addresses them as day-to-day tasks in your role as community development worker in your own organisation.

8. Be aware of the politics
   - Once the form of the initiative is clearer, revisit your analysis of your stakeholders' interests and concerns. Egan[19] suggests it helpful to identify who are our partners in this change, who our allies, who are fellow travellers, fence sitters, loose canons, opponents, adversaries, bedfellows – and who are the voiceless.

9. Empower others to act on the vision
   - Everyone is a change agent. Occasionally some of us fall back into the trap of thinking we have to do everything ourselves, the myth of heroic leadership! Empowering people to act for themselves needs time for all to explore and adopt the vision. It also needs support so that they can grow and develop their capacity to act.

10. Plan in order to overcome resistance
    - There will be resistance even though you have done your best to be sensitive and strategic. Don't be surprised or hurt by it! We address this more fully later.

11. Plan for and create 'quick wins'
    - People need to see outcomes for their efforts to change. Sometimes they will be in charge of this, sometimes they will need your steer – so ensure that experiments or pilots, for example, are given the best chance of success by being directed to areas where change may be easier and accompanied by appropriate (and replicable) resources.

12. Celebrate success and own the emerging challenges
    - Communication in youth work organisations, which often operate from a variety of bases with a predominance of sessional staff poses problems – and demands a high profile. Communicating successes in your change initiative – as well as in the work generally – is a vital link in reinforcing the positives and in developing an upbeat and can-do culture.
    - Where problems do arise the change leaders must own them and act upon them.

Reflection

Think about a change that you have recently implemented. Use the 12 points described to reflect upon it and to identify any places where you might do things differently.

---

18 Kotter, J.P. (1990) *A Force for Change: How Leadership Differs From Management*, New York: The Free Press.
19 See footnote 16.

Changing organisational cultures

One of the key roles of senior managers is to build and sustain the organisation's culture. The skill of managing the culture and managing change in the culture is therefore very important.

Generally you will inherit a culture. A head of a youth service described the culture as 'A proactive, can-do and positive mentality to developing the service, including responding to new demands'. Another might be wrestling with a culture of decline, low morale, low energy and passivity in the face of little support at a political level.[20]

Change is notoriously slow and often difficult to embed. Transforming Youth Work talks of 'encouraging a culture of self-assessment' and later 'local authorities will want to build a culture of continuous improvement'. So how does this occur? The literature of management development highlights the following as ways in which the leaders 'ensure that the beliefs and values that they embody permeate the entire institution'.[21]

● Personal modelling. We suggest that, despite or even because of, the anti-authority stance of some youth workers, they pay particular attention to what management does, often waiting to catch it out so that they can say 'I told you so'! Does how you as a senior manager spend your time have any correlation with your stated values? Peters and Waterman used the phrase 'management by walking about'. How do you demonstrate to full and part-time staff your commitment to their face-to-face work? Project visits can be time-consuming and empty rituals for youth work managers – but if the questions you ask and the things you do on such visits support your development agenda and core values, they are time well spent.
● Quality monitoring and enforcement. Quality stems directly from vision and values. Is your quality assurance a bureaucratic nightmare and a control system, or does it explicitly reinforce a creative approach to the key tasks of the organisation?
● Staff induction. How do you ensure that the full and part-time staff joining your organisation share your service's values? There are untapped seams of potentially very able staff out there. How do we tap into them, present our jobs in a way that will attract them and then induct and support them to the full, once appointed?
● The use of language to symbolise particular institutional attributes and create shared meanings. What key concepts have you found yourself using in reports, in supervision sessions, in your input into whole organisation staff meetings? Are they clear and do they reflect the culture you are seeking to develop?
● Telling the story. Much of culture is communicated as the continuing story of the organisation. This is the everyday description of events that reveals what is important, what has value and so on. The story needs to be continually re-told and refreshed. The way the story is told can be changed – using we (not us and them), celebrating rather than blaming, seizing opportunity (rather than responding to threat), challenging cynicism etc.
● Managing in a way that fits the culture – engaging, supportive, challenging, emphasising co-learning, working to an agenda driven by clarity of organisational purpose and underpinned by shared values.
● Engage effectively with the organisation's 'culture bearers'. All organisations have 'culture bearers'. Nias argues that they are often 'the main custodians of the organisation's past, the repositories of its humour, the stage managers of its presentations, they play a central but supporting role in its ceremonies, understand and attend to the detail

---

20 See footnote 4.
21 Peters, T. and Waterman, R. (1982) *In Search of Excellence*, New York: Harper and Row.

which helps to ensure the smooth and efficient translation of values into action'.[22] Who plays this role in your organisation? Find them, nurture them where possible or, if they represent the old ways you are trying to change, deal with them.

Ralph Kilmann[23] suggests a five-stage approach to culture change:

Reflection

How do you describe the culture of your organisation? What is your evidence?

How is the organisation seen in its stories, heroes, myths and artefacts?

Who are the custodians of the culture? Is the culture they promote positive – is it the same as the one you wish to see in place?

Is the culture as you would like it to be? If not, what steps could you take to change it?

1. **Surfacing the actual norms.** Organisational members list the actual norms (expected behaviours in the organisation) that they believe currently influence their attitudes and actions.
2. **Articulating new directions.** Group members discuss the current direction of the organisation and the behaviours necessary for success.
3. **Establishing new norms.** Group members develop a list of new norms that would have a positive effect on the organisation.
4. **Identifying culture gaps.** Identify areas in which there is a major difference between actual norms and those that would impact on organisational effectiveness.
5. **Closing culture gaps.** Agree new norms and design means of reinforcing them, such as developing reward systems to follow the new cultural norms.

While more mechanistic, the collectiveness of this approach might appeal to youth work organisations if the trust can be established, particularly in stage 1, to elicit open responses.

Managing individual change

The models above focus on change in the organisation as a whole. Managers face a second challenge – how to enable individuals in the organisation to change and develop. People are very often resistant to change. Typical reasons identified in the literature include:

- Self-interest: *'There's nothing in it for me. I might even lose out.'*
- Misunderstanding and lack of trust: *'It's management again following their own agenda. They're never concerned with the real work with young people.'*
- Different assessments of the virtues of change: *'That's not what we should be putting our energy into at this stage. There are loads of higher priorities.'*
- A low tolerance for change e.g. they fear they will be unable to learn new skills and behaviours even though they might agree with it in principle: *'I'll never be able to relate to the young people they say we should be targeting.'*
- They see the change as an indirect criticism of the status quo for which they may feel responsible: *'Can't they see we've been doing our best – with very little help from them, I might add.'*

Individuals or groups go through different stages in relation to significant change. The stages are similar to the grieving cycle described by Elizabeth Kubler Ross.[24] and that the manager needs to adapt her or his style and way of working with the staff member to fit the different stages of the process (see figure 4.4).

There is no simple formula for managing individual change. High quality, accurate listening is vital, as is the capacity to respond flexibly: giving information, facilitation/support, negotiation, participation/ involvement or, in extreme circumstances, explicit or implicit coercion. We look at the range of styles a manager might adopt in Chapter 5.

---

22 Nias, J. (1989) *Staff Relationships in the Primary School*, London: Cassell.
23 Killmann, R. (1985) *Gaining Control of the Corporate Culture*, San Fransisco: Jossey Bass, © 1985, Jossey Bass; reprinted by permission of John Wiley & Sons Inc.
24 Kubler, Elizabeth (1969) *On Death and Dying*, New York: Collier.

Feelings matter. They affect our capacity to change and to respond to others' needs and wants during change. Many managers have led failed change processes for lack of attention to feelings. Change involves a range of feelings, both positive and negative.

Figure 4.4: A cycle of personal change

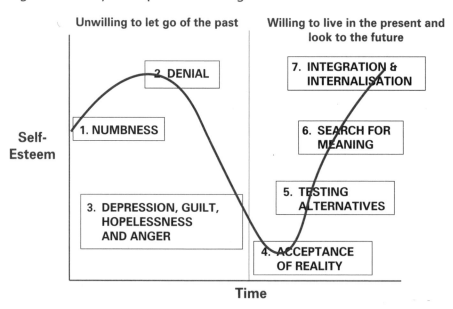

Reflection

What are the main issues and problems you have faced in managing change in individuals?

Look at the cycle of change shown in figure 4.4. Does this accord with your experience of managing change in individuals? Explore the management style and approach you have adopted for staff at different stages in the cycle. In what ways might you change your approach to be more effective?

The 3Rs of emotional literacy provide a useful mental checklist when working with staff who are responding to change:[25]

● **Register** that there are feelings at play.
● **Recognise** what those feelings are (and also, perhaps, where they stem from).
● **Respond** appropriately.

Some managers may find it difficult to focus on the importance of emotion in the workplace – preferring to focus on the task alone. It is worth noting that the rise of interest in emotional literacy has come from the commercial world, and is driven by the usual hard-nosed concern for business efficiency and effectiveness. Effective managers have been found to be emotionally intelligent.[26]

It is very easy for youth work organisations to get caught in the action trap, partly because most youth workers are activists but also, perhaps, because we are uncertain of what really makes for quality and so take refuge in quantity and 'being busy'. Accurate intervention to bring about effective change needs careful collective consideration. Managers need both to preserve reflection time for themselves individually and as a team, and also encourage it in those they manage.

Poor management of individual change can lead to serious problems – both for the individuals concerned (affecting their health and motivation) and for the organisation (leading to disputes, conflict and sometimes legal action). These can be hugely time consuming and detract from the delivery of the organisation's services to young people

25 Orbach, S. (1999), *Towards Emotional Literacy*, London: Virago.
26 Goleman, Daniel (1995) *Emotional Intelligence*, New York: Bantam.

Chapter Five:
Modern management

Introduction

This chapter explores the role of the modern manager. It sets out current thinking and looks in detail at critical aspects of the manager's role, including leadership, leading staff teams, managing the organisation's values and managing diversity.

We also look at the task facing the manager in influencing 'up the line' to line managers, the new political structures resulting from modernisation of local government, or to the board of trustees in voluntary organisations.

The chapter focuses mainly on the centre and right hand side of the management model, building your understanding of yourself as a manager and leader. It looks at how these capacities are used in setting the strategy and standards for the organisation and in motivating your staff. This chapter covers:

- Management
- Leadership
- Leading staff teams
- Managing upwards
- Managing the organisation's values
- Managing diversity, equality and equity

Figure 5.1: The experiential cycle

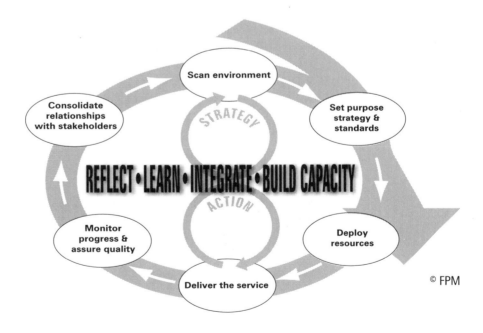

Management

We can define management as '... the attainment of the organisation's purpose in an effective and efficient manner through planning, organising, leading and controlling organisational resources.'[1] Or put another way: 'achieving the organisation's purpose through and with other people'.

The senior manager takes broad responsibility for the work of the whole of the organisation, or of a substantial part of it. In local government the senior manager lives at the interface between the elected politicians who make the policy decisions and the officers who implement them. In voluntary organisations the senior manager straddles the space between the board of trustees, which governs, and the staff team which puts the board's decisions into action.

This calls for skill in understanding the workings of the policy-makers (elected councillors or trustees) and the wider policy environments in which they work, combined with the capacity to lead and delegate effectively to the staff team so that the work gets done.

Like all senior managers, senior youth work managers work between a rock and a hard place. They do very little, if any, of the practical youth work for which they have been trained. Their main focus is strategic, although many senior mangers continue to deliver a considerable amount of operational management. They are no longer one of the 'workers' but do not have complete authority. They are accountable to another manager, or directly to a board or elected councillors. The role is to be caught in the middle. For many, this aspect of a senior management role is never comfortable; for some it is downright miserable.[2]

Our definition separates management into two main parts:

The task

Making sure the purpose (and therefore the task of the organisation) is clear. Achieving the organisation's purpose through ensuring that it has the capacity to deliver its purpose. This includes: managing, building and sustaining the organisation's values and culture; setting aims and objectives; planning; allocating resources; setting standards; developing systems to monitor progress; making sure that information flows effectively around the organisation; harvesting learning and managing knowledge; building relationships with stakeholders; and promoting and accounting for the organisation.

The people

Securing the commitment of others to get the work done: leading, inspiring, motivating, building relationships, building and sustaining teams, developing the organisation's values and culture among its people, rewarding effective work, negotiating.

These two dimensions run through much of the literature on management and leadership. They are interdependent. To be effective a manager needs to be able to vary her or his emphasis on task or people depending on circumstances.[3]

The two roles take place in a wider context – the world outside. It is part of the manager's role

---

1 Based on definition by Daft, R.L. and Marcic, D. (1995) *Understanding Management*, Orlando, Florida: Dryden Press, p7.
2 See 'Do You Really Want to Be a Manager?' in Richard Daft (2000) *Management* (5th edn), Orlando, Florida: Dryden Press, p20.
3 See for example Hersey, Paul and Blanchard, Kenneth (1993) *Management of Organisational Behaviour: Utilising Human Resources*, Englewood Cliffs, New Jersey: Prentice Hall, p197.

to scan and make sense of this and identify how changes will impact on the organisation.

If the role of the senior manager is to do whatever needs to be done to make sure the organisation achieves its purpose, whilst being true to its values and responsive to change in the external environment, three things result:

1. The manager must have a very clear picture of the purpose and values of the organisation. This means understanding the wider context in which the organisation is working and working effectively with those who ultimately decide on the purpose of the organisation – elected members or boards of trustees. In a value led service, such as work with young people, the glue that holds the work together is a shared set of values. The manager must be seen to live up to those values, otherwise authority will be eroded.

   'The most important question in any organisation has to be, 'What is the business of our business?' The answer to this question determines what the organisation should do and what it shouldn't do. The question must be revisited often because the answer can change swiftly. Determining the business of the business is the first step in setting priorities. This is a major leadership responsibility because, without priorities, efforts are splintered and little is achieved.'[4]

2. The manager has an enormous range of roles to play and tasks to fulfil: from setting the organisation's goals, through inspiring and motivating staff, building and sustaining networks of influence, monitoring progress and accounting to others for resources deployed.
   - Managing really is an endless task of engaging in new conversations and opportunities with all the anxieties and uncertainties they bring.'[5]

   The only way I can describe my role is like being a juggler desperately keeping a huge number of objects in the air. I seem to be facing two audiences at once – one above me and one below me. Both audiences are throwing new objects at me, for me to juggle. If I keep the objects in the air people sometimes applaud, but more often I get blamed for dropping things. As I juggle I find the ground I am standing on being altered, or I am asked to move to another room, still juggling. And just when I think I have got a good rhythm going some consultant will arrive, ask me why I am juggling at all, and suggest I should stop and spend more time thinking strategically.' A senior youth work manager

   - The multiple roles played by managers were explored by Harvard professor, Henry Mintzberg[6] who studied what managers actually do. He identified ten roles as described in table 5.2. Interestingly, he puts leadership as part of management. We will explore this later. He stressed that managers need to be effective in all the roles. More senior managers may spend more time on the interpersonal and informational roles, although it is rare to find an escape from the tyranny of disturbance handling!

3. The manager needs to have considerable skill in reading and analysing situations (the frameworks explored in Chapter Four will help with this) so as to play the most effective role at that particular moment to advance things towards achieving the organisation's purpose. This calls for great flexibility. This is by no means a modern idea:

'Similarly, he should encourage his citizens to believe that they can go about their business

4   Judith Bardwick, founder of a US consultancy firm, in Frances Hesselbein, Marshall Goldsmith and Richard Beckhard (eds) (1996) *The Leader of the Future*, San Franciso: Jossey Bass, p134.
5   Streatfield, Phil (2001) *The Paradox of Control in Organisations*, London: Routledge.
6   Mintzberg, H. (1972) *The Nature of Managerial Work*, New York: Harper and Row.

undisturbed, whether it be trading, agriculture or any other profession, so that one man is not afraid to increase his wealth for fear that it might be taken from him, and another is not afraid to start a business for fear of excessive taxes. For a Prince should prepare rewards for those who want to do these things, or for anyone who thinks of any way to make his city or state greater. In addition, at the appropriate times of the year, he should entertain the people with celebrations and performances. And since all cities are divided into guilds or family groups he should bear these groups in mind, meeting with them periodically, showing himself to be humane and munificent whilst, none the less, always firmly retaining the majesty of his position, for this must be maintained at all times.'[7]

Table 5.2: What managers do

Category	Role	Typical activities of senior youth work managers
Interpersonal roles (leading and managing the people)	Leader	Direct the staff team, motivate and inspire commitment to high quality work, ensure that organisation has capacity to deliver.
	Figurehead	Symbolic role in representing the organisation, symbol for the culture of the organisation. Acts as champion for work with young people with the elected members or board; champion for youth work with others outside the organisation.
	Liaison	Connects the organisation to those with an interest in it. Connects the elements of the organisation and ensures that it is linked to the outside world.
Information roles (maintaining and developing the information network)	Monitor	Seeks out information about the wider environment, scans journals, receives internal information, reports, accounts, etc. Keeps in contact with work by 'walking the floor'.
	Disseminator	Ensures that information flows up, down and across the organisation.
	Spokesperson	Gives information about the organisation to people outside and inside who need it (for example to elected members, the board, the press, other service providers, young people).
Decision roles (managing action and day-to-day operations)	Enrepreneur	Identifies and creates new possibilities for work, generates new ideas for improvements; managing change.
	Disturbance handler	Sorts out crises; 'fire-fighting' role; mediates in disputes between staff.
	Resource allocator	Sets priorities for resources allocation; ultimate say in where resources are allocated for day-to-day work with young people.
	Negotiator	Represents organisation in its negotiations with others – rest of local authority, other departments, contractors, partnerships, trades unions, etc.

Adapted from Mintzberg, 1972 (see footnote 6)

7   From Nicollo Machiavelli's classic work *The Prince*, witten in 1513. See Machiavelli (1995, translated by Stephen Milner) *The Prince*, London: Phoenix.

Reflection

Reflect on Mintzberg's description of management – is your managerial life as disjointed as he describes? What strategies do you use to overcome this?
Think about your role as a manager in relation to demands, choices and constraints. How much of your work is spent responding to demands as opposed to being proactive in creating space to make choices? What do you do actively to manage constraints, and push them back?

Examine John Kotter's idea of fluid work agendas (see page 80). Do you operate using similar fluid agendas and building key networks to get things done? What are the strengths and weaknesses of this way of working?

Mintzberg found that in their actual work, chief executives differed drastically from the popular image of reflective, systematic planners. In particular, he found:

● **An unrelenting pace** – the managers began working as soon as they arrived in the office and kept going throughout the day until leaving in the evening. Coffee was drunk and lunch eaten during meetings (an average of eight per day). When not in meetings, they handled up to 36 pieces of mail per day (this was before e-mail!), as well as other communications. Any free time was taken up by anxious subordinates.
● **Brevity, variety and fragmentation** – managers handled an astonishing variety of issues each day, and many were surprisingly brief (half completed in less than nine minutes). Work sessions at the desk and informal meetings averaged ten and fifteen minutes respectively. The managers experienced continual interruption from telephone calls and subordinates. Because of the fragmentation and interruptions, many managers saved their major brain work for times outside the normal day.
● **Verbal contacts and networks** – managers showed a strong preference for verbal contact rather than written communication. For obtaining and transmitting information, they relied heavily on networks (cooperative relationships).

Mintzberg's work (on CEOs in the USA) is confirmed by other studies: Rosemary Stewart[8], studying one hundred managers, found that in four weeks each of them had, on average, only nine half-hour periods without interruption. She described the manager's job as being made up of constraints, choices and demands. She comments that, the manager's job is made up of a mix of doing what you have to do (meeting demands), deciding what to do from an array of options (making choices) all within the context of things that define and limit the job (constraints). The balance of the three elements differs between managers' jobs, although the individual has some discretion in shifting the balance (by pushing back constraints, for example).

Figure 5.3: Constraints, demands and choices

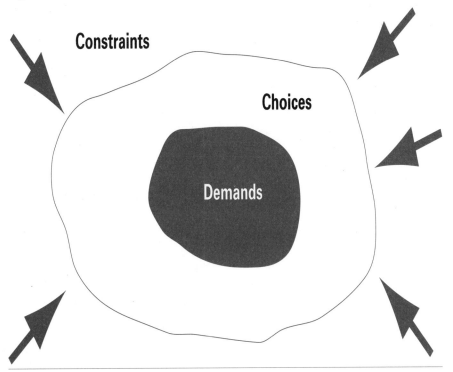

8 Stewart, R. (1982) 'A Model for Understanding Managerial Jobs and Behaviour', *Academy of Management Review*, vol. 7, pp7–13.

Fluid work agendas

So how do managers cope with highly fragmented lives? John Kotter, Professor of Leadership at Harvard University, found that many coped by developing fluid work agendas[9] – loosely connected sets of goals and tasks that the manager is attempting to accomplish. Typically these address immediate, as well as the longer-term job responsibilities, and are used alongside the formal organisational plans.

Kotter found that, in general, managers work hard to establish key networks to enable them to put their work agendas into action. By making use of work agendas and networking strategies, the managers in Kotter's study were able to engage in short, seemingly disjointed conversations and still accomplish their missions.

Senior youth work managers typically face similar pressures of interruption and fragmented work patterns. They may also have considerable room for choice in how they carry out their work, within a framework of constraints and demands (such as plans, standards and other regulatory requirements). It is worth looking at whether you are using your own work agenda, and whether this helps you to maintain your sense of purpose in your fragmented working time.

Personal development in response to uncertainty

The sense of a manager responding to demands ('feeding the beast') whilst making strategic choices, within a context of constraints, has echoes in many prescriptions for personal development. How do we as individuals avoid simply reacting to events so as to exercise choice in, and influence over, our lives? American writer Stephen Covey[10] describes a model for developing personal effectiveness using interlocking circles of influence and concern.

Covey argues that effective people focus attention and effort on the things that they can influence, and in so doing tend to gain more influence. Reactive people are characterised as being focused on the circle of concern. They start with problems and difficulties over which they have no control, seek to place blame and avoid responsibility.

Figure 5.4: Circles of influence and concern

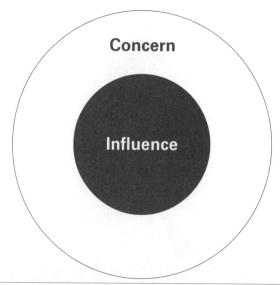

9   Kotter, John (1982), *The General Managers*, New York, Free Press.
10   Covey, Stephen (1992) *The Seven Habits of Highly Effective People*, London: Simon and Schuster.

The way youth work managers react when confronted with change (such as the development of Connexions, the Transforming Youth Work agenda, or the outcomes of the Children Bill) can follow Covey's patterns of behaviour. We have observed some managers who respond by gathering information and looking for ways to influence the change. They seek to seize the agenda, so that their vision of effective services for young people could be advanced. Others have taken the reactive route. They adopt stances of inaction (we can't do anything until we know more about it all ...), negativity (it won't work, they don't understand what we do, etc), through to feeling threatened and victimised.

Reflection

How do you sustain a core of your work (and life) over which you feel you have influence in the face of increasing external concerns?

Leadership

The very highest leader is barely known by men.
Then comes the leader they know and love.
Then the leader they fear.
Then the leader they despise.
The leader who does not trust enough will not be trusted.
But of the best, when their work is done, the people all remark 'We have done it ourselves'.

Translated from Lao Tzu, Chinese Taoist philosopher, c 600 BC

There has been a significant change in how we understand organisations, from orderly, hierarchical and machine-like to 'learning organisations' – flat, fluid and flexible organisations that continually learn, change and develop in response to customers and the fast-changing, complex and often chaotic, external environment.[11]

Managers in all sectors are being asked to embrace this complexity and uncertainty rather than seek to control it. The simplistic approach of 'command and control' from the top down (or centre out) is being replaced in all sectors by new styles of managing that emphasise empowering those staff closest to the service user to make decisions for themselves, so that services can be responsive and flexible. In particular there has been a growing emphasis on the leadership aspect of the manager's role. Managers are expected to be able to lead in new ways, to enable their staff to work well in the new complex environment.

We start with the idea that leadership is a function that managers will be expected to carry out (from the Mintzberg roles of the manager). Leadership can occur outside of managerial relationships. Leaders need not be managers, but managers are increasingly expected to be effective leaders.

Reflection

Start thinking about leadership by answering the question: 'why would anyone want to follow you?'

You therefore need to have a clear idea of what leadership is and how you can deploy your capacities and talents to greatest effect as a leader. Leadership is often characterised as something whose presence you can recognise but is in essence hard to define. I asked my 11-year-old son what he thought made a good leader and he identified 'someone who makes you want to do things, and who helps you when you need it'. Pause for a moment to conjure up your view of a good leader.

Andrew DuBrin[12] describes leadership as 'the ability to inspire confidence and support among the people who are needed to achieve organisational goals'. Management guru and writer Peter Drucker puts it slightly differently:

---

11 See for example Pedler, Mike and Aspinwall, Kath (1988) *A Concise Guide to the Learning Organisation*, London: Lemos & Crane.
12 DuBrin, A. (1995) *Leadership: Research Findings, Practice and Skills*, Boston: Houghton Mifflin.

'The only definition of a leader is someone who has followers. Some are thinkers. Some are our prophets. Both roles are important and badly-needed but without followers there can be no leaders'.[13]

He identifies four features of effective leaders, based on his observations of leaders in organisations:

1. They have followers – people decide to follow them.
2. The followers do the right things to achieve the organisation's goals. An effective leader is not necessarily popular, loved or admired. Results are the hallmark of leadership.
3. Leaders are highly visible. They set examples.
4. Leaders take responsibility for their organisations. They celebrate the work of their followers, and do not blame others when things go wrong.

Drucker suggests that what makes a leader (characteristics or traits) is so varied that it defies tidy categorisation. He does identify consistent behaviours he has observed in leaders.

They energetically pursue the question: 'What needs to be done to achieve our goals?' and identify specific things they can do to make a difference.

They constantly return to the question: 'What is the purpose of all this? What are we aiming to achieve?'

They have a high level of tolerance of diversity and variety, coupled with a fiendish level of intolerance about performance standards and values.

They are not afraid of strength in their staff and associates – they surround themselves with people who are good at what they do.

They live up to their own standards.

Background: thinking about leadership

Traits

Reflection

Rate yourself against Drucker's observed features and behaviours of effective leaders.
Do you know whether others who work with you would rate you in the same way? How might you find out?

Early work on leadership used the approach of natural history: seeking to identify the distinctive features of great leaders. This led to the development of 'great man' or 'trait' theories – leaders being born not made, leaders having certain characteristics, and so on. Research has failed to demonstrate that there is a recipe for a good leader, although the trait theories are surprisingly resilient. They appear to run counter to meritocratic ideas and offer a hint of reassurance to the hereditary principle. If leaders are born, not made, then sooner or later we should be able to breed them!

The great risk of the 'big leader' syndrome is that followers stop thinking, questioning and arguing, and just follow. This is dangerous as it creates dependency in the organisation and may create an environment in which people stop asking questions. Hannah Arendt[14] explored the rise of totalitarianism in Hitler's Germany and Stalin's Soviet Union. She argues that isolation, loneliness and a sense of powerlessness are prerequisites for the rise of dictators and tyrants and, ultimately, totalitarian states. The same may be true of tyrants in organisations.

13 Hesselbein, Frances, Goldsmith, Marshall and Beckhard, Richard (eds.) (1996) *The Leader of the Future*, San Francisco: Jossey Bass.
14 Arendt, Hannah (reprinted 1968) *The Origins of Totalitarianism*, Orlando, Florida: Harcourt.

For practising leader-managers trait theories are singularly unhelpful. Whilst you can alter your behaviour, you cannot change your basic traits.

Behaviour/style

More recent work has focused on the behaviours found in effective leaders. This has led to both academic research and a flurry of 'how to' books, each giving a prescription of which behaviours will make you a better leader.

Much of the writing about leadership has, as mentioned at the beginning of the chapter, used two inter-dependent dimensions:

● orientation towards people and relationships (soft); and
● orientation towards the goal or task itself (hard).

Effective leadership is a combination of skills, the capacity to read situations and personal qualities (such as integrity) that mean others will follow. The idea that leadership style is contingent grew from work that saw a wide range of valid leadership styles. Tannenbaum and Schmidt[15] described a continuum of leadership styles, shown below.

Figure 5.5: Continuum of leadership styles

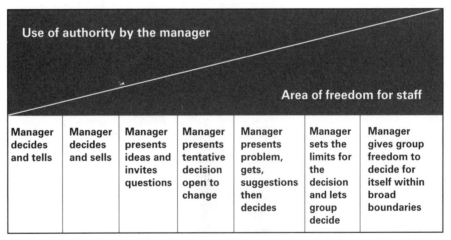

Manager decides and tells	Manager decides and sells	Manager presents ideas and invites questions	Manager presents tentative decision open to change	Manager presents problem, gets, suggestions then decides	Manager sets the limits for the decision and lets group decide	Manager gives group freedom to decide for itself within broad boundaries

Adapted and reprinted by permission of Harvard Business Review from
'How to Choose a Leadership Pattern' *by Tannenbaum and Schmidt May/June 1973*

They argued that leaders adopted a wide range of approaches and styles, depending on how much authority/power they retained and how much was delegated to staff.

This led on to contingency theories of leadership:[16] there is no right way, it all depends on circumstances. What is emphasised consistently is the need for effective leaders to read situations well (both the task and the people) so as to deploy their skills and capabilities to best effect. Returning to the Tannenbaum and Schmidt model above, it is possible to consider a situation and adopt a leadership style from the continuum which appears most appropriate to the situation. This forms the basis for the situational approach to leadership.

Thinking about your leadership style, like many areas of academic discourse, creates a

---

15 Tannenbaum, R. and Schmidt, W. (1973) 'How to Choose a Leadership Pattern', *Harvard Business Review*, May/June.
16 See, for example, Fiedler, F.E. (1967) A Theory of Leadership Effectiveness, New York: McGraw-Hill and footnote 3.

problem of chicken and egg. Which comes first: developing people or getting on with the task? Does the situation create the leader or the leader the situation?

Charles Hampden Turner[17] provides a simple tool for reconciling such strategic dilemmas. The two 'horns' of a dilemma are drawn as two axes at right angles to each other. Rather than either/or this allows the manager to explore both at the same time. The diagram looks at task/people.

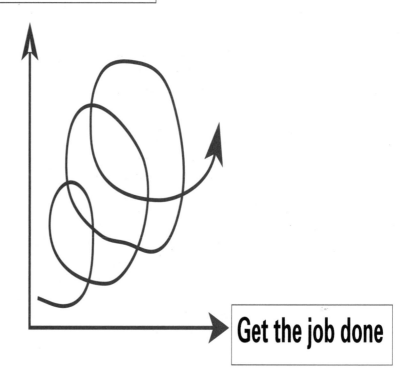

Get the people right

Get the job done

Reflection

Explore your leadership style using the models described. Are you comfortable across the whole spectrum of styles described by Tannenbaum and Schmidt?

An effective manager will continually adjust her or his leadership style between the two polarities. Ineffective managers get stuck in a single position.

Transformational leadership

Managers of modern services are increasingly urged to adopt a 'transformational' leadership style. This emphasises inspiring and motivating people to do things for themselves – 'influencing staff for whom one is responsible, by inspiring them, or pulling them towards the vision'[18] – rather than command and control. Transformational leaders 'earn' their influence on their followers. They lead through consent and commitment rather than through control and sanctions.

The transformational leadership style has been distinguished from transactional leadership – which corresponds in many ways with good operational management. There has been considerable debate about the difference between leadership and management. John Kotter[19] suggests the differences are as set out in the table on the next page.

17 Hampton Turner, Charles (1990) *Charting the Corporate Mind*, Oxford: Blackwell.
18 Alimo-Metcalfe, Beverly (1995) *Effective Leadership*, Luton: Local Government Management Board.
19 Kotter, J.P. (1990) 'A Force for Change: How Leadership differs from Management' New York: the Free Press, in Andrew J. DuBrin (1995) *Leadership – Research Findings, Practice and Skills*, Boston; Houghton Mifflin Company, p4.

Table 5.6: Differences between leadership and management

Leading role (Transformation)	Managing role (Transaction)
Sets direction; develops vision and strategies to achieve vision.	Plans and budgets; establishes detailed steps and timetables to achieve results; allocates resources.
Aligns people to do things; communicates vision and strategy to all those whose cooperation may be needed.	Organises and staffs; sets up structures; delegates authority for implementation; develops policies and procedures; creates monitoring systems.
Motivates and inspires people to overcome major political, bureaucratic and resource barriers to achieving the vision.	Controls and solves problems; monitors results against plans.
Produces change sometimes of dramatic nature; may create disorder but also new ideas, products, etc.	Key results expected by various stakeholders; predictability and order.

Adapted from Kotter, 1990

Abraham Zaleznik[20] described clear differences between leadership and management. He argued that they were so different that each needed a different type of person (suggesting a trait orientation in his thinking!). This might be seen as the start of a rather sterile debate which seeks to separate leadership (powerful, active, visionary) from management (dull, servile and bureaucratic). Our view is that both sets of behaviour need to be present in an effective organisation.

Leadership is needed at all levels in an organisation. One of the tasks of senior managers is to create a culture in which everyone can lead within their own areas of responsibility. This translates as a process of empowering management and is at the heart of modern thinking on leadership.

Organisations are often over-managed and under-led.[21] They may be good at handling the daily routine, but not at questioning whether the routine should be done at all. The Best Value regime introduced a requirement to challenge whether a public service was needed at all, and if so to question whether its current form was the best way to do it. This is an encouragement towards greater leadership.

So what are the behaviours that distinguish effective transformational leaders? Research in 1995 by the Local Government Management board[22] identified 12 characteristics of effective transformational leaders, as identified by their staff:

---

20 Zaleznik, Abraham (1977) 'Managers and Leaders: Are They Different?', *Harvard Business Review*, March/April.
21 Bennis, W. and Nanus, N. (1985) *Leaders: The Strategies for Taking Charge*, New York: Harper Row.
22 See footnote 18.

Table 5.7: Leadership characteristics identified by local government staff

Behaviour	Details
Actively supports staff development	Is sensitive to needs and aspirations; gives space and time for people to develop and learn – creates a learning culture, active learner her/himself.
Shows self-confidence	Inspires confidence in others through being self-confident, determined and credible.
Communicates clearly	Makes sure the vision is shared and owned by all; involves others in creating and developing the vision; encourages strategic thinking; creates a sense of 'corporate identity'.
Empathic	Listens; supports; is loyal; praises; celebrates.
Empowering	Trusts staff to take decisions; delegates authority.
Wins confidence of the elected members	Understands and is seen to understand the concerns and interests of elected members; delivers plans and outcomes; devotes time to building key relationships and links.
Shows integrity	Has robust personal values and standards.
Shows intellectual capacity	Good grasp of broad and complex issues; can see big picture as well as detail; open to new ideas.
Makes good use of time	Has energy and drive; uses it well; manages time effectively.
Politically skilled	Secures support from key stakeholders.
Takes risks	Encourages reasonable risk taking; actively seeks innovation and challenges to the status quo, if this will lead to a better service.
Self-aware, has humility	Open; honest about own strengths and weaknesses; able to change, but not blown whichever way the wind is blowing.

This can be added to four 'unexpected qualities' of leaders identified by Goffee and Jones.[23] They agreed that leaders need to have vision, energy, authority and strategic direction, but found they also:

1. **Selectively show weakness:** by exposing some vulnerability they become more approachable and humane.
2. **Rely heavily on intuition:** they gather soft data all the time, and are willing to trust their feelings about it as a basis for action.
3. **Manage with 'tough empathy':** they empathise passionately and care about the work employees are doing, but at the same time are realistic and willing to give difficult feedback.
4. **Reveal their differences:** make a strength out of what is unique and special about themselves.

Goffee and Jones also point out that leaders do not necessarily just deliver results. They excel at inspiring people and winning hearts and minds. They may sow the seeds for exceptional results but these may occur later and may require a less transformational leader at the helm.

This leaves senior youth work managers with some significant challenges with respect to leadership. They need to:

- understand the nature of leadership, and how they themselves see it;
- be aware how they themselves react and behave when leading;
- read the environment, their people and events so as to make strategic choices about the most effective leadership behaviour to adopt; and
- act with integrity and be authentic, because few people will follow a phoney.

Emotionally Intelligent Leadership

The American psychologist Daniel Goleman observed that the most successful people were not necessarily the most intelligent or talented but tended to be those who had the greatest capacity to deploy their emotions (and connect with the emotions of others) in the most effective way to achieve what they wanted[24]. He used empirical research to build up a competency model of how people made effective use of their emotions. He called this 'emotional intelligence' and identified four dimensions:

Reflection

Re-read the descriptions of transformational leaders. Identify your strengths and weaknesses against them. Draw up a plan of how you might enhance your skills in three main areas which you think you could improve. Reflect on Arendt's thinking. Does your leadership style actively address the issues of isolation and powerlessness she raises?

23 Goffee, Robert and Jones, Gareth (2000) 'Why Should Anyone Be Lead by You?', *Harvard Business Review*, September–October
24 Daniel Goleman (1996) *Emotional Intelligence: why it can matter more than IQ.* London, Bloomsbury.

Personal Competence
How we manage ourselves

1. Self-awareness
- Emotional self-awareness: reading own emotions, recognising their impact, using instinct and intuition
- Accurate self-assessment: knowing strengths and weaknesses
- Self-confidence

2. Self-management
- Emotional self-control
- Transparency: honesty, integrity and trustworthiness
- Adaptability
- Achievement: driven to improve and meet inner standards
- Initiative: seizing opportunities
- Optimism: seeing the positive

Social Competence
How we manage our relationships

3. Social awareness
- Empathy: sensing others' emotions, 'walking in their shoes'
- Organisational awareness: reading what's happening in the organisation
- Service: recognising and meeting client, user or customer needs

4. Relationship management
- Inspirational leadership: motivating with a compelling vision
- Influence: using a range of tactics
- Developing others
- Catalyst of change
- Conflict management
- Building bonds
- Teamwork and collaboration

A person can develop competence in all of these areas. The four dimensions provide a useful starting point to explore your own perception of your emotional intelligence (and that of those you work with).

Goleman went on to apply his thinking on emotional intelligence to leadership[25]. He drew on research findings that demonstrate that organisations are more effective when the emotional climate is positive (smiles and laughter really do boost performance). Other research showed that emotional distress has a powerfully negative effect on people's ability to work (both for themselves and with others).

Goleman identified six leadership styles (see table over). He argued that an effective leader will have a preferred or dominant style, but will develop the skill to use all the styles when appropriate. He quotes Aristotle to illustrate the challenge of applying each style effectively: 'to be angry with the right person, to the right degree, at the right time, for the right purpose and in the right way – this is not easy.'

Four of the styles are emotionally 'resonant' – they help to build a positive mood and climate. Two are 'dissonant' – they have a negative effect on the emotional climate and if used without extreme care can cause damage to the organisation. The styles are described on the next page.

---

25 Goleman, Daniel; Boyatzis, Richard and McKee, Annie (2002) *Primal Leadership: realizing the power of emotional intelligence*, Boston, Mass., Harvard Business School Prress.

Style	How it builds emotional resonance	Impact on emotional climate	Underlying emotional intelligence competencies	When to use
Visionary (Authoritative)	Moves people towards shared dreams	Strongly positive	Self-confidence, empathy, change catalyst	When clarity of vision and shared purpose is at a premium – at times of change, building a new venture, etc.
Coaching	Connects what the person wants with the organisation's goals	Very positive	Developing others, empathy, self-awareness	To help people improve performance by building their capacities
Affiliative	Connects people to each other and builds harmony	Positive	Empathy, building relationships, communication	To build team, heal rifts and conflict, motivate at times of stress
Democratic	Involves people in decision making, respects and values their input	Positive	Collaboration, team leadership, communication	To build consensus, get valuable input from staff or stakeholders
Pacesetting	Sets and meets challenging and exciting goals	Often very negative (because not well used)	Conscientiousness, drive to achieve, initiative	To secure good results from an already motivated and competent team
Commanding (Coercive)	Calms people by giving a clear direction in a crisis or emergency	Often extremely negative (because not well used)	Drive to achieve, initiative, self-control	In a crisis, to turn things round, deal with emergencies, tackle problems

To conclude this short exploration of leadership, it is worth returning to Hannah Arendt (see page 82). Whilst she was writing nearly half a century ago, the relevance of her thinking is still great. If staff are isolated from each other, and feel powerless, they are more likely to follow 'great leaders' without question. Isolation and powerlessness lead people to consent to small, often casual acts which, taken together, create a climate in which serious harm can result, by accident or design. The challenge for leaders is not therefore to secure followers as such, but to build organisations in which followers think for themselves, adhere to values and principles and have power to intervene when things appear to be wrong.

For many of the young people with whom youth services and organisations work, isolation and powerlessness may be a common experience. This makes it even more important that the leaders of the service or organisation do not repeat and reinforce behaviours which emphasise their sense of powerlessness and isolation.

The senior manager has a critical role to play in making sure the organisation is clear about its values and in managing in ways that reinforce the values. We explore this next.

Leading staff teams

One of the key tasks of a senior manager is to build and lead really effective teams of staff – in particular your own management team. This is a key test of your leadership skills and the application of appropriate leadership styles.

Much research has been carried out into what makes an effective team. Although there have been a number of attempts to distinguish between teams and groups, the terms are often used interchangeably. Katzenback[26] defines a team as 'a small number of people with complementary skills who are committed to a common purpose, performance goals and an approach for which they hold themselves mutually accountable'. He proposes three litmus tests for a 'real team'.

1. There must be results from working together which could not be achieved by the team members working on their own. This is not the same as open discussion, debate, decision making or delegation of authority. He puts forward the view that collective work products for top teams are rare except in times of crisis or major change.
2. The leadership role must shift depending on the task. Whichever manager has the knowledge or experience most relevant to the task in hand assumes the leadership role.
3. Team members must be mutually accountable for the team's results – 'we hold each other accountable' rather than ' the boss holds us accountable'.

Reflection

How does your management team measure up to Katzenback's litmus test?

Katzenback goes on to say that these tests are rarely met by senior management teams where the membership is made up of all those who report to the most senior manager.

Perhaps the most important aspect of a team is not whether it defines itself as a team, a group or a network, but whether it has a clear purpose, which adds real value to the organisation. Many teams flounder because no one has really explored what they are supposed to add.

Managers face three key issues regarding their teams:

● Clarity of purpose.
● Composition – who is in it, and what do they bring.
● How the team operates together.

Purpose

Most management teams meet to share information, allocate work, check progress and maintain working relationships between the members. Many also set aside time each year to work jointly on the overall strategy for the organisation (or unit), review and planning.

---

26 Katzenback, J. R. (1997) 'The Myth of the Top Management Team', *Harvard Business Review*, Nov/Dec.

The rationale for management teams usually emphasises the value added by creating a space for senior managers to focus on matters of strategic importance. The picture is of lean and efficient meetings where each item has a clear purpose and is advanced by discussion. This splendid aspiration is regularly scuppered by:

- no clear purpose (to misquote Descartes – 'we meet therefore we are');
- no proper agenda;
- the endless agenda (so long you never finish it);
- descent into detail;
- ascent into matters of fundamental principle (without any real purpose);
- diversion into analysis;
- discussion without evidence or appropriate information;
- discussion with too much evidence and information, so the purpose is lost;
- catch up behaviour (because people have not read the papers);
- collective amnesia (where things go round and round as everyone seems to forget what happened the last time it was discussed);
- non-delivery by team members (tasks not done, no accountability to the team);
- sabotage and hijacking; and
- no learning and development.

Reflection

Review your management team. Is its purpose clear? What value does it add? Is it fit for its purpose?

This is hardly rocket science, but huge amounts of expensive time continue to be wasted in pointless meetings.

Composition

Teams are affected by their members. You may have little influence over the membership of your management team. You have to work with whoever is in the team. However, you may be in a position to set up project or task groups whose membership is under your control.

There are several useful frameworks for analysing the membership of a team. Analysis provides information that may explain some of the problems that occur and may enable the team to identify new behaviours to improve joint working. We explore two main frameworks for analysing team composition below.

Meredith Belbin found effective teams were made up of people whose strengths and weaknesses complemented one another: the right combination of 'imperfect people' can make 'perfect' teams'.[27]

Belbin identified eight main roles which contribute to the ideal team. In each role there are strengths and weaknesses that need to be balanced by other roles in the team. These roles are shown in the table overpage.

---

27 Belbin, M. (1981) *Management Teams: Why They Succeed or Fail*, Oxford: Butterworth Heinemann.

Table 5.8: Belbin's team roles

Role	Attributes	Allowable weaknesses
Company worker	Conservative, dutiful, predictable, with organising ability, common sense, hardworking.	Lack of flexibility, unresponsiveness to unproven ideas.
Chairman	Calm, self-confident and controlled, with a capacity for treating all potential contributors on their merits and a strong sense of objectives.	Ordinary intelligence and creative ability.
Shaper	Highly strung, outgoing, dynamic, with drive and a readiness to challenge inertia, ineffectiveness or self-deception.	Prone to provocation, irritation, impatience.
Plant	Individualistic, serious, unorthodox, with genius, imagination, intellect, knowledge.	Up in the clouds, inclined to disregard practical details or protocol.
Resource investigator	Extroverted, enthusiastic, curious, communicative, with a capacity for contacting people and exploring anything new; an ability to respond to challenges.	Liable to lose interest once the initial fascination has passed.
Monitor-evaluator	Sober, unemotional, prudent, with judgment, discretion, hard-headedness.	Lacks inspiration or the ability to motivate others.
Team worker	Socially oriented, rather mild, sensitive, with an ability to respond to people and situations and to promote team spirit.	Indecisiveness in moments of crisis.
Completer-finisher	Painstaking, orderly, conscientious, anxious, with a capacity for follow-through; perfectionism.	A tendency to worry about small things; a reluctance to let go.

In Belbin's view, members of teams perform most effectively in the roles that are natural to them. Analysis of the role people gravitate towards in teams can help to identify weaknesses and to enable team members to work together to cover the roles that are weak or absent.

The Team Management Systems (TMS) approach created by Margerison and McCann[28] identifies eight team roles which reflect personality type as correlated to work behaviours:

Reporter–advisers

Reporter-advisers are good at generating information and gathering it together in a way that makes it comprehensible. They are usually patient and prepared to wait to make decisions until they know as much as possible about the work to be done. They may seem to procrastinate but prefer to wait until they are sure that the advice given is accurate. Reporter-advisers are invaluable support members for a team, concerned to make sure the job is done correctly and that all relevant information has been provided.

Creator–innovators

Creator-innovators will have a number of ideas which may well contradict and upset the existing way of doing things. They are very independent and wish to pursue ideas regardless of the present system and methods. It is important to have ideas people on every team and to give them the opportunity to talk through their views.

Explorer–promoters

Explorer-promoters are excellent at taking up an idea and getting people enthusiastic about it. They will find out what is happening inside and outside the organisation and compare new ideas with what others are doing. They are good at bringing back contacts, information and resources to help move ideas forward. They see the big picture but are often poor on details. They can push an idea forward but may not be good at organising and controlling it.

Assessor–developers

Assessor-developers look for ways to make an idea work in a practical way. They will produce a prototype or run a pilot. They like to develop innovation to the point where it can work but are not interested in producing it on a regular basis. They will want to move on to another project.

Thruster–organisers

Thruster-organisers like getting things done. Once convinced that an idea is worth pursuing they will set up systems and procedures to turn the idea into working reality. They like goal and role clarity and will push to ensure deadlines are met. They can be very impatient and are prepared to ruffle feathers in order to get things done.

Concluder–producers

Concluder-producers place emphasis on producing to a standard on a regular basis. They

---

28 Margerison, C. J. and McCann, D. J. (1995) *Team Management: Practical New Approaches*, Kemble, Cirencester, Glos.: Management Books 2000.

like working to set procedures and doing things systematically. They like to use existing skills rather than continually changing and learning new ways.

Controller-inspectors

Controller-inspectors enjoy detailed work and making sure facts and figures are correct. They are careful and meticulous and like to pursue a task in depth making sure the work is done according to plan in an accurate way. They are valuable in auditing and quality work or in dealing with contracts

Upholder-maintainers

Upholder-maintainers take pride in maintaining the physical and social side of work. They may be the conscience of the team and provide support and help to team members. They hold strong views about the way the team should be run based on their convictions and beliefs. If upset, they can be obstinate and defend their interests. However, when they believe in what the team is doing they can be a source of strength and energy and often make good negotiators.

These eight roles need to be present in an effective team, together with a ninth – that of Linker. The Linker is not a separate role, but a set of activities that must be carried out in conjunction with the other roles if the team is to work effectively. The activities include:

- maintaining quality standards;
- allocating work;
- setting objectives;
- delegating;
- developing the team;
- active listening;
- communicating;
- building team relationships;
- problem solving and counselling;
- participative decision making; and
- managing the interface between the team and others.

Margerison and McCann argue that it is important that all eight team roles can be covered when required. A balanced team will be able to cover exploring, controlling, advising and reporting aspects of work.

Greater use is being made of personality profiles (including Myers Briggs, see Chapter one) to help new teams make the transition into working together effectively. The pace of change in working life is such, that attempts are being made to speed up or by-pass Tuckman's [29] forming, storming and norming and performing stages of team development. A clear assessment of the team's strengths and weaknesses is likely to help it to get up to speed more quickly and to function more effectively.

The operation of the team

An effective team includes a range of features: [30]

Reflection

Use the Belbin or TMS analysis of team roles to carry out a quick audit of your team. Are all the roles covered? If not what do you do about it?

To what extent are you able to make use of team member profiles in selecting members of your management team?

---

29 Tuckman, B. W. (1965) 'Development Sequence in Small Groups', *Psychological Bulletin*, 63 (6).
30 Yancy, M. (1998) *Work Teams: Three Models of Effectiveness*, Denton: Center for the Study of Work Teams; Campion, M. A., Medsker, G. J. and Higgs, A. C. (1993) 'Relations Between Work Group Characteristics and Effectiveness' *Personnel Psychology*, 46, pp823–850; Guzzo, R. A. (1986), 'Group Decision Making and Group Effectiveness' in P. S. Goodman (ed), *Designing Effective Work Groups*, San Franciso: Jossey Bass; Hackman, J. R. (1990) *Groups That Work (and Those That Don't)*, San Francisco: Jossey Bass.

1. The purpose of the team is clear and understood by all.
2. The team owns its own goals and is committed to them.
3. There is a focus on achieving results.
4. The atmosphere is open and supportive, with a focus on learning. Humour is widely used to lighten the mood, create energy and relieve tensions.
5. The team is able to develop many alternatives when problem solving.
6. Members feel that they are equally valued.
7. There is a focus on team, rather than individual performance.
8. There is diversity among the membership.
9. Relationships between members are strong.
10. Communication between team members and with those outside is frequent and effective.
11. Team members work with an appropriate amount of information. This avoids arguments rooted in ignorance and enables the team to focus on facts and issues rather than personalities.
12. All members participate and are listened to; no one dominates.
13. Ideas and behaviours are challenged, in order to get better results.
14. Leadership is shared and moves around the team members – each taking a lead on particular things.
15. Issues of power and control have been openly discussed and resolved. Initially this is through seeking consensus. If this fails the most relevant senior manager makes the decision guided by input from the rest of the group or through putting the matter to a vote.[31]

Reflection

Use the list of 15 characteristics to evaluate with the team any potential action.

The team leader is responsible for getting the team to work effectively. He or she will be in a position of authority over all or some of the other team members. This calls for skill and flexibility of leadership style. At times the team will need to be given a clear lead (directive), at others the leader may step back and give the lead to someone else. The team leader may also need to coach some team members, challenge others and provide gentle support to others.

Katzenback[32] describes four myths about teams:

1. **Teamwork naturally leads to better performance.** He argues that there has been too much emphasis on processes such as communication, cooperation, collaboration and compromise, and too little weight given to the outcomes of teamwork.
2. **Teams should spend more time building consensus.** This assumes that building consensus is synonymous with reducing conflict and that less conflict somehow leads to more team-like behaviour. Katzenback argues that real teams thrive on conflict, a view that is borne out by research findings (see below).
3. **The senior group should function as a team whenever it is together.** This implies that every task is a team opportunity. Some tasks are best completed by individuals or by groups with a single leader who delegates elements of the task.
4. **If the team agrees, it must be a sound decision.** Somehow the collective judgment and experience of those in the team always makes up for a lack of more specific and relevant skills.

Good teamwork involves challenge and occasional discomfort. Without conflict groups lose their effectiveness and may even suffer from what Janis[33] described as 'groupthink'. Groupthink is defined as 'a mode of thinking that people engage in when they are deeply

31 Eisenhart, K. M., Kahwajy, J. L. and Bourgeois, LJIII, (1997), 'How Management Teams Can Have a Good Fight', *Harvard Business Review*, July/August.
32 Katzenback, J. R. (1997) 'The Myth of the Top Management Team', *Harvard Business Review*, November/December.
33 Janis, I. (1982), *Groupthink: Psychological Studies of Policy Decisions and Fiascos*, Boston: Houghton Mifflin.

involved in a cohesive group, when the members' strivings for unanimity override their motivation to realistically appraise alternative courses of action'. The manager has to build a culture in which it is possible to 'disagree without being disagreeable'. It is vital that any conflict is productive and does not degenerate into damaging interpersonal warfare.

Not all problems will be best dealt with by teams. The effective team leader differentiates between tasks best carried out by the team (where teamwork adds value) and those that are most effectively carried out by individuals or smaller groups.

Managers must consider whether the expenditure of time needed to get 'real' team performance is worth it. At times a better alternative may be for the manager to adopt a leadership style to the right end of the Tannenbaum and Schmidt continuum. Groups with a single leader can be fast, efficient and powerful when the person in charge really does know best. There are other times when the organisation needs the team to work much more collaboratively.

Winning commitment from the team or group

Much of what is called team working is little more than a coordinating and communicating mechanism among groups of staff who are responsible for different aspects of an activity. This approach to 'team working' is valuable as long as its purpose is clear and individual expectations are met. It is important to recognise that in looser groups and networks, power and influence can become diffused and may or may not be used for the benefit of the organisation.

We have all observed the hokey cokey in groups and networks – members all come together in the dance then step back and do their own thing. They all come back together with another burst of organisational fervour, then away they go and do what they want, without reference to the group. Agreements are not honoured, deadlines not met and colleagues not backed up. One of the hardest things for independently minded professionals to do is actually to join a team, as it brings with it a loss of autonomy and freedom.

The matrix in figure 5.9 is useful for exploring the membership of teams, groups and networks. It is neither safe nor sensible to assume that all the members arrive with equal and positive motivation.

Figure 5.9: Motivation/energy matrix

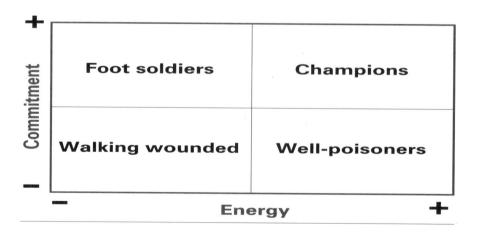

Reflection

Think about the composition of your management team using the matrix above.

Do you have any walking wounded or well-poisoners? If so what leadership style will you adopt to ensure that the team can move forward and limit any negative impact they might have?

Clearly those with high energy levels are likely to be powerful and influential individuals. Those whose motivation is high but whose energy is low are vital for getting the work done, keeping the whole operation going. The people who often consume disproportionate amounts of energy are those with low motivation (limited commitment to the team and/or the organisation). Where their energy is high they represent a real threat and challenge (the well-poisoners). Where their energy is low they often drag others down with them.

Team structures

The traditional management team structure is hierarchical:

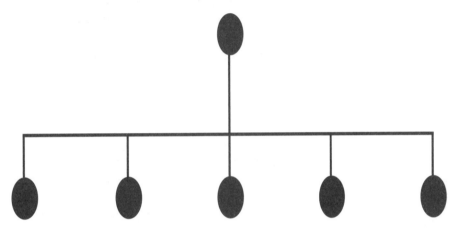

This has the advantage of clarity, and emphasises the positional power of the team leader. It also assumes that the other managers are carrying out a similar type of role (usually managing a function such as finance, personnel or human resources, marketing and promotion, service delivery or research and development). The drawback is that many teams are not made up of managers carrying out discrete functions. They may include a number of general managers whose task is the delivery of a part of the whole service – usually on a geographical area basis.

This often leads to another structure – the matrix:

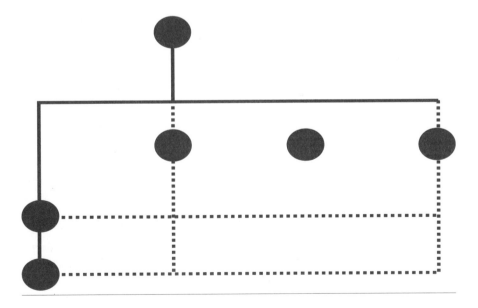

Here the two general (area) managers (vertical circles) work in a matrix as part of the team, in which they must establish relevant relationships, meetings and agreements with the three functional managers (horizontal circles). (For example, in a national voluntary organisation the functional managers might be Directors of Marketing, Finance, and Human Resources, with the general managers each being responsible for half of the service operations). This requires considerable skill and can take a lot of time. It can produce an informed team within which members are able to negotiate with each other to ensure that they are able to deliver the service. The manager often plays a coordinating role, with stronger leadership reserved for establishing the team's purpose, objectives and standards and for monitoring progress. The matrix can break down through becoming too complex, or if members bypass the matrix and go straight to the manager for decisions. If you are leading a matrix structure you must become very good at resisting such approaches.

The last team structure we will look at is when the team is really a means of coordinating a number of loose task and project groups.

Figure 5.10: The loose group team

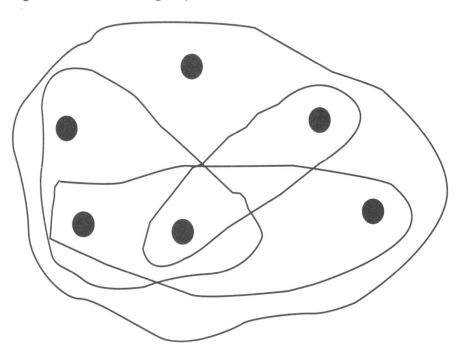

In the diagram there is an overall team, led by the team leader. The overall team sets the overall targets, standards etc. for the rest of the team. The work is actually done in a number of loose groupings, some short lived, others more permanent. This way of working allows considerable flexibility, but requires clarity of purpose and discipline by team members if it is to work. The fluid and fast changing nature of the workplace means that this sort of flexible arrangement is becoming increasingly common.

Clear lines of accountability

Involvement in cross-organisational, multi-agency and partnership working means individuals find themselves in a variety of teams with a range of reporting lines. Lines of responsibility and accountability can become vague and blurred. The individual may report to different managers for different parts of his or her role. This can result in conflicting priorities which leave the individual feeling stressed and isolated. The approach to line management becomes task oriented with no one manager having overall responsibility for providing support.

To avoid this situation, it is important to put effective supervision in place. The individual should have a lead manager who establishes clear lines of communication with all other managers involved (a type of matrix arrangement). He or she will have responsibility for managing the overall workload and performance management and for arranging appropriate professional development opportunities. Such an approach has resource implications, which can be dealt with through the activity-based approach discussed later.

Managing upwards

Senior managers account for their work, upwards (to their line manager, direct to councillors or their boards) as well as laterally, to peers and colleagues in other organisations, departments etc.

The fact that managers manage downwards, upwards and sideways, all at the same time, may explain the common feeling of being pulled every which way, juggling competing demands and never really having time to do anything as well or as thoroughly as you might like.

Managing those over whom you have no formal control or influence requires a strategy and the deployment of a range of skills. In essence it is a process of stakeholder management and requires a clear understanding of the stakeholders' interests and concerns, mandate and authority. We will explore stakeholder management a little more in Chapter Ten.

Figure 5.11 shows a range of relationships the senior manager is likely to have. It also suggests the sense of pressure from above, below and sideways.

Figure 5.11: Range of relationships of senior manager

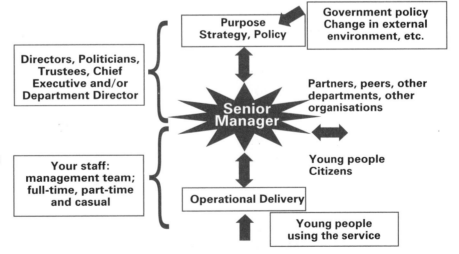

Reflection

Does figure 5.11 correspond to your own sense of your job?

Developed from work by John Thurlbeck, Sunderland Youth Service

The strategic questions the manager needs to be able to answer include:

1. Who do I account to? (line manager, politicians, board of trustees)
2. What is their role and their accountability?
3. What is their authority over me?
4. What are their key interests and concerns?
5. What information do they need from me to do their job?
6. What sort of relationship do I need to develop with them to do my job?
7. What sort of leadership style is likely to be most effective in securing the relationship I need?
8. How will I judge the effectiveness of the working relationship (what success criteria will I use?

Democratic renewal and council structures

There is concern over low levels of turnout in local council elections (in some wards voter turnout has dropped below 10 per cent of the electorate). The UK Government has taken steps to renew local democracy. It wants to see clearer accountability and more efficient decision making.

The Local Government Act 2000 required all local councils in England to change their structure as one step towards achieving this. The essence of the change is to create a smaller, more focused body which is responsible for the executive functions of the council – delivering a strategy that implements the council's policies and delivers better public services. The full council remains responsible for overall policy, budgets and scrutiny of the work of the local authority. The old committee structure is replaced by a smaller executive structure linked to a number of scrutiny panels. A few committees remain covering 'semi-judicial matters' such as licensing and planning. The executive structure must conform to one of three main models:

1. Leader and cabinet in which the council elects a leader, and appoints a small cabinet.
2. Mayor directly elected by the public, with a cabinet appointed by the mayor.
3. Mayor directly elected by the public, with a council manager appointed by the council who runs the council.

Democratic renewal has led to a majority of councils adopting the leader and cabinet model.

The change in structure directly affects senior managers in the youth service and in local voluntary organisations. In the past managers needed to build a relationship with the relevant committee, to secure political support for youth work. In the new structures managers would need to develop relationships with the cabinet member who champions youth work, or the mayor and council manager. Managers will also need to build relationships with relevant scrutiny committees.

Governance of voluntary organisations

The changes in local government are mirrored by trends in the voluntary sector. There is widespread demand for charities and organisations which spend public money to be more open and accountable. Whilst there has been no legislation on governing structures, many charities have taken decisions to reduce the size of their boards, so that they can be more effective at governing the charity. A growing number of organisations have developed a second, larger body to work alongside the board. These forums enable a larger number of people to discuss broad policy and to ask questions about the conduct of the charity.

Managing the organisation's values

Tom Peters and Robert Waterman, the gurus of 'excellence', argue that the first task of managers is to manage the organisation's values.[34] They argue that the purpose and culture ('the way we do things round here') of the organisation flow directly from these values. Rather than assuming that values are shared, the job of the manager is to make sure that people know about, understand and share a commitment to them.

Senior managers in both statutory and voluntary youth work organisations are being bombarded by a range of external demands to account for what they do, meet funding requirements and work with other agencies in partnerships. All these demands have the potential to draw the organisations away from their core purpose and values. Instead of asking 'why should we jump at this?' managers may give up and just respond with 'how high do you want us to jump?'

So what values would you expect to see in an effective organisation that works with young people? Mary Marken[35] identifies the following as central to the work of higher performing local authority youth services:

- Young people are valued as equal partners.
- Equality and equity are valued.
- There is an understanding of and commitment to effective youth work.
- Fun is valued as an integral part of learning.
- Qualities of integrity, tenacity, flexibility, creativity and humour are valued.
- Individual staff and the whole organisation value 'constant learning'.
- Individual staff and the whole organisation see themselves as part of a wider set of services to young people.
- Collaboration is valued.
- Feedback is welcomed and encouraged.

Value	Expressed in action in my organisation
Understanding of and commitment to effective youth work	
Fun is valued as an integral part of learning	
Young people are valued as equal partners	
Integrity, tenacity, flexibility, creativity and humour are valued	
Individual staff and the whole organisation value 'constant learning'	

34 Peters, Tom and Waterman, Robert (1982) *In Search of Excellence*, London: Pan.
35 Marken, Mary (2000) *Higher Performing Youth Services*, Leicester: The National Youth Agency, p18.

Value	Expressed in action in my organisation
Learning from experience	
Equality and equity are valued	
Valuing staff	
Individual staff and the whole organisation see themselves as part of a wider set of services to young people	
Collaboration is valued	
Feedback is welcomed and encouraged	

Example: Using the 7S model to explore a value

Many organisations that work with young people claim to value young people's views and participation in decisions. We can use the 7S model to explore this (see page 45). Place this value in the 'shared values' circle at the centre of the model. By looking in each of the other circles, we can explore the implications of this shared value:

Structure: Are young people's voices heard at all levels of the organisation and in all its parts? How? Could this be improved?

Systems: Do the systems help the active involvement of young people in decision making? What are the implications for young people of financial regulations (eg reimbursing young people's expenses for involvement, rewarding such commitment in kind), communication systems, the timing of meetings, the monitoring and evaluation system etc.

Staffing: To what extent are young people involved in recruiting and selection issues? Do we employ young people on an ad hoc or contracted basis? To what extent are young people involved in staff development or aspects of staff management?

Skills: What skills are needed for the active involvement of young people – and have we asked young people to help us identify them? Is the organisation skilled-up for the active involvement of young people or do we need to add to our skills?

Style: Is the style – both the management style or the culture of the organisation – one which encourages and supports the active involvement of young people – and what would be the characteristics of such a style/culture?

> **Strategy:** How can we ensure that developing the quantity and quality of active involvement over the next three years is a key strategic objective? Will young people be actively involved in developing the strategy in the first place?
>
> For a fuller exploration of this see *Hear by Right*,[36] which uses the 7S framework as a basis for standards for young people's involvement in democratic decision making.

Managing diversity, equality and equity

Britain is a diverse society. Effective youth work organisations must have an effective approach to operating in a diverse society, so that all young people have access to services and all parts of the community are reached and can be involved.

Diversity is relatively easy to understand – a society made up of many different groups, interests, races, faiths and so on. Effective management of diversity involves a commitment to provide services and be open to all.

Equality is widely used in discussion of diversity as in 'there should be equality'. Equality implies 'the same' – but the same as what? Much of the debate on equality happens without any attempt to clarify meaning.

Equality is defined as the condition of being equal: 'identical in quantity; of the same value; adequate; in just proportion; fit; equable; uniform; equitable; evenly balanced; just'. Equity relates more to a sense of justice: 'moral justice; the spirit of justice which enables us to interpret laws rightly; fairness'.[37]

The debate on equality is highly political. It usually blurs two distinct aspects of the issue:

1. Equality of opportunity: that all should have the same chance to do and experience things in life.
2. Equality of outcome: that we should all share equally in the results of our collective endeavours. That the same work should lead to the same rewards.

If equity rather than equality is used, 'equal' and 'the same' tend to be replaced with 'fair' or 'just', which implies a recognition that, while people are not the same, differences should not lead to injustice.

Using the term 'diversity' takes us in a different but related direction. Diversity implies a recognition that things are diverse and complex. The task of the manager is to manage in such a way that diverse groups and individuals are treated fairly and have fair access to opportunities.

Managers of youth work organisations have two key areas for action to secure fair treatment and opportunities: employment practice (internal) and youth work practice (the service offered to young people).

---

36 Wade, Harry; Lawton, Anthony and Stevenson, Mark (2001) *Hear by Right – Setting Standards For the Active Involvement of Young People in Democracy*, Leicester: The National Youth Agency.
37 *Chambers 20th Century Dictionary.*

It is essential that organisations are able to attract staff from all sections of the community. Quite apart from any moral imperative, to do otherwise is to limit your pool of available talent and restrict your organisation's chances of success. Youth work organisations need to have links with the whole community to be effective, and are expected to have staffing that reflects this. Your organisation will have an equalities policy and practice guidelines regarding employment. These take account of legislation to prevent unfair discrimination in employment. It is vital that you and your staff are aware of the procedures and carefully follow them.

The current context

To be effective in tackling the issue of equality and justice in your organisation you need to be aware not only of the internal policies and procedures, but also the external context within which you operate. It is a key requirement of a strategic manager's role to remain aware of and alert to the current policy environment.

The wider context within which you are managing has a profound impact on the role and approach you need to adopt as a manager. This is explored in Chapter 6.

Chapter Six:
The impact of the external environment

Introduction

Managers need to be aware of the environment (context) within which they work. This includes both the internal environment (the organisation within which the manager operates) and the external environment. Both are in a state of constant change and evolution. We explored the internal environment of the organisation in Chapter Three.

This chapter looks at the main features of the external environment that affect managers of youth work organisations in both the voluntary and statutory sectors. This is the scanning role in the model below. The role involves finding out what is going on outside, understanding it and analysing how it might/will affect the organisation in which you are a manager. This chapter covers:

- Scanning the external environment
- The changing world of young people
- The changing face of public services
- The changing third sector
- The changing wider world
- Changes affecting organisations that work with young people
- So what does this have to with me?

Figure 6.1: The experiential cycle

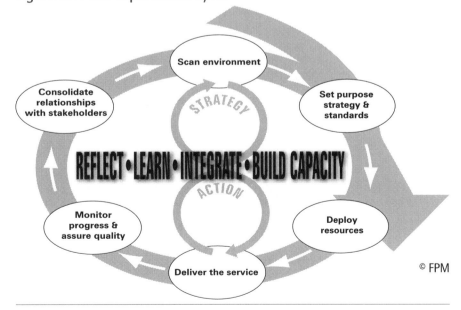

Scanning the external environment

Managers can use a variety of tools to help them scan the external environment. Perhaps the best known is the PEST (or PESTLE) analysis. This looks in turn at changes in the Political, Economic, Social, Technological, Legal and Environmental fields that may affect the organisation.

The paragraphs that follow are based on a PESTLE exercise, but draw out particular themes which seem most relevant to youth work managers in voluntary and statutory organisations. These are: changes in the world of young people; changes in public service provision; changes in civil society; changes in the wider world and changes directly affecting organisations that work with young people.

It is worth also reflecting back to the Mintzberg idea of levels of strategy (see page 61). The issues discussed below are largely at the level of deep ocean currents, although one or two may be mid-ocean currents.

The changing world of young people

The Social Exclusion Unit Policy Action Team (PAT) 12 report[1] provides a thorough review of the changing world of young people. Young people today face a markedly different situation to their predecessors, and one that is rapidly changing. Many of the changes experienced have been positive: most young people are better educated, more wealthy, physically healthier and live longer. However, there are also changes – particularly in the nature of the labour market, family relationships and social structures – that mean young people face new risks and challenges:

- Far more jobs are now only open to those with qualifications. Most young people therefore spend more time in learning, and there are fewer opportunities for those without skills.
- The disappearance of traditional sources of employment and less likelihood of a 'job for life'. While some welcome the prospect of periodic job change and acquiring new skills to learn throughout a working life, for others it is a threat.
- Longer dependence on parental support as young people enter work, marry and leave the parental home later in life.
- Earlier and more intense exposure to high risk behaviour, including experimentation with alcohol, smoking, drugs and sex, and exposure to violence.
- Social and media attitudes encouraging pre-adolescents and adolescents to be seen as older than they are and behave accordingly.
- Greater likelihood of experiencing breakdown in their own relationships with one in four marriages likely to end in divorce.
- A more diverse population of young people, with many of those from black and minority ethnic backgrounds facing unfair discrimination on racial grounds. Those from minority ethnic groups often experience greater poverty, poorer public services and, in some cases, specific challenges like the need to learn English or recover from the trauma of being a refugee.

Many young people experience:

- family life characterised by disrupted relationships, poverty and worklessness;

---

1   PAT 12 Report (2000) *Young People*, London: Social Exclusion Unit

- education provision that does not meet their needs;
- a way of life lacking stimulation, enjoyment and challenge;
- serious health problems and problem behaviours;
- difficulty finding a decent place to live or money to live on; and
- a much greater chance of being both victims of crime and perpetrators of crime.

Young people from black and minority ethnic groups face these problems disproportionately – not least because many live in disadvantaged neighbourhoods, as well as facing the additional effects of racism.

At the same time the support mechanisms on which adolescents have traditionally depended have been weakened in some significant and overlapping ways:

- For many young people, family ties have become more fluid or more fragile. One in four children born in the 1970s experienced the break-up of their parents' marriage by the age of 16. One in 12 children currently live in step-parent families and around one in five live in single parent families, three times the number in 1971. Over the last ten years, contact with grandparents and other relatives also fell.
- Community ties may also be of less help to young people than previously, particularly where a whole neighbourhood has suffered entrenched long-term unemployment and so role models and informal networks are either limited or provide a negative influence.
- There is less access, in schools and elsewhere, to help with problems in learning or personal life because of limitations on resources and the priority given to the most acute problems.
- There is growing inequality in income and employment. In 1995-96, one in three children grew up in poverty, compared with one in ten in 1979. One in five households has no family member in work.

The result of all these changes is that:

- a significant minority of young people experience a range of serious problems and acute crises in adolescence;
- the numbers affected are in many cases worse than other comparable countries; and
- too many of the trends have been in the wrong direction (ie it is getting worse!).

The Policy Action Team focused on two repeating themes which affect a significant minority of young people, disproportionately concentrated in the poorest areas:

1. The complex disadvantage faced by certain groups of young people such as those who grow up in care, in poverty, in deprived neighbourhoods or who do badly at school.
2. The inadequate response young people have often had from a fragmented set of services that do not organise around their needs.

The PAT identified the need for action in three areas to develop a joined up and comprehensive approach to these issues:

Gaps in individual services – there is not enough emphasis on prevention; services are not delivered in ways that recognise the specific needs of disadvantaged young people; and services need to be provided wherever they are needed, not haphazardly or on a restricted basis.

Allocation of resources – resources are not reaching those most in need. There is evidence that the State spends 14 per cent less on young people in the most deprived areas, than on the average young person.

Fragmentation of policy-making and service delivery – the absence of a 'big picture' and somebody to pull it together nationally, locally and at the level of the individual. Instead, at least eight UK Government departments have an interest in policies and services for young people, and at least four local authority services work directly with young people. At the level of individual young people, responsibility is also fragmented.

The PAT made four proposals:

1. Create a new cross-government approach to youth inclusion and structures to ensure that the UK Government designs and delivers its contribution effectively.
2. Shift the emphasis from crisis intervention to prevention.
3. Make individual services better. Have action on: support for families; budget for prevention; and an overhaul of professional training.
4. Adopt a new approach to designing and delivering services based on consulting and involving young people and on evidence about what works for them.

The UK Government has responded to these recommendations with a raft of policies and initiatives including a Minister for Youth, establishing the Children and Young People's Unit in the Department for Education and Skills; establishing the Connexions Strategy and Service, Transforming Youth Work, Sure Start, the Children's Fund, tax credits, Jobseekers Allowance and incentives for staying on at school or college and, most recently, the Children Bill and its supporting documentation Every Child Matters: Next Steps.

The changing face of public services

As the PAT 12 makes clear, there is a growing need and demand for public services to be more responsive to need and more accountable to users. This takes place in a context in which there is continuing pressure for services to provide 'value for money' or 'best value'. UK Government has increased spending on public services in the early years of the new millennium following years of restrictions and cutbacks.

Governments across the world have found their power to control the affairs of state being eroded by globalisation. There is pressure to limit public spending (eg to be part of the European Union; to keep taxes low and encourage the economy). Restricting public spending also relates to changes in the marketplace, with people spending a smaller proportion of their lives in employment. Recent concerns about pension provision reflect this. The public has become used to the idea of choice, increasingly critical of services felt to be inadequate, with a consequent rise in the voice and power of the consumer.

Governments are exploring ways to make public services more flexible and responsive.[2] In the marketplace effective organisations attract and generate resources to grow and provide more services. The introduction of markets and quasi-markets into public services is one mechanism that has been and continues to be tried. In the UK the Government has consistently emphasised pluralism – that services must be provided by a range of providers so that users have greater choice and costs are reduced by competition. UK Government is seeking the active involvement of the third sector as a partner in delivering public services

---

2   Osbourne, D. and Gaebler, T. (1992) *Reinventing Government: How the Entrepreneurial Spirit is Transforming the Public Sector*, Reading, MA: Addison-Wesley.

to increase pluralism. It is experimenting with new types of third sector organisation (such as Public Interest Companies). All this is not without some disquiet from parts of the existing voluntary sector, which fear for their independence, and loss of capacity to campaign for change on unpopular issues.

It is not straightforward to apply the ideas of the market to voluntary and public service organisations. They do not necessarily increase their income through improving their services or delivering more services. Public services tend to be paid for by UK Government (local or national) rather than the user. Creating demand for services more often leads to rationing unless further public money can be freed to meet the demand (often based on political criteria rather than need). Figure 6.2 explores this dilemma. Route A is commonly cited for public and voluntary sector organisations which do not secure more resources by providing more or better services.

Figure 6.2: Impact of resources on service development

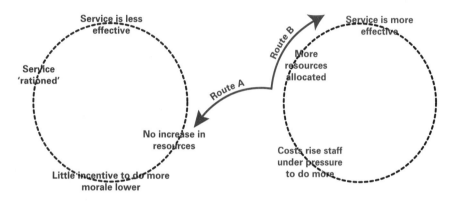

The White Paper *Strong Local Government – Quality Public Services* (December 2001) signals the continuing desire of the UK Government to find ways to break the rationing cycle. It seeks to give local authorities greater freedom to invest, charge, spend and develop services which respond to need. To support the changes proposed, UK Government will continue to reward the best service providers (through public service agreements, Beacon status, more resources and more freedom) and shame the worst. The paper also emphasises joined up working between the sectors.

The public, private and voluntary sectors appear to be converging in their approaches to planning and delivering public services. For managers, one of the consequences is the requirement to manage relationships with a much wider range of stakeholders than they had previously.

John Bryson, a US professor of planning and public affairs, points out[3]:

'When such fundamental public functions as tax collection, health, education, and welfare services and weapons' production are handled by the private and non-profit sectors, then surely the boundaries between public, private and non-profit sectors are irretrievably blurred. The blurring of these boundaries means that we have moved to a world in which no one organisation or institution is fully in charge, and yet many are involved or affected or have a partial responsibility to act. This increased jurisdictional

3   Bryson, John, M. (1995) *Strategic Planning for Public and Nonprofit Organizations: A Guide to Strengthening and Sustaining Organizational Achievement*, San Francisco: Jossey Bass.

ambiguity requires public and non-profit organisations (and communities) to think and act strategically as never before. Strategic planning is designed to help them do so.'

From bureaucracy to new public management

Public services have been traditionally organised through bureaucratic organisational forms. Rules and procedure were emphasised. This culture tends to focus on **input measures** (economy and efficiency) rather than the achievement of **results** for service users. Many have used a command and control culture, in which power lay at the centre, and woe betide anyone who questioned the source of the power.

Current thinking has been influenced by developments in physics, mathematics and biology that suggest that uncertainty is the norm, chaos can produce order and organisations are part of wider, complex open systems.

In response, a new approach to public service management is developing. It has followed the lead of the commercial world in dismantling tall organisational hierarchies. This usually means removing layers of middle management and pushing traditional middle management responsibilities down the line towards first line managers, thus creating a flatter structure. In the commercial world this has usually been accompanied by a delegation of decision making power down the line, linked to very clearly stated targets and performance standards . There has been a shift away from checking on inputs – what people do – to monitoring the results of their actions. Managers are given more leeway to decide on the means, but the ends are clearly defined from above.

The dilemma faced by managers is not to decide 'either flat or tall' structure, but to achieve an effective balance between systems/procedures and delegated power to take decisions and be flexible. There is no right way to structure the organisation – it depends on what it is trying to do (purpose), when, where etc.

There has been a rise in the strength of the managerial culture[4] – working with clear explicit, processes to achieve measurable results against agreed explicit targets. This contrasts with historic forms of professional management in which the professional was trained to a high level and then largely left to use his or her judgment in the delivery of services. This can be characterised as a shift from 'Trust me (I am a professional)' to 'Prove it (and if you cannot I will sue)'.

Professional services did not typically set explicit targets and were not easily open to public scrutiny. For example, in the last decade medical practitioners, teachers and public administrators have all come under pressure to move to a more managerial culture. Youth workers, whilst still a young profession, face the same pressure. It is no longer acceptable to talk of mysterious relationships and development without making explicit what is being done and what results have been achieved.

So, public sector management is about systems and structures that can deliver a range of functions (prescribed or permitted by statute) and enable appropriate agencies to provide services. Services for young people have their basis in the 1944 Education Act. Years of lobbying are beginning to make headway towards clear agreement as to what constitutes an adequate and sufficient youth service (the youth work 'pledge' and new standards currently in development).

---

4   See Charles Handy for an exploration of different organisational cultures. Handy, Charles (1993, 4th edn) *Understanding Organisations*, London: Penguin, pp181–209.

Ten distinctive elements of a new model of public sector management have been identified:[5]

1. **Catalytic** – steering rather than rowing. Steering (policy and regulation) is separated from rowing (service delivery and compliance). Many different methods of service delivery are used including: contracts, vouchers, grants and tax incentives. The best method is chosen to provide the most effective services at the most reasonable cost. This is visible in the development of executive agencies (such as the Vehicle Inspectorate or the Prison Service) and 'small business units' (such as the Connexions Service National Unit, or the Sure Start Unit) which have targets, budgets and considerable executive freedom. These are distinct from the policy and regulatory elements of government.

2. **Community owned** – empowering rather than serving. Control of services is pushed out into the community. Communities are funded to solve their own problems and become independent. The New Deal for Communities initiative exemplifies this principle.

3. **Competitive** – injecting competition in services. Service deliverers must compete for UK Government business based on quality of performance and price. The Best Value regime incorporates competition as one of the four 'C's. It replaced the (fairly ineffective as judged by the Audit Commission) requirement for Compulsory Competitive Tendering (CCT). UK Government has taken this principle further by introducing competition between local authorities, through league tables, with extra rewards going to those that perform best, most notably through the inception of its Comprehensive Performance Assessment for Local Authorities process.

4. **Mission driven** – in place of rule driven government. Each agency is given the freedom to pursue its mission, with managers free to choose the most effective way to deliver within the overall mission of the authority and legal bounds. Internal regulations are reduced, unnecessary rules removed and procedures simplified, for example budgets, personnel and procurement. The requirement under the Local Government Act 1999 for local authorities to produce a Community Plan exemplifies this principle. The Community Plan provides the over-arching mission for all the services in the area. Service providers are expected to align their missions to the Community Plan and then be free to get on with improving their services.

5. **Results oriented** – funding outcomes (results) not inputs. Concern is no longer with 'did you follow the correct procedures?' but with 'have you achieved the right results?'. This goes hand in hand with setting targets in relation to results. Ideally targets should be set locally, with community involvement. The introduction of Best Value Performance Indicators, along with numerous inspectorates, each setting its own targets, has led to a heavy 'top-down' approach in England with criticism of the volume of performance measurement required. Emphasis appears to be shifting towards self-assessment and the idea of continuous improvement (as evidenced by results). UK Government has created opportunities under Public Service Agreements (PSAs) for authorities to gain some additional freedoms, flexibilities and funds in return for meeting more ambitious service delivery (and improvement) targets.

6. **Customer driven** – meeting customer needs rather than service needs. Service users are treated as customers. This means putting the service user at the centre of the service. Providers are expected to find out what service users think of the services.

---

5   See footnote 2.

They are expected to consult and involve them (increase their voice) and whenever possible to make sure that service users have a choice. The Best Value regime again exemplified this. Service users (and non users) were given a statutory expectation that they would be consulted. Along with an increasing voice in this way, service users (such as parents and children) have been encouraged to seek choices (such as in schools). One local authority has appointed a customer care officer, whose task includes acting as a mystery shopper using the services the authority provides.

Reflection

Consider your role as a manager. Can you detect a shift away from old-style professional and administrative management towards the new public management? What opportunities might this open up? What are the threats?

If you are a manager from a voluntary organisation, consider what impact the new public management is likely to have on your organisation and its work with young people. What are the opportunities this might open up? What are the threats?

7. **Enterprising** – earning not spending. The emphasis moves towards generating resources that can be invested in better services. Fees are charged, a return on investment is expected, incentives such as enterprise funds, challenge funds (where for example half the money provided by UK Government has to be matched from local sources) and so on are used to encourage managers to generate income. Another example was the Standards Fund – a central fund that enabled local youth services to develop their own initiatives to drive up standards. This was incorporated from 2003-2006 into the Transforming Youth Work Development Fund.

8. **Anticipatory** – focusing on prevention rather than cure. Local government is expected to think ahead and plan services to meet predicted need, or to eradicate need altogether, rather than respond to particular events and crises. This puts an emphasis on a manager's thinking and planning strategically, being able to step back from day-to-day work to look ahead, and on longer term planning and budgetary systems (which escape the tyranny of annual planning). There is a growing emphasis on active management of risk across all areas of the organisation.

9. **Decentralised** – moving from hierarchy to participation and teams. Greater discretion for decision making is pushed down the line to those staff who have direct contact with customers. The principle of subsidiarity is followed, ie decisions are made nearest to the ground unless they are better made higher up. Managers empower employees by flattening the chain of command and making sure that people are aware of what authority they have to act. Hand in hand with this empowerment, managers must establish clear processes for reporting back and accountability.

10. **Market oriented** – levering change through the market. The market is used where it has strengths to offer the provision of public services. For example, using tax incentives to encourage organisations and individuals to behave in ways that solve societal problems. Local government might find a way to encourage small organisations to create ideas to solve the problem of household waste rather than continuing to deliver a centralised bureaucratic waste disposal system.

The changing third sector

What is the third sector?

The third sector is made up of organisations whose purpose is not private gain and which are not in the public sector (and therefore directly under the control of elected politicians). It contains a wide variety of organisations, whose only shared characteristic seems to be that they are not of the public sector nor are they for private gain: charities, mutual and self help organisations, housing associations, community businesses, universities, religious bodies, sports clubs, community groups and so on.

6   For discussion of the ICNPO see Kendall, Jeremy and Knapp, Martin (1966) *The Voluntary Sector in the UK*, Manchester: Manchester University Press.

There is no single standard definition of the third sector. The International Classification of Non-Profit Organisations (ICNPO[6]) was developed by Lester Salamon at Johns Hopkins University in the USA, in the 1990s. This is an important benchmark, but confines itself to classifying organisations by the field in which they operate (such as health, environment or housing).

The ICNPO standard can be refined by combining it with two other dimensions[7]: **who benefits** from the activities of the organisation (which individuals, institutions and/or the environment); and **what the organisation does**. The functions are usually divided into four main types: providing funding; providing services; campaigning, lobbying and advocating; and representation.

Charities and other civil organisations have been described as the cornerstone of democratic societies.[8] They are associated with the maintenance of 'community' in all its varied forms. The New Labour UK Government has promised a more inclusive, fairer, but still enterprising society. There are high expectations that charities and other civil organisations will have a new and vigorous part to play working alongside government and commerce in building this new society. The UK Government introduced a new Voluntary Sector Compact[9] in 1998 following extensive consultation and discussion with voluntary organisations. This established, for the first time, an explicit framework for government and voluntary sector to work together. Since then local authorities have been encouraged to agree their own local compacts.[10]

The *Report on the Future of the Voluntary Sector in England*[11] described how voluntary organisations are being asked to perform more and more tasks on behalf of UK Government. It argued for recognition of the independence of voluntary organisations but warned that

'... this freedom has to be coupled with the recognition that taking on new roles and relationships also involves accepting responsibilities: in particular, clear accountability for performance.'

Blurring of boundaries

In the olden days we had a simple division of organisations into three sectors – voluntary, private and public – as shown in figure 6.3.

In this model the private sector (and to some extent the public sector, through nationalised industry) generates wealth, from which taxation (and borrowing) provides the money for the public sector to provide public services. Civil society is funded by individual and company donations, and by grants or contracts with the public sector.

Figure 6.3: Three sectors

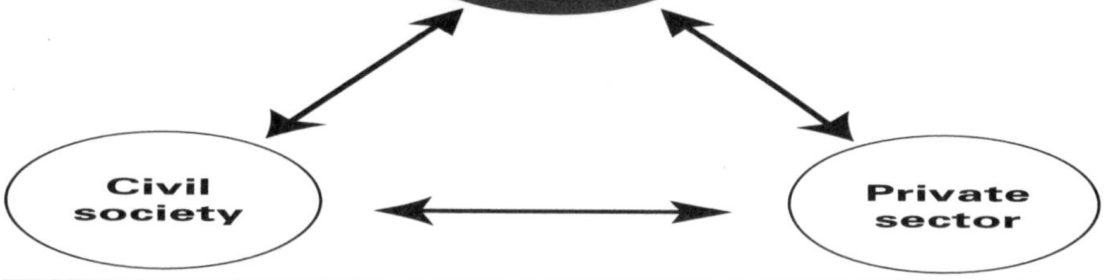

---

7 See NCVO (2001) *Voluntary Sector Almanac 2000*, London: NCVO Publications.
8 For example Salamon, Lester (1995) *The Global Associational Revolution: The Rise of the Third Sector on the World Scene*, Demos: London.
9 For details see NCVO website: www.ncvo-vol.org.uk
10 See NCVO (2000) *Local Compact Guidelines: getting Local Relationships Right Together*, London: NCVO.
11 Deakin, Nicholas (1996) *Report of the Commission on the Future of the Voluntary Sector*, London: NCVO.

The model seems wholly inadequate to describe the current complexity. It perpetuates ideas of boundaries and divisions between the sectors, which are misleading and unhelpful.

It seems more useful to describe the activity using just two dimensions (from Rob Paton[12]) – whether they are for private or public benefit, and their size.

Figure 6.4: Organisations and individuals in society

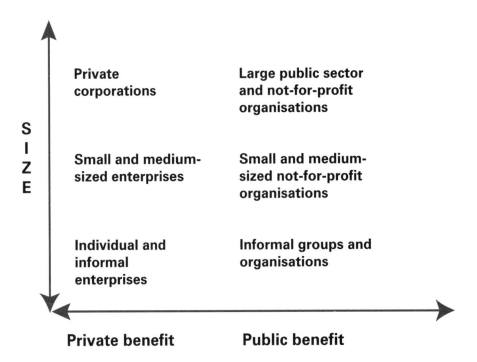

Adapted from Paton, 1992

The boundaries between the organisations and individuals shown in figure 6.4 are blurred and shifting. Many organisations which exist for private benefit are rapidly developing community links, employee involvement, social responsibility programmes and sponsorship of charities and community groups etc. The National Health Service, a public body, is the largest single involver of volunteers in the UK. Charities, such as Age Concern and Oxfam, have well-developed commercial subsidiaries. Building societies and mutual insurance societies, which arguably had social objects in mind at their inception, have been widely privatised.

In the charity world there is remarkable segmentation by size. Over two-thirds of charities are small, with incomes of less than £10,000 per year. Nine out of ten charities have annual incomes of less than £100,000.

Medium sized charities whose annual incomes are between £100,000 and £1 million make up only 7.3 per cent of all charities, but account for a quarter of the sector's income.

Large charities, with incomes of more than £1 million per year make up only 1.5 per cent of the sector, but account for 65 per cent of its annual income.

12 Rob Paton in Julian Batsleer, Chris Cornforth and Rob Paton (ed) (1992) *Issues in Voluntary and Non-Profit Management*, Wokingham: Addison Wesley.

Impact of the market

Charities have had to adapt to operating as part of complex, changing markets. There has been an emphasis on efficiency and competitiveness, and a sharp growth in the use of the marketing tools and techniques imported from the business world.

Service providing charities, in particular, have been affected by the creation of markets and quasi markets in the public sector. The nature of quasi markets is important to charities that are contractors to statutory bodies. Marilyn Taylor[13] identifies a number of differences between quasi markets and conventional markets. Objectives and ownership are less clear; providers are not driven by profit; purchasing power may not be in the form of cash; the customer may not make purchasing decisions.

A considerable volume of service provision has been contracted out to charities from the state, and charities have had to learn to operate as contractors in a market economy. This has brought with it enormous cultural and operational change in organisations.

There has been a move away from relatively unspecific grant giving, towards tightly specified grants and contracts. Linked to this has been the development of criteria for measuring the quality of services provided by charities, particularly on contract to other bodies.

The fragmentation of statutory services and the growth of contracting has led to a blurring of traditional distinctions between state services, voluntary sector services and private provision. Charities are in open competition with other organisations and aspects of their organisational structures have evolved to address or reflect this. Contracts are won not on the virtues of the charity's values and ethos, but on the basis of best, most cost effective match to the purchaser's specification.

The third sector as service provider

Contracting out of public services and plural provision continues. The UK Government conducted a far reaching review of voluntary organisations with a view to identifying and remedying barriers which prevent them from providing public services. This so-called cross-cutting review[14] has led to a raft of initiatives to build the capacity of voluntary and community sector organisations. In particular, the review embeds in UK Government policy the principle that voluntary organisations providing public services should be expected to receive from the UK Government the full cost of providing the service including full organisational overhead. The Best Value regime has accelerated the involvement of voluntary organisations as service providers as it has required commissioners of services to explore comparative costs from a variety of providers and to encourage competition.

Charities are part of a market for social, health and other services. Direct public funding through grant aid is unlikely to increase and may continue to decline. UK Government is actively seeking ways to enable more charities to enter partnerships with central and local government. Charities themselves are arguing for fair treatment, the implementation of the new deal regarding core costs, and to be treated as valued equals. For many smaller organisations, often dealing in isolation with a local authority youth service, a way forward in addressing this search for equity in partnership is to form a strategic alliance with others within the sector. This is therefore an additional focus for the manager to consider

---

13 Taylor, Marilyn; Hoyles, Lesley; Lart, Rachel and Means, Robin (1992) 'User Empowerment in Community Care', in *Studies in Decentralisation and Quasi Markets*, Bristol: SAUS.
14 Cross Cutting Review on the role of the voluntary and community sector in service delivery (2002), HM Treasury.

from a strategic perspective, scanning the external environment for the opportunities that are presenting themselves that link their delivery to the agenda of the day.

Third sector organisations will continue to win substantial contracts to provide care services in areas formerly the preserve of the public sector. The questions raised by Barry Knight in 1993 over the tensions between providing services on a large scale and campaigning for social change are likely to be an item of considerable discussion.[15]

How can charities be effective at both, within the confines of one organisation?

The trading role of charities seems set to continue to expand, raising questions of the ethics and legal basis of charitable trading as well as questions from non-charitable competitors about unfair competition.

Professional branding and marketing

Voluntary organisations are investing more in building strong brand images, which they are using to sell their services and attract funds. The old relationship in which the charity trustees relied on the goodwill, gifts and grants from others is changing. Newer developments include direct selling (for example Age Concern's flowers, Oxfam's developing world products) and indirect selling through licensing deals (such as the use of charity logos on credit cards and the use of the National Trust's name on soups for sale in major supermarkets). Charities' trading and commercial activity is likely to grow. This may pose problems for the relationship between charities and their partners, such as arguments over intellectual property rights or branding.

Accountability and quality

The 1992 and 1993 Charities Acts, along with wider public debate on accountability such as that prompted by the Nolan Report on standards in public life and the Cadbury Report on the financial aspects of corporate governance, has led to detailed scrutiny of charity governance. This includes the nature of governance itself, the role of trustees, the capacity of trustees to carry out their role effectively, and the relationship between trustees and the newly emergent charity professionals. Charities are under greater pressure than ever before to account explicitly, not only for the money they spend but, more importantly, for the impact they are having in achieving their objects.

There is increasing expectation that charities will provide their stakeholders, including the general public, with information that is transparent, readily accessible and understandable.

Third sector organisations are expected to be able to demonstrate value for money in all their activities. They must be able to demonstrate explicitly the quality of their services, both to their users and to their funders.

Change in civil society itself

Britain along with most other parts of the world has over the past ten years experienced a growth in people's participation in voluntary organisations.[16] Whilst civil organisations appear to be growing, they are not doing so uniformly. Membership of traditional civil

---

15 Knight, Barry (1993) *Voluntary Action*, London: CENTRIS/Home Office.
16 See footnote 8.

organisations, including the church, trades unions, working men's clubs and women's institutes is in decline. However, involvement in newer, often looser forms of organisation – particularly single-issue campaigns (such as road protests and environmental action) – appears to be rising. Many of these campaigns seem to be premised on the belief that political processes will not effect the necessary changes citizens hope for to improve society.

Alongside this has been a marked growth of interest in the importance of civil society and in the mechanisms through which people participate. Part of this new interest has been prompted by concerns about the capacity of individualistic societies to compete with those which have retained strong community cultures. New thinking includes communitarianism,[17] and the idea of social capital.[18]

This has been in parallel to an increasing apathy and disenchantment with mainstream politics. Professor John Stewart at the Institute of Local Government at Birmingham University has set out an agenda for changes in the organisation and management of local government.[19] The Commission for Local Democracy has explored similar territory.

We appear to be on the edge of significant change in the way in which the state, organisations and individuals relate to each other. There is a recognition of complexity and the need for much more fluid systems to involve both citizens and organisations in planning and decision-making.[20] It is unclear what shape this new set of relationships will eventually take!

The changing wider world

Globalisation

There is a rapidly escalating trend towards what has been called 'the global village'. National governments appear increasingly less powerful in the face of the global marketplace. Also they have to address the needs and demands of regional administrations within their territories.

At the same time, developments in rapid mass communications have made it possible for individuals to interact directly with large suppliers of goods and services and to expect to receive products and services tailored to their needs. This process is mirrored amongst providers of services, whether private or not for profit, where there appears to be a paradoxical movement towards very large organisations covering vast areas within which there are localised and specialised business units. These units have the advantage of being close to their local customers and tuned to their local customers' needs.

Accompanying both these changes has been the impact of information technology. Computers, the internet and international computerised banking systems have all contributed to global communication effected within minutes at the press of a button.

Consumerism

The importance of consumer rights – ultimately exercised through the courts – has risen. The

17 The term was coined in Thurow, Lester (1993) *Head to Head: the Coming Economic Battle Among Japan, Europe and America*, New York: Warner.
18 Putnam, Robert (1995) 'Bowling Alone: America's declining Social Capital', *Journal of Democracy* 6, pp65–78.
19 Stewart, J. (1995) *Innovation in Democratic Practice*, Birmingham: University of Birmingham, Institute of Local Government.
20 An example in a local authority context is Arthur Battram's excellent pack *Learning from Complexity*, from the Local Government Management Board. A more academic treatment is Kickert, W. J. et al (1997) *Managing Complex Networks – Strategies for the Public Sector*, Sage: London.

growing use of charters for users of public services has accentuated this trend. The public has been encouraged to be discriminating about demanding of those who provide services.

There has also been a growth in movements of people who use welfare services, usually linked to ideas of civil rights and justice. The demand for user involvement and representation continues to grow.[21]

These developments have brought with them the threat of litigation if services are not up to standard. They have also brought pressure to develop effective mechanisms to consult with and involve users and consumers in the running of services.

Demographic changes

The demographic changes faced by the United Kingdom in common with most other western democracies have been well documented. Not only will people be living longer and for the most part, more healthily into old age but people may also be retiring earlier. The working population is likely to continue to shrink whilst productivity rises.[22] This seems to be coupled with greater pressure on those in work, and a growing reluctance by those in work to support, unquestioningly, those who are not – a less tolerant and caring world?

The gap between the rich and the poor continues to grow. The role of the state or other mediating agencies will be important in redistributing wealth. There will be a growing problem of financing old age.

The demographic impact of large-scale migration, including asylum seekers, is a growing issue.

Changes in social institutions

The institutions and structures which symbolised British society and which were once taken for granted, are in transition. The monarchy, systems of government, the professions, the police, schools, work, religion, church, marriage and family are all being questioned, rethought and redrawn so as to be relevant to a modern, multi-cultural society. Women's changing role in the home and workplace, the working lives of all parents and geographical mobility are also impacting on social and family life. The composition of households is also changing, for example, more and more Britons live alone. Personal privacy is more highly valued and sought after. Society is described as becoming more atomised and individualistic.

Equality and diversity

The New Labour UK Government has made a priority of bringing the excluded back into the mainstream of society. All organisations have been affected by the development of equality and diversity strategies in society and the workplace. Legislation has meant that a certain standard of anti-discrimination practice is now expected. A climate of expectation regarding the needs and demands of minority groups has developed.

Global climate change and environmentalism

The climate appears to be changing. World governments are working towards the

21 Robson, Paul et al (1997) *Consumerism or Democracy? User Involvement in the Control of Voluntary Organisations*, York: Joseph Rowntree Foundation.
22 Hobsbawn, E. (1994) *Age of Extremes: the Short 20th Century*, London: Penguin.

implementation of far reaching agreements to limit environmental damage and avert a possible catastrophe. The speed of change is slow.

The UK Government is introducing an increasing number of measures to limit environmental damage. Impact on the environment is an important management standard in all sectors.

Young people in particular appear to identify closely with the demand for a cleaner, healthier, biologically diverse and sustainable future.

Changes affecting organisations that work with young people

Organisations working with young people in England are directly affected by three main policy developments: the Connexions Strategy and Service; Transforming Youth Work, particularly the *Resourcing Excellent Youth Services* publication; and the Children Bill and its associated publication *Every Child Matters: Next Steps*.

Reflection

Consider the trends identified.
Would you add any or emphasise any in particular?
What is the likely impact of these wider trends on your organisation?

All three developments flow directly from the work of PAT 12 (see page 106) that, in turn, drew from its own analysis of change in the wider external environment as it affects young people.

They seek to ensure that services to all young people are improved (universal services) and that agencies become more effective in targeting services towards those young people most in need. The need to include young people in decision-making is emphasised, as is the need for evidence of good practice, continuous improvement and service quality.

It is essential that senior managers have read and analysed the key documents on these policies.

So what does this have to do with me?

The trends and changes described above have a direct impact on managers of youth work. For example:

1. There will be proportionately fewer young people as the impact of demographic change is felt. Will this affect the young people with whom you work?
2. The demand for evidence-based practice will rise. Can your organisation provide evidence of need for the services it runs and evidence of impact that will satisfy UK Government funders?
3. Parts of the statutory youth service have already been, or are in the process of being, outsourced away from direct local authority control. This has taken a variety of forms including:
   ● Wholesale transfer to a Connexions partnership.
   ● Retention of a small strategic commissioning core with all delivery outsourced to third sector organisations.
   ● The delivery of local authority youth services in areas outside their own.
   ● Setting up a new charitable company to run the youth service.
4. Voluntary organisations are being encouraged to take on more delivery of youth services – what will the affects of this be? In many areas more youth work is being

delivered by voluntary organisations and other public agencies than by the statutory youth service.

5. The market for youth workers has become more competitive. There is a national shortage of qualified youth workers (the Youth and Community Workers' Union estimates that England is short of approximately 4,000 qualified youth workers). Recruitment and retention have become big issues. How are these affecting your organisation?

6. There appears to be a growth in specialist work with young people – such as in the environment and in relation to business development whilst generic work is growing less fast. Will this affect you?

7. There will be more frequent and thorough inspection. Organisations will be expected to meet demanding standards.

8. Organisations are likely to be required to produce evidence of their commitment to the environment. What impact will this have on you?

Reflection

Consider this list and add any of your own strategic dilemmas.

Chapter Seven:
Managing your resources strategically

Introduction

This chapter explores the role of the manager in managing and deploying resources to best effect towards achieving the strategy. We focus on the key resources of money, people and information.

The chapter looks at some key ideas and concepts and focuses on the particular dilemmas facing senior managers in youth work organisations. We conclude with a short coverage of risk management.

This chapter is firmly located in the lower right hand quadrant of our model – deploying resources to deliver your organisation's strategy. The chapter covers:

- Allocating resources
- Costing services
- Budgets and financial plans
- Managing your people
- Managing information
- Managing risk

Figure 7.1: The experiential cycle

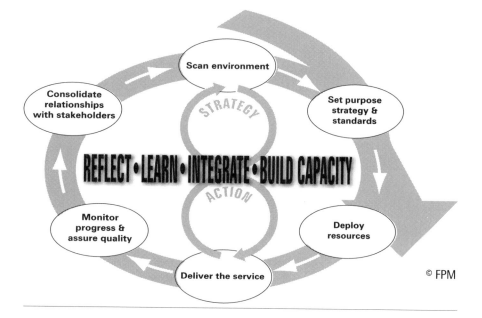

Allocating resources

Organisations use a range of resources to achieve their strategic objectives. When a strategic plan is drawn up, resources need to support the strategy.

Many organisations use an incremental approach to resource management – last year's resources plus a bit more – which can lead to the resources becoming increasingly out of line with strategy.

Example

A county youth service had allocated resources to community colleges, based on historic precedent. The resources did not mirror needs in the county. Each year each institution would bid for last year's resources plus a bit more. It took several years to change this historic allocation and incremental approach to one based on evidence of need.

We describe in the following paragraphs a model for resource allocation. We are conscious that whatever the model may say, the budget for many youth services or youth work chapters of voluntary organisations, has typically been imposed externally, based on historic considerations, not coupled with need and not easily open to bargaining. It has been under constant threat (or reality) of erosion, so the norm has been to defend a dwindling resource. Around the fringe of this main budget, managers have seized new money in whatever form it became available, from challenge funds, new initiatives and partnerships. In voluntary youth organisations resource allocation is often even more basic: it is dependent on what money has been raised or is likely to be raised, rather than need. We consider the allocation model worth exploring as it provides a baseline from which to think.

Resource planning involves two main sets of decisions:

1. Broad decisions on how resources should be allocated between functions, departments divisions or separate units.
2. More detailed decisions on how resources should be deployed within any one part of the organisation to support the strategies.

Two important factors affect the approach to resource allocation:

1. The amount of change required in the resource base to fit the strategy – either change in the aggregate level of resources or significant shifts between resource areas.
2. The extent of central control of the allocation process.

These factors can be expressed as a diagram (see figure 7.2) and lead to four main approaches:

- Formula, often with some room for bargaining and fine tuning. This usually leads to disagreements about its validity and fairness and many formulae are too rigid to support strategic development.
- Free bargaining, where each service head or manager negotiates for the necessary resources on an individual basis. This is rarely seen in its true form because it is too disruptive and time consuming. An alternative approach is to relax the rules on virement (flexibility in using money allocated to one budget heading, on another, eg

saving money on wages and using the money for activities), giving each area some degree of discretion about how it deploys its resources.

● Open competition, where areas bid for resources. This is usually constrained to bidding for new or additional funds.

● Imposed priorities, where resources follow strategic priorities eg top-slicing for new ventures or freezing staff replacements – any vacancies are released to the area with the most pressing needs.

Figure 7.2: Approaches to allocating resources

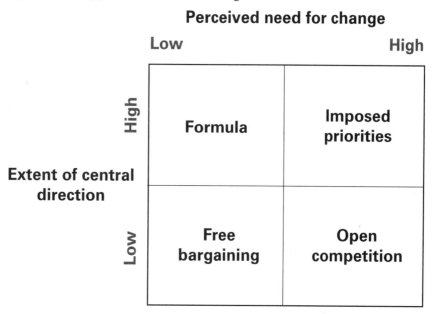

From: Johnson and Scholes, 1993

Reflection

How are resources allocated to the youth service in your authority or how does your organisation allocate resources to support youth work?

How far is the resource allocation a given, based on a formula, and how far is it open to bargaining?

To what extent has or could the review process lead to the reallocation of resources?

Where resources are static or declining, reallocating resources will require some areas to reduce in absolute terms to maintain other areas and/or support new developments. It is sometimes possible to achieve reductions by amalgamating related areas or activities, although this is extremely difficult in a small organisation or service. In this case budget reductions usually result in some part of the service having to go. UK Government appears to be seeking ways to create greater flexibility of resource allocation by relaxing the rules about local authorities working outside their area. For example, a number of youth services and organisations might be able to make cost savings by sharing core functions.

Extreme forms of resource reallocation are possible only in times of crisis and usually mean closing down one part of the organisation or even whole organisations.

Reviews in general and Best Value reviews in the statutory sector provide an opportunity for resource reallocation. The history of Best Value suggests that reviews have not led to significant increases in funding to support youth work, although positive results do appear to strengthen the platform for promoting youth work and may yield more resource in the longer term.

Charging for shared resources (overheads)

One of the particularly difficult and contentious issues involving resource allocation is the mechanism used to charge for shared resources, or central services given to service providing areas. There are three common methods:

- Indirect charging through an overhead recovery charge. This approach is fairly arbitrary, in that there may be no relationship between the charge and the use made of the central service. This is a common approach for many local authorities and voluntary organisations.
- Direct charging for services as used. This puts the onus on the central service to earn its budget and is used for services such as recruitment, property maintenance, printing or legal services. This is done by some local authorities and some larger voluntary organisations.
- Direct **charging by passing managerial responsibility to a designated division**, which then cross-charges other users. This is not popular because it can result, for example, in a head of service becoming responsible for printing.

Direct charging methods keep accountability and responsibility together but may lead to bureaucracy. Many organisations confine charging to two main areas:

- Internal services that can be delivered in a genuine customer/supplier way (e.g. IT), through service level agreements (SLA) (or recharging without any SLA!).
- Major items of overhead, where an incentive is needed to encourage areas to think more strategically, eg floor space. For example, a local authority that adopted the approach of charging a notional rent for the floor space occupied by each department found itself with spare accommodation, which is rented out to other organisations.

The approach used to charge out central overheads has a direct effect on the cost of service delivery. The different approaches used by local authorities have made comparisons of unit costs and spending per head almost meaningless. To enable more meaningful comparisons to be made the Chartered Institute of Public Finance and Accountancy (CIPFA) has published *Best Value Accounting Code of Practice 2002*[1] after consulting local authorities on the best way forward.

In the next few pages we explore the basics of costing. Costing your service is fundamental both to budgeting and to judgments about its competitiveness and whether it constitutes best value.

Costing services

Costing is the process of gathering information to enable you to say how much it costs to deliver a service. Accurate costing enables managers to:

- decide at what level to seek finance in order to achieve their objectives and targets (or ensure that their activities can be financed from the budget they have been given);
- decide at what price to sell their services, if they are contracted by other agencies, or to compare, in a Best Value review, with the price of other service providers (price is the cost plus whatever is added to build a surplus or profit); and
- see where savings could be made if particular parts of the service delivery process were carried out differently.

There are four main elements:

---

1 CIPFA *Best Value Accounting: Code of Practice 2002*, London, Chartered Institute for Public Finance and Administration (from website www.cipfa.org.uk).

1. **Direct costs** – those that can be attributed in full directly to the delivery of the service, eg cost of actual staff time, cost of materials used, cost of heat and light used, transport costs, equipment and insurance.
2. **Indirect costs or overheads** – incurred whilst delivering the service but cannot be directly attributed to that product or service, eg management time, proportion of organisation costs to support the service (eg finance, human resources or legal), proportion of building or other capital costs.
3. **Fixed costs** – do not change (in the short-term at least) with the level of activity eg rent, rates, salaries, some insurance costs. Stepped fixed costs are fixed between certain ranges of activity. At a critical level of activity the costs step up to a new plateau, eg supervision costs in a children's day centre might be fixed for supervising one to five children, but a sixth child may require an additional child-carer to be employed.
4. **Variable costs** – vary in direct proportion to the volume of the activity, eg the cost of providing learning materials for an IT programme will be directly proportional to the number of people on the programme. Some costs are semi-variable, as they include an element of both fixed and variable costs, eg telephone costs contain a fixed element (the line rental) and a variable element (call charges).

Variable costs include **opportunity costs**. These are the cost of the sacrifice made when a choice of one course of action precludes the pursuit of an alternative course. For example, if managers spend a day planning, there is an opportunity cost of the loss of the whole team's typical daily work as well as the cost of their time on the day. The opportunity cost to managers of taking part in external partnerships needs to be carefully considered.

Variable costs also include **marginal costs** – the additional costs arising from the delivery of additional units of service. For example, if a tutor is running a course for 16 learners, adding two should make very little difference to the overall costs of running the event. Generally, the higher the amount of an activity the lower the marginal cost.

Figure 7.3: Fixed and variable terms

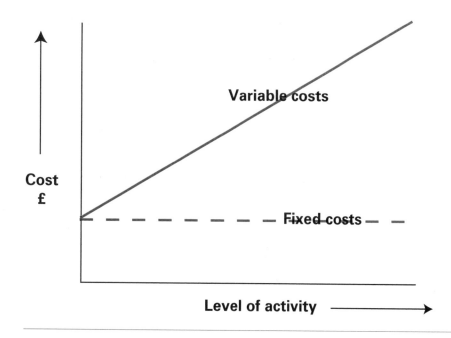

Managers also need to be aware of which costs they have direct control over: the controllable costs. To a great extent, any costs outside the controllable costs are of limited immediate interest to the manager. Many quite senior managers have in reality limited control over most of their costs. For example, staffing is typically the main cost and it is possible to reduce staff costs by increasing staff productivity (making best use of their time, using technology), delaying appointments, making posts redundant and replacing expensive staff with less expensive (ie usually less qualified or experienced) ones.

Different strategies for costing

Costing is not an exact science. It involves making judgments. Judgments about the cost of an activity may result from three broad strategies or approaches:

Full costing

Full costing adds the direct cost of delivering the service to a proportion of the total overheads. The 'centre' of the organisation charges the various units that provide services for a proportion of the overheads. In complex organisations this may take place at more than one level (eg a local authority may have a corporate overhead, departmental and unit or divisional overhead). The overheads can be classified in different ways. CIPFA classifies local authorities' overheads into four categories:

● support services eg payroll, personnel, finance;
● corporate management;
● service management; and
● regulation.

This is a useful checklist, which could also be applied to voluntary organisations.

Full costing in public authorities (and many voluntary organisations) sets out the full cost of delivering a service or activity at the start of each budgetary period. It may be difficult to vary the budget during the year. This makes it relatively inflexible. A service that does more than is expected will usually be unable to get additional resources, and so may have to be rationed.

This contrasts with organisations that generate income directly from their activities. In these organisations, once the full cost of the overheads has been covered, further activity helps to generate a surplus. This further activity is usually costed in a different way using marginal costing.

Marginal costing

In marginal costing, the direct costs of providing a particular activity (direct labour, direct materials and direct overheads) are subtracted from income generated by the activity. Whatever is left over is used as a contribution to the general organisational overhead. At a certain point the overhead is covered and break-even is reached. Any additional activity generates surplus.

Figure 7.4: Marginal costing

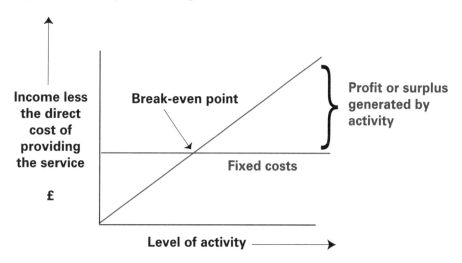

Marginal costing covers the overhead of the particular activity first then begins to generate a surplus.

Activity based costing

The third approach to costing identifies the total cost related to a specific activity. The activities are priced to recover the total cost and, if appropriate, make a profit. This is the method used by many professionals and tradespeople, including lawyers, management consultants, plumbers and personal fitness coaches. It requires detailed record keeping of time spent in activities as well as a very accurate system for apportioning overheads to each unit of activity.

Example

An Ofsted inspector might spend 1.5 hours travelling for a 2.5 hour visit to a youth facility. To cost the work we would need to know:

* total cost of one standard hour of the inspector's time
* total cost of the travelling time.

One standard hour
The standard hour of labour is a calculation in which the total salary and other costs of employing the inspector plus an additional amount to cover both fixed and variable overheads (eg rent, rates, insurance, management time) is divided by the number of contact hours in any one year. Note that the contact hours are not the same as the number of hours a person could work in the year. This method of calculation is called full charge out rate recovery. In a commercial company there will be an added element to provide profit.

Travelling time
The cost of travel will include salary, the cost of transport (such as mileage rates or the cost of vehicle leasing).

Dilemmas with costing

The way that a manager approaches the costing of her or his services can have profound implications. If the costings are inaccurate or use false assumptions, the financial basis of the service can be undermined. We have identified a number of common costing dilemmas for managers in services and organisations that work with young people:

Doughnut costing

All the organisation's activities are costed on a marginal cost basis. This means activities cover their own costs but are not expected to contribute to the organisation's overall overheads (core costs). The result is a doughnut, with activity surrounding a core which has little or no resources. This can lead to slow breakdown of management, as the core managerial roles always take second place to the task of delivering the marginal activity. This is very common in small organisations, classic symptoms include minimal or absent management systems, little time spent on overall strategy and a sense of frantic activity as staff search for resources for the next round of activities. The price of the services as charged to others is kept low, creating an artificial market, as the necessary investment in the core of the organisation is lacking.

In local government the management deficit at the core may be made up by inputs from the centre. This input still costs money and is being paid for somewhere in the system. The cost will eventually be passed on to each service. As local government services are contracted out, the size of the corporate centre in relation to the smaller service activities can grow to be disproportionate. This can lead to heavy overheads for the remaining services, accelerating the pressure for more outsourcing.

In voluntary organisations doughnut costing can make services look like good value. This is a fool's paradise as it is not sustainable. It is often linked to separate lobbying for 'core funding'. There would be no debate about core funding for service providers if their costings included an accurate contribution to the core overheads. The Association of Chief Executives of Voluntary Organisations has produced a useful booklet on core costs in voluntary organisations.[2]

House of cards

This is similar to the doughnut in that all costing is activity based. Here, however, the organisation has made an effort to cover a proportion of core costs from each activity. Problems arise if one of the activities fails. The loss of its contribution to the core may lead to the core becoming unsustainable and the whole financial structure collapsing like a pack of cards. The solution lies in building sufficient contingency resources into the costings to cover a reasonable level of this risk.

The shock of the full

When managers carry out a thorough full costing exercise, linked to the organisation's strategy, this may produce a considerably higher unit cost for each activity than previously. How does the organisation sort this out with its funders, commissioners and so on, who are notoriously unsympathetic to such price hikes? 'If you could provide the service at cost

---

2   ACEVO (2001) *Funding our Future: Core Costs Revisited.* From website www.acevo.org.uk

A last year, why can't you do so again this year (and how about a 2-3 per cent reduction while we are talking?)'

Investment and sustainability

In commercial organisations the cost of developing the management core is often met in the first instance by raising investment from outside. These investments have to be repaid, with interest, so the contribution of each activity to the overheads will rise. This sort of investment has been less obvious in the public and voluntary sectors – although the pursuit of 'core funding' is analogous. The difference with 'core funding' is that the organisation rarely costs its activities to make the core sustainable after the initial investment.

Unit costs and price

Reflection

Consider the approach your service or organisation uses to costing its activities. Are you confident that the unit cost of each activity provides you with coverage of the full cost of delivering the activity?

The unit cost is the cost of providing one unit of the service. To be sustainable your organisation must budget on delivering a certain number of units of activity at full cost. Additional activity might be costed on a marginal basis (although this can create a problem as the same activity may appear to cost two different amounts).

The price charged for the activity (to funders or commissioners) would be the full cost plus an amount for long-term investment and contingency.

Resource planning at service level

Although service level resource planning is detailed, it should be conceived in a strategic manner. It is important to understand how the detailed resource plan underpins the strategy. There are three key questions:

1. **Resource identification** – exactly what resources are needed to deliver the strategy and how should these be configured? There is a tendency to consider the new strategy on the basis of old expectations or existing ways of operating, rather than in terms of what is required in the future.
2. **Resource deployment** – how can existing resources be reconfigured to support the strategy and new resources fitted in?
3. **Added value** – how will the total resource fit together to add the greatest value?

The answers to these questions depend on the quality and clarity of the organisation's strategy. Many organisations that work with young people do not get past question 1, as they pursue an open ended strategy. The idea of adequacy and sufficiency in statutory youth services or clear and quantified targets in voluntary organisations can overcome this.

Resource plans

Key elements of a resource plan are shown in figure 7.5.

Figure 7.5: Resource plan – key elements

The plan should address:	Through one or more of . . .	Planning tools:
• Critical success factors • Key tasks • Priorities • Testing assumptions		• Budgets/financial plans • People's plans • Project plans

From: Johnson and Scholes, 1993

- **Critical success factors** are those factors on which the strategy depends for its success: for example, the need to improve staff skills or reduce costs. Keep these to a manageable list – no more than six. These are explored in more detail later in this chapter, when we look at information.
- Identify the **key tasks** essential to the delivery of each critical success factor. Allocate management responsibility for each of the key tasks.
- Establish **priorities**. Which tasks need to be done before others and which have priority because of their importance?
- Clarify **assumptions**. All plans are based on assumptions about what will happen. If these are not valid, you will need to adjust the plan. For example, your plan may be based on the assumption that new staff will be recruited. If this is not possible, the plan must be adjusted. This is an important stage in identifying the risks attached to your strategy. Approaches to risk management are dealt with later in this chapter.
- The **budget** should express your plan in financial terms. It is likely that only one year will be shown in detail, with further years covered in broad outline.
- The **people plan** should identify the number of people and the types and levels of skills needed. This will lead to recruitment, training and development plans.
- The **project plan** lists key tasks in priority order and establishes a timetable for implementing the strategy. If suitable milestones are built in, the project plan can be used as a mechanism for reviewing progress.

As senior managers you may delegate much of the detailed operational planning to your staff. However, it is essential that you are able to provide them with a clear framework for their planning and to adopt an effective leadership style. Some staff may need to be directed, some coached, some given gentle support and others may need to be left to get on with the task with you acting as a critical friend.

Providing your staff with clear critical success factors, with clear targets can free them to develop appropriate plans to meet the targets.

Budgets and financial plans

Johnson and Scholes[3] describe a budget as the financial model of the resources required to implement the strategy. 'One of the very real difficulties experienced in budgeting is the extent to which the process actually helps the reallocation of resources to fit future strategies. This is because the budgeting process is usually tied into the power structure in the organisation. The types of reallocation that may be necessary at both the corporate and operational level may well prove extremely difficult due to historical vested interests.'

Budget allocations are crucial for the implementation of strategies and plans but

---

3   Johnson, G. and Scholes, K. (1997) *Exploring Corporate Strategy*, Hemel Hempstead: Prentice Hall.

Reflection

Consider the approach your service or organisation uses to costing its activities.
Are you confident that the unit cost of each activity provides you with coverage of the full cost of delivering the activity?

'budgeting typically tends to be short-term, incremental, reactive and oriented towards accountability, rather than long-term, comprehensive, innovative, proactive and oriented towards the accomplishment of broad purposes, goals or priorities'.[4] This view is echoed in a report published in 1999 in which the Audit Commission called for a change in the approach to service and financial planning in local government.[5] Historically the priority has been to deliver services within tight financial constraints. This led to an emphasis on economy and efficiency rather than effectiveness (doing things right – or guarding your own back – rather than doing the right things for the service user).

Best Value reviews explore how well policy priorities reflect community needs and spending decisions. As the PAT 12 report points out (see page 106), there is concern that resources still do not go to those who most need them. Changing community needs are likely to be best met by a revision of spending priorities over the longer term. This calls for focusing the mainstream on priorities rather than developing discrete, short-term initiatives to tackle particular needs. The Neighbourhood Renewal Unit captures this change of emphasis in its recent publication *Bending the Spend*.[6] This will move authorities away from the incremental budgeting of the past.

Incremental budgeting assumes the expenditure patterns of the past are valid for the future. It creates a gap between budgeting and planning, which is unhelpful in implementing strategic plans. Mintzberg[7] argues there is a great divide between them because planning for control and planning for action are fundamentally different. Performance control consists of two hierarchies, budgets and objectives, while action planning consists of two additional hierarchies, strategies and programs. Bringing the two hierarchies together is not an easy task but new approaches to budgeting, which will be dealt with later in this chapter, go some way towards it.

Bryson recommends a number of strategies that managers can adopt to lessen the impact of incremental budgeting:

- Have strategic planning precede the budget cycle. This can help, but has been used by many organisations without any noticeable impact. The planning and budget cycles remain separate instead of being integrated.
- Leaders and managers can seek to influence budgeting in strategic directions. The short-term incremental nature of budgeting can be a source of opportunity rather than constraint for the strategically minded public and non-profit leader. The system is a natural setting for organising a series of small wins informed by a sense of strategic direction.
- Pick your budget fights carefully. Given the number of players that budgeting attracts, it is not possible to win every battle. Attention should therefore be focused on those battles which are crucial to moving the desired strategy forward.

The Audit Commission is insistent that a much more radical solution is needed in local government. It maintains that the duty to deliver Best Value will need to be backed by sound service and financial planning which will help to:

- identify community needs and allocate resources to meet them;
- focus on strategic decisions to bring about real improvements in service performance and delivery; and
- move away from year-on-year negotiations over detailed budget changes.

---

4   Bryson, J. M. (1995) *Strategic Planning for Public and Nonprofit Organizations: a Guide to Strengthening and Sustaining Organizational Achievement*, San Francisco: Jossey Bass.
5   Audit Commission (1999) *Planning to Succeed: Service and Financial Planning in Local Government*, London: Audit Commission.
6   Neighbourhood Renewal Unit (2002) *Bending the Spend: Harnessing the Power of Public Spending to Build Better Neighbourhoods*, London: Audit Commission.
7   Minztberg, H. (1994) *The Rise and Fall of Strategic Planning*, New York: Free Press.

Figure 7.6: Achieving Best Value

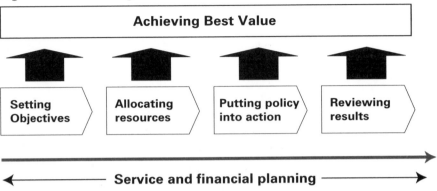

Adapted from Planning to succeed: service and financial planning in local government, Audit Commission, 1999

The Audit Commission recommends a single policy and resource allocation cycle, to ensure that the allocation of resources flows from changing service needs and priorities. It identifies four key elements:

● **Setting priorities and objectives.** This requires an appropriate forum including all relevant stakeholders – Local Strategic Partnerships are being groomed for this role, but may face difficulties actually delivering it! (see Chapter 10). These discussions need to take place early in the planning cycle.

● **Coordinating the process.** Setting a timetable to review spending against policy priorities. The budget then ensures that resources flow to meet the agreed priorities. The earlier the budget process starts, the less likely it is to be simply an incremental exercise and the more likely it is to reflect strategic service considerations.

● **Making informed choices.** Each service aligns its plans and spending to the overall strategy. Service plans should include a clear description of how the service provided meets the priority needs.

● **Scrutinising and reviewing progress** against plans.

The result should be an integrated approach to planning as is shown in figure 7.7.

Figure 7.7: An integrated approach to planning

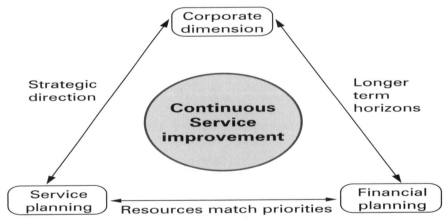

Adapted from: Planning to succeed: service and financial planning in local government, Audit Commission, 1999

Alternative approaches to budgeting

Dissatisfaction with traditional approaches to budgeting is not confined to the public sector or even to the United Kingdom. Ashworth and Connelly[8] state that traditional budgeting tends to:

● be inordinately time consuming for the benefits achieved;
● involve an excessive number of iterations;
● accept existing expenditure levels as the starting point of 'negotiations' and therefore encourage incremental cost build-ups;
● result in arbitrary cost slicing or cost reduction, with everyone taking an equal share of the budget allocation cutback; and
● be focused primarily on the resource inputs, which tend to be expressed almost exclusively in financial terms.

The weaknesses of incremental budgeting have led to two other approaches:

Zero based budgeting

Zero based budgeting (ZBB) is defined by CIMA (Chartered Institute of Management Accountants) as 'a method of budgeting whereby all activities are re-evaluated each time a budget is formulated. Each functional budget starts with the assumption that the function does not exist and is at zero cost. Increments of costs are compared with increments of benefit, culminating in planning maximum benefit for a given budgeted cost'.

The key to successful implementation of ZBB is a questioning attitude that challenges existing practices and expenditures. The idea is simple, but the process can be extremely disruptive unless it is tempered with pragmatism. The process of Best Value review creates a cycle that will encourage every service to conduct a zero based budgeting exercise at least every five years.

Activity based budgeting

ZBB has been superseded, to a large extent by activity based budgeting (ABB). This is based on activity based costing (see page 127) and aims to identify the cost of providing each activity or service.

Activity based budgeting supports continuous improvement and has been adopted by local authorities in a number of European countries. It recognises that:

● activities generate costs, so the aim is to manage the activities (rather than the costs). In the long run costs will be managed and better understood;
● not all activities add value, so it is essential to differentiate and examine activities for their value adding potential; and
● the majority of activities are driven by demands and decisions beyond the control of the budget holder. Activity based costing allows the manager to identify the parts of the budget over which he or she really has control.

---

8 Ashworth, G. and Connelly, T. (1994), 'An Integrated Activity-Based Approach to Budgeting', *Management Accounting*, vol. 2, issue 3, pp32–36.

Activity based budgeting:

- makes a clear link between strategic objectives and resource allocation;
- relates all costs to actual activities; and
- makes it easier to recognise the cross-organisational (or multi-agency) nature of some activities, and to be clear about their costs.

PBB is often referred to as a separate approach, but it can be an integral part of a full ABB system where it is used to decide on improvement priorities. The approach is one of comparing costs with contribution to achieving objectives and choosing those which yield the best return for the costs involved. The aim of priority based budgeting is to allocate resources according to a defined set of criteria that reflects the organisation's strategic aims. The use of activity and priority based approaches is recommended by the Audit Commission as a way of integrating service and financial planning.

Moving from inputs to results

The trend in budgeting has been an attempt to move from a focus on inputs (traditional approaches) to outputs (activity based approaches) and outcomes (priority based approaches). The US public sector (and also some parts of Europe) has developed the 'results based budgeting' approach. Rather than focusing on programmes, activities, input and productivity indicators such as how many people are served through the programmes or whether programmes are meeting their performance standards, decision makers ask questions about how well their investments are achieving the priority policy goals and outcomes they have articulated.

Asking whether investments are making the desired difference in people's lives is a bigger and more important question than whether a particular agency or programme is working properly, whether it is expending a certain level of effort and complying with specified rules. Such an approach requires a significant shift of emphasis to seeing the big picture and the impact of services on things that matter to people. The case study below gives an example from Holland of this sort of process.

Case study – Tilburg City Council (in Holland)

The council wanted a system that clearly linked its spend to outcomes for service users. Political leaders were particularly concerned to make resource allocation decisions informed by the impact of those decisions on their constituents.

Action

The budgeting approach is based on rethinking the work of service units in terms of 'products' (results) delivered to customers. More than 230 products have been identified. Product descriptions distinguish between the activities carried out, the product that they lead to and outcome targets (the policy effect). These elements are defined and measured each year. This process of definition and measurement involves staff and in turn, informs individual performance targets. Costs are assigned to products and the budget is constructed on this basis. To complement the budget process, an audit is carried out every four years, which looks at budgets within a wider context, including social changes that affect services, service quality and customer orientation.

Results
- Political leaders have well-founded information and costs for making decisions.
- Citizens are better informed about how money is spent and how services perform.
- Managers and staff have more opportunity to be innovative and creative in meeting customers' needs.
- Services are more responsive to changing needs.

The results of citizens' surveys show a steady increase in the level of user satisfaction. Tilburg has balanced its budgets since the late 1980s, and has had six years of budget surpluses.

Budgeting and the service leader

There are lessons to be learned from the alternative approaches to budgeting. Activities results in costs and budget management is not possible without a strong focus on the efficiency and effectiveness of these activities. An awareness of the costs of the various activities you control and of the underlying reasons for those costs is the first step in effective budgeting and resource management.

Ten questions about allocating your resources

Reflection

Work through the ten questions. Do you have sufficient information to answer them? Do you have the power to make changes that would deliver your strategy more effectively?

How far are you hamstrung by history – for example inheriting a significant spend on activities that are either not effective (not delivering your priorities) or not efficient (not making best use of resources)?

If this is the case, what are you, as a leader, doing to tackle the issues?

1. What are your strategic priorities?
2. Who will pay for you to deliver the priorities? (How well do your priorities fit with those of your funders, commissioners or paying customers?)
3. What is the full cost (including overheads) of delivering all your activities? (This includes internal servicing activity such as developing staff, managing information and finance etc, as well as direct service delivery).
4. How well do the activities fit with your strategic priorities (if they do not, how will you change them)?
5. How efficiently are the activities being carried out? How do the unit costs compare with other providers, other organisations and authorities? How could improvements or savings be made?
6. What new or different activities need to be carried out?
7. Who should be involved in the activities (to be both efficient and effective)? Are the right people involved now?
8. What is the total resource needed to deliver the strategy?
9. Where will the resource come from?
10. If there are shortfalls how will they be accommodated? Are you making enough use of others' resources (through partnerships etc.)?

Influencing resources outside your control

It is not enough to consider the resources you control directly, you should also identify

135

those held by others whose use you may be able to influence. Increasing involvement in collaborative working can provide the opportunity to influence the deployment of resources in other organisations in a way that contributes to achieving your objectives. It is important that partnership activities are reviewed in relation to the costs involved versus the contribution to achieving core objectives. This is explored in more detail in Chapter 10.

Seeking new resources

Managers in both statutory and voluntary organisations need to be able to find and secure new sources of funding. There is a great deal of money available but accessing it successfully requires a strategic approach.

Project funding has been a fact of life for many years and it is important to view funding for specific projects with some rigour. There has been a tendency to chase project funding without considering the relationship of project activities to the 'core business'. This can divert the organisation away from its purpose. Project funding must contribute to the core overheads, otherwise you will end up with doughnut costing and destabilise the organisation.

The manager needs to be aware of public funds (including European funds), charitable funds and resources in the private sector. Securing funding requires a clear case for why funding your agency will help the funders to achieve what they want. All the foregoing discussion of strategy, purpose, objectives plus information on need and likely impact is relevant.

Managing your people

Organisations that provide services to young people rely on the quality and performance of their staff. It follows that the skill of managing your people is fundamental to being an effective manager. There is not the space in this Book to cover the subject of managing people in any great depth; we are mainly concerned with the role of the manager in leading, motivating and inspiring her or his people. We have already looked at some aspects of this in relation to the management of teams in Chapter 5.

In these few paragraphs we aim to provide a short overview of the key management concepts relating to people management, clarify their relevance to managers in organisations that work with young people and surface some questions and dilemmas.

What is people management?

The terms 'people', 'personnel' and 'human resource' management are used almost interchangeably, both in practice and in the literature. In this book we will adopt the meaning used by the Personnel Standards Lead Body: 'to enable management to enhance the individual and collective contributions of people to the short and long-term success of the enterprise.'

Personnel management has often been criticised for being focused on policies and procedures such as payroll, recruitment, disciplinary and grievance. rather than having any strategic role. The rise in the use of the term 'human resource management' (HRM) accompanied a changing attitude to staffing – people could provide the competitive advantage and were a resource to be invested in and maximised, rather than a cost. HRM emphasises the importance of the people to the achievement of the overall strategy and marks out a more strategic role for people management. It seeks to embed effective people management at the heart of the delivery of the organisation's strategy. A number of key characteristics have been attributed to HRM,[9] namely, that it is a more comprehensive approach to the organisation and management of people at work, with an emphasis on:

- The integration of the people with general business management and the reinforcement of the desired organisational culture, aimed at 'unlocking' goals such as 'flexibility' and 'commitment'.
- The common interests of employer and employee in the success of the business to release the potential for initiative and commitment.
- A coherent set of relationships between human resource practices (eg between recruitment, induction, training and salary structures), and between those practices and the organisation's strategic aims and objectives.
- The role of the line manager, both at the strategic level and in the effective delivery of HRM policies, eg conducting team briefings, holding performance appraisal meetings, target setting, introducing quality initiatives.

Fowler observed that, 'In a nutshell, HRM represents the discovery of personnel management by chief executives.'[10]

Preoccupation with organisational culture

Modern people management places great emphasis on the management of the organisation's culture, as we discussed in Chapter 2). Many organisations, in response to intensifying competition have sought to create deliberate shifts in organisational culture. One of the most quoted case studies is that of British Airways who set out: 'To reorientate the corporate culture from one driven by internally generated concepts of what constituted professionalism and standards, to one which is driven by the expectations, standards and needs of our customers.'[11]

This preoccupation is now widespread in the public sector, where there has also been a sharp shift towards the interests of the service users and away from the interests of the public service professionals. The levers for securing cultural change are very visible: mission statements; linking training to the corporate strategy; corporate planning; developing quality assurance schemes. This approach sees the organisation in terms of a culture (see earlier discussion on page 42).

Principles for effective people management

There are many recipes for managing people. Pfeffer[12] specifies a set of seven critical people management principles:

- Security of the employment relationship.
- Putting in a lot of resources to recruit the right people in the first place.
- High expenditure on training and development.
- Extensive use of self-managed teams and decentralisation.

9   Storey, J. (ed.) (1995), *Human Resource Management – a Critical Text*, London: Routledge, pp3–32.
10 Fowler, A. (1987), 'When Chief Executives Discover HRM', *Personnel Management*, January, p3.
11 Bruce, M. (1987), 'Managing People First – Bringing the Service Concept to British Airways', *Industrial and Commercial Training*, March/April.
12 Pfeffer, J. (1998), *The Human Equation: Building Profits by Putting People First*, Cambridge Mass: Harvard Business School Press.

● Wage levels that are high and strongly linked to organisational performance.
● Reducing status differentials.
● A willingness to share information up, down and across the organisation.

The Harvard Model of HRM

Reflection

To what extent does your organisation follow the policies identified by Pfeffer?

At a more analytic level the Harvard Model of HRM is useful (see figure 7.8). It was developed by a team at Harvard Business School and sets out the components of a strategic approach to managing people. It draws from the 'soft' end of the management spectrum, with an emphasis on development, culture and commitment.

Figure 7.8: The Harvard HRM Model

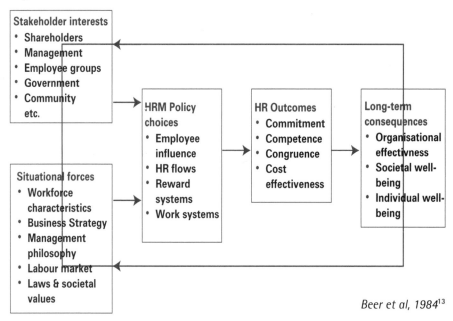

Beer et al, 1984[13]

The model combines understanding of the stakeholders' interests with understanding the forces affecting the organisation in the external environment. Analysis of these leads to the establishment of four core HR policy choices:

Reflection

Look at the Harvard model. Does your organisation achieve the four Cs of HR outcomes set out in the model? If not, what might be improved?

● **Employee influence** – how will staff be involved in decision making? What level of partnership does management want to build with its workforce?
● **HR flows** – the flow of people into, through and out of the organisation. This includes how the organisation approaches recruitment and selection, performance review, training and development. Do you recruit ready skilled people or grow your own? Do you seek long-term commitment or short periods of employment, etc?
● **Reward systems** – how does the organisation reward its staff? This includes both pay and conditions and more intrinsic rewards such as training and development, advancement, pensions, car schemes and so on. The debate lies mainly between advocates of performance related pay (opponents argue that its impact is often short term) and advocates of creating a culture in which people want to perform for a whole variety of reasons.
● **Work systems** – how is the work organised? How do staff fit into the system? What is the impact of new technology on the workplace?

---

13 Beer, M., Spector, B., Lawrence, P. R., Quinn-Mills, D. and Walton, R. E. (1984), *Managing Human Assets*, New York: Free Press.

The strategic HR policy choices should lead to staff being committed, competent, congruent (i.e. all working to the same ends) and cost effective. This in turn leads to benefits for the organisation, the staff and society as a whole.

Challenges for youth work managers

Dispersed and part-time staff

Youth work is typically carried out by staff who work in dispersed locations, often with a large proportion of part-timers. It is difficult to bring the staff together at any one time. Part-timers are often expected to spend nearly all their time in face to face work, with little space for team meetings, supervision, personal and professional development and so on. The task of building a strong and coherent culture for your organisation is therefore difficult. The checklist in Chapter 4 (page 68) provides some ideas.

One of the major blocks to progress is often as simple as poor costing. Many services have not costed sufficient resources to allow staff to develop and learn. The costs involve not only the time of the staff themselves, but also the cost of cover (if needed), additional management time and expenses.

Recruitment and retention

Some organisations have made all the right moves regarding training and development and are still struggling to recruit suitable staff. This reflects wider labour market changes, in particular an emerging demand for qualified youth work professionals to work within a number of other sectors. There is a growing problem recruiting experienced full-time staff, and an even greater one, across England, in attracting part-time staff. You may be very limited in how you can respond. What can you change in the way you employ your youth work staff?

Balance of staff skills

Reflection

What are the main challenges you face in aligning your people to the organisation's strategy? Have you explored all possible ways to overcome them?

Many youth work organisations limit the effect of their professional staff through lack of administrative support. This either means that either administrative functions do not get done or that professional youth work staff spend time on tasks that do not use their skills and which they may not be very good at. This is often a major hurdle when seeking to improve information gathering and flow. Looking at the whole human resource may lead managers to conclude that a small reduction in the total number of youth worker hours, in order to employ an administrative assistant, may actually lead to an increase in the number of contact hours by the youth workers with young people. The example below illustrates the point.

Small voluntary providers may have little or no resources to assist the development of skilled and motivated staff in a culture of learning and performance. One solution may be to build stronger strategic alliances with other agencies and organisations (such as the youth service or other voluntary organisations).

Example: Gaining more administration without losing contact time

During the annual review of provision in a department of an FE college two key issues were identified: a lack of surplus money and the target of gaining top grades for quality had not been met.

Inadequate administration was found to be a major contributing factor. This resulted in a failure to claim all available funding and in programme documentation not being completed to the standards required by the awarding bodies. Each group of programmes has a manager who is responsible for achieving agreed targets in relation to income and quality. These managers have an annual time allowance for programme management, which reduces their available contact time with students.

Initial discussions with the group of programme managers highlighted the need for additional administrative support. The managers felt that the time allocated was inadequate and a significant number said they were not really interested in 'driving a desk'. A number of options were debated, including increasing the time allowance for programme managers. This was rejected because it would be extremely difficult to find appropriately qualified part-time staff to cover the additional teaching hours this would throw up. The preferred option was to appoint an administrator dedicated to providing support for programme management. The proposal was approved but with a proviso that there was no increase in overall expenditure.

The programme management activities were analysed. The activities were split into two categories: those which could be carried out by an administrator and those which required detailed knowledge of the curriculum and students. The split was roughly 60:40. Given that a lecturer's contact hour costs roughly three times an administrator hour, this was clearly not the most effective use of scarce resources.

Programme managers agreed to a reduction of 40 per cent in their annual time allowance, which released the budget needed to pay for a full-time dedicated administrator. The programme managers were happy because they had proportionately more time to carry out those activities which required the use of their skills, knowledge and experience. It also meant that they had more contact time available, reducing the need for part-time staffing which was extremely difficult to find. A full-time administrator was employed, who continues to provide valuable support to all programme managers.

Reflection

Consider the example. Could you envisage similar events in a youth work organisation?

Tackling poor performance

One of the blocks to building a culture of high performance is under-performance of staff. This may be for a variety of reasons, ranging from a need to learn and develop skills to outright sabotage. The main vehicle for managing performance is a staff supervision and appraisal system which is directly linked to the achievement of the organisation's overall purpose and particular targets. This needs to be supported by regular informal communication which re-inforces the values and culture of the organisation. This amounts to the manager making sure that the 'story' of the organisation or agency is kept alive and fresh and does not degenerate into a series of unrelated individual stories.

The supervision process must balance effectively meeting the organisation's requirement for performance (clear targets and standards) with meeting the staff member's requirements for support, learning and development. Under-investment in supervision creates risk of patchy performance. It is not just a case of putting the system in place – all staff have to be able to use it and make it work, which brings a training cost.

To manage poor performance, the manager must first have established with the worker exactly what work (outputs and outcomes) is expected and to what standard. Without this, the worker is entitled to make the assumption that they can do what they like since they have not been told otherwise. Once the framework for performance has been established, the manager may be faced with making a judgment that on the information available to her or him, the member of staff is not meeting the standard of work as agreed.

Typically, this involves a one-to-one interview at which the manager:

- Identifies and makes explicit to the member of staff the concerns about their performance. This must be based on evidence and be specific. It is no good making general statements about attitude and so on.
- Explores the member of staff's perceptions of the concerns raised.
- Identifies what needs to be done to improve performance to meet the standards expected. This includes raising the capacity or capability of the member of staff. It may include recognising that there are external factors (such as ill-health, family or other commitments) which are preventing effective performance. It may also highlight that the poor performance stems from an unwillingness on the part of the staff member to do the job as required.
- Agree an action plan, including dates by which improvements in performance will be achieved and clear criteria for judging what those improvements are to be.

If the staff member fails to achieve the action agreed in the action plan, then the manager will have no choice but to move into disciplinary proceedings with the ultimate sanction of dismissing the member of staff. All organisations should have detailed disciplinary and grievance procedures. It is essential that the manager follows these to the letter of the law. If you are unsure seek professional HR advice.

Managing information

Managers need information to know how well the organisation is performing – is it on track to deliver its strategic priorities? The manager's monitoring role cannot be carried out without information. Neither can you develop your strategy without the right information on need and changes in the environment. The challenge is to get the right information, at the right time and in the right form. Too much information will be unmanageable, too much detail distracting, irrelevant information – however interesting – will be wholly unhelpful, information that is too late will be completely useless.

Information has been defined as 'data that has been processed into a form that is meaningful to the recipient, and is of real perceived value in current or prospective decisions'.[14] Senior managers rely very heavily on verbal information (despite the quantity of written information with which they are presented).[15]

We need the equivalent of the gauges on the dashboard of a car. These provides the driver with enough information to drive safely and reach the destination on time. You would have less confidence as the driver if there was only one gauge (for example, just showing the engine temperature) or if there were so many you did not have time to read them all and could not make any sense of what they were telling you. The business world has been criticised for using one gauge – profit – when wider information is needed to inform managers about progress in the organisation.[16] The public and voluntary sectors have been criticised for having too much information on inputs and activities and not enough about results (actual progress).

Managers need to have information that will tell them quickly how well the organisation is doing in delivering its strategy. For this to work the strategy needs to be expressed in terms of measurable priorities and targets. Information must then be gathered to allow progress to be measured and reported. Information is also needed about the people to whom you provide the service, the environment you are working in and so on. This seems simple. So why have so many organisations struggled to get the right information in a form that helps deliver the strategy? Why does it so often prove difficult to engage the staff in gathering information and providing evidence of progress?

Too often staff are asked to produce information over too short a time frame, in ways that are not clear, focused on activities rather than results and cannot be compared over time or with other information. The motto tends to be 'if in doubt provide more'. The consequence is to be lost in detail. The solution appears to be to relate all the information gathered to the targets that will deliver the strategy. Staff need to be involved in this process and in this way are more likely to see information as central to their work rather than peripheral.

The 'balanced scorecard' approach[17] offers a way to tackle these problems and to develop a very practical way of linking your reporting of action to the strategy that is supposed to be driving it. The approach is based on the idea that an organisation needs to have information covering all the activities critical to achieving its strategy. This includes, for example, information on: the results of the work (for service users/customers), finances, staff who provide the service and relationships with key stakeholders. For organisations working with young people you would expect to see explicit reference to young people's involvement.

In figure 7.9 each of the four scorecards represents a strategic priority area, with impact on young people being the overarching priority. The bullet points represent the success criteria – what the organisation needs to achieve if it is to deliver the strategy successfully. Each success criteria provides the basis for setting a target and agreeing how performance will be measured. The emphasis on measurement is a feature of the balanced scorecard. Under each heading the managers and relevant staff agree specific targets for the year or each quarter. They also agree how the progress towards the target will be measured, using concrete and verifiable measures (rather than subjective judgment).

14 Davis, G. B. and Olsen, M. (1985), *Management Information Systems: Conceptual Foundations, Structure and Development*, 2nd edn., New York: McGraw-Hill.

15 For example, Mintzberg, H. (1973) *The Nature of Managerial Work*, New York: Harper and Row.

16 Kaplan, Robert, S. and Norton, David, P. (1996), *The Balanced Scorecard – Translating Strategy into Action*, Boston Mass: Harvard Business School Press.

17 Ibid.

Figure 7.9: A balanced scorecard for a youth work organisation

Impact on young people

- Proportion of target group involved
- Outcomes for young people: learning and development achieved
- Outcomes for wider community
- Satisfaction with service
- Involvement in the organisation's decisions

Operational excellence

- Performance to budget
- Performance against benchmarks outside
- New resources attracted
- Effective systems
- Compliance

Vision & Strategy

Relationships with stakeholders

- Satisfaction
- Value added by partnerships
- Level of support
- Achievement of external targets
- Proportion of stakeholders engaged

Staff excellence

- Recruitment
- Sickness and retention
- Training and development
- Learning and sharing best practice
- Performance against outside standards (eg IIP)
- Staff satisfaction

If we take one heading from the example: 'Young people's satisfaction with the service'.

- **Target:** 80 per cent of young people using the service to consider the service to be good or better.
- **Method of gathering information:** feedback questionnaires every six months to a sample of young people and/or small group discussions facilitated by peers (not youth service staff).

Relevant staff members are made responsible for providing this information. Most of the work goes into agreeing the target and measurement and in gathering the data. Reporting can be a single line.

Some organisations use a colour code to provide even more immediate information. For each target the managers and staff agree what level of performance corresponds to:

- Green (on target or better).
- Amber (falling behind a little – needs small adjustments).
- Red (considerably below target – needs significant change and action to address).

If this colour system (red, amber, green – sometimes shortened to RAG) is used, management information can be simplified to the list of main targets for the balanced scorecard, with a box alongside each coloured appropriately. The manager can get a picture of progress at a glance. The system can provide the manager with an organisational dashboard.

The national voluntary organisation Encams (formerly the Tidy Britain Group) uses a version of the balanced scorecard. The central management information provided to the

Board is a single A4 sheet with the colour coding against the strategic success criteria for the organisation. The Board can then focus its attention on areas of red and amber (for which it might seek further information) rather than fiddle with activities that are progressing according to plan.

Reflection

How closely does the balanced scorecard approach resemble your organisation's way of gathering and communicating information on progress towards the strategy?

Does the model suggest ways you might streamline your systems?

The balanced scorecard can only work if managers:

- establish clear strategic priorities;
- use the priorities to agree a small number of appropriate and measurable success criteria;
- develop clear targets for each of the success criteria;
- assign responsibility for achieving each target to named managers or staff; and
- agree straightforward ways to measure progress towards each target.

The system ensures that the information gathered is directly related to the strategy and that the minimum of information is passed up the line.

Like any other change, implementation of the scorecard requires significant investment so that everyone is involved, understands the system and is able to use it. If no investment is made it becomes yet another fad which will be talked about rather than make any difference.

Information to develop your strategy

As well as information to monitor progress towards the strategy, managers also need information that will help with the development of the strategy itself: to plan the organisation's strategic priorities.

This comes from a variety of sources and provides a picture of the internal and external environment of the organisation. An organisation working with young people might need the following sorts of information:

- **Geography:** area served, characteristics using indices of poverty and affluence.
- **Demographics:** eg numbers of young people of a given age in any given year; breakdown for each year by gender and ethnicity; comparisons of the population of young people with those in other locations on key data eg performance in school, unemployment, crime, teenage pregnancy, health, drug misuse, truancy and school exclusions. Numbers of young people in priority target groups. Sources: census data; data on deprivation; planning data – all available from local councils' planning departments or central government departments.
- **Policy framework:** relevant UK Government policies, priorities and targets; relevant local government policies, priorities and targets. See the policy supplement for a digest – from central and local government. Short cut by gathering a number of relevant statutory plans – these nearly always include a summary of the policy framework.
- **Political decision making:** information on the key decision makers affecting the organisation and the decision making processes .
- **Other relevant services:** map and audit of the other organisations and agencies providing similar services; audit of partnerships. Comparative figures for costs of services.
- **Stakeholder views:** information about what the users and other stakeholders want from the service. Information on public attitudes. Many general surveys are now

carried out for local government and are usually public.

● **Internal information:** to give a picture of the current spend and allocation of resources in relation to the priorities of the organisation. Also feedback from users and stakeholders, comparative costs of service provision against benchmarks, projected income, growth and an analysis of risks.

We have looked at how this sort of information is used to develop the strategy in Chapter 4. Critical questions are:

● What will you do to ensure that this information is readily available when you need it? This means developing a system for getting the information in the form that you want. This may raise some difficult questions: you may be part of an organisation that cannot (or will not) gather information in the required form; the information may not exist (eg there is great reliance on census data, but this is limited).
● Who will be responsible for collecting the information? This raises resource implications. There will be grounds for looking at ways to share this function with other similar organisations, through collaboration and partnerships. It seems foolish for numerous organisations in the same area to duplicate a large number of the information gathering functions. Other agencies such as The National Youth Agency may already provide some of the information you need.
● How will you keep the information 'fit for purpose' and avoid gathering so much that it becomes useless? This is part of designing the system.
● How will your information requirements link to your IT system?

The result of answering the above questions will be a clear management information system (MIS). This does not need to involve IT (although it probably will) as the technology should serve your purpose, not be an end in itself. The management information system collects, processes and distributes the information required for managers to make decisions. It should be designed to be cost-effective, so that the value of management time saved is greater than the cost of the system. Additionally, the information provided should be valid, reliable and up to date.

Many management information systems fail to fulfil their purpose of supporting decision makers.

Earl and Hopwood point out that there is a tendency for the use of IT to lead to an increasingly technological perspective on the way information is processed by managers. This leads to increasingly formal systems and bureaucratic procedures which 'neither fit nor suit the realities of organisational activity'.[18] A good MIS includes information from all four quadrants in the table below.

Table 7.10: Four quadrants

	Routine	Non-routine
Official	● Formal MIS ● Service planning and control	● Budgeting and finance ● Task groups ● Liaison roles
Unofficial	● Political activity	● Organisation grapevine ● Informal discussions

18 Earl, M. J. and Hopwood, A. G., (1980) 'From Management Information to Information Management', in *Information Systems Environment* (eds. H. C. Lucas, et al) New York: North-Holland.

Some decisions are routine, while others are in response to particular problems or opportunities. Often these require special cooperation between managers or organisations. Informally exchanged information between managers who trust and respect each other is extremely important; in some organisations political activity and power is important in certain decisions. The role of a formal information system is clear for official routine decisions, but it cannot enable universally better decision making. Even if their limitations are recognised, many formal systems fail to meet managers' needs for information to support routine decisions because they are not designed with the needs of the end users in mind.

Getting information out

The senior manager has a particular responsibility to ensure that information flows fast and freely down and out of the organisation – to staff, to young people who use the services, to other stakeholders. An ad hoc approach is unlikely to be successful. Careful consideration needs to be given to the various groups' information needs and to the best way of communicating the information to each group. Oral briefings are needed as well as written communication which may not be read or may be misunderstood. These can operate on a cascade system, although care needs to be taken that the message does not become distorted on route or the process routine and sterile.

> ## Example: Cascade briefing
>
> A large voluntary organisation working with young people developed a cascade briefing system. The senior management group met each month. Within 24 hours the main action points and key items of information were available on the organisation's intranet news group; they were also posted on noticeboards. The intranet allowed access to detailed information for those who wanted it. In addition, every operational team leader was expected to pass on the messages to her or his staff, either at team meetings or through individual contact. Information coming back up the line was gathered against targets using an adapted balanced scorecard.
>
> A short information bulletin (no more than two sides of A4) was sent out to key external stakeholders, usually on a quarterly basis. A similar bulletin was made available to young people. There were plans for young people to develop their own key message system (both electronic and paper).
>
> Senior managers were expected to spend a proportion of their time walking their patch, explaining what was happening and hearing staff views.

Reflection

What strategy do you use to ensure that information gets out to your staff, young people and stakeholders?

What do you do to make this system live and avoid overloading people with useless information?

There is no evidence to suggest that there will be a reduction in the information flooding experienced by every senior manager. Indeed, some researchers predict there will be a 30-fold increase over the next ten years. The risk is that important information may get lost in the morass, while time is wasted wading through irrelevant material. The need for an effective information strategy has never been greater.

Information overload

The survey report *Quality of Working Life*, published by the Chartered Management Institute and UMIST in February 2001suggested that 82 per cent of managers in the UK believed that the volume of information they had to handle has greatly increased over the past three years, and 54 per cent of the sample claimed to suffer from information overload.

In his 1999 book, *Information Overload*, David Lewis[19] distinguishes between information and exformation, which he describes as all the irrelevant information that comes our way. He proposes a number of filtering techniques for selecting information that requires attention. He recommends performing a mental audit of the content of each piece of information by asking:

- What if anything do I know about the source?
- Is the information current or likely to be updated soon?
- How will reading any of this help me?

There is a great potential for information overload in the public sector, particularly in local authorities because of the sector's many and varied responsibilities.[20] It is likely that the increase in partnership working will add to the volume of information that reaches the average manager. The London Borough of Lewisham has adopted an approach which is based on distinguishing information from exformation. At its heart is the creation of a culture among employees in which each individual acts as an information filter. Everyone takes responsibility for sharing only relevant information, rather than burdening others with data of no real value.

Knowledge management

Most organisations are only dimly aware of the huge amount of knowledge that lives in the minds of their people. Lew Platt, Chief Executive of Hewlett Packard, has articulated it in the phrase 'If only HP knew what HP knows, we would be three times as profitable'. It has become more of an issue as information (rather than technology or process) has become one of the main sources of competitive advantage in the business world. With large organisations tending to break down into smaller fragments, much of this implicit knowledge is leaking out, as staff leave (quite often to sell the knowledge back as consultants or contract workers).

Knowledge is information within people's minds. Nonaka and Takeuchi[21] argued that knowledge is either explicit or tacit. Explicit knowledge can be codified – it is recorded and available and is held on databases and intranets within organisations. Tacit knowledge exists in people's minds. It may be difficult to articulate in writing and is acquired through personal experience. The key challenge of knowledge management is how to turn tacit knowledge into explicit knowledge.

Knowledge management has been defined as 'the capabilities by which communities within an organisation capture the knowledge that is critical to them, constantly improve it and make it available in the most effective manner to those people who need it, so that they can exploit it creatively to add value as a normal part of their work'.[22]

Youth and community work has been criticised for being ineffective at capturing and sharing the knowledge it has built up. There is often a sense of re-inventing the wheel rather than learning from past knowledge. Partnership working opens up huge opportunities to share best practice and increase the fund of knowledge available to all public service providers. These opportunities could be significant in terms of the information garnered

19 Lewis, David (1999) *Information Overload: Practical Strategies for Surviving in Today's Workplace*, London: Penguin.
20 Russell, P. (2001), 'In-Box Clever', *People Management*, vol. 7, issue 7.
21 Nonaka, I. and Takeuchi, H. (1995), *The Knowledge Creating Company*, New York: Oxford University Press.
22 Davenport, E. and Hall, H. (2002, in press) 'Organizational Knowledge and Communities of Practice' in B. Cronin and D. Shaw (eds.) *Annual Review of Information Science and Technology*, Medford, NJ: Information Today.

relating to the four youth service benchmarks alone and managers should strive to build on the platform this information can provide.

Knowledge management is different from the task of gathering and storing information. The organisation needs to have effective information management systems in place as these help to support knowledge management. It is a much wider process of sharing and capturing what the people in the organisation have discovered, learned and achieved. How might senior managers lead this process?

Action to improve knowledge management

1. Create a culture in which it is the norm to share good practice, celebrate successes and learn from failures (see page 72).
2. Make time available for staff to share and learn from each other – this means face-to-face interactions focused on learning and sharing.
3. Discuss and develop a wide range of ways to share learning (such as meetings, workshops, marketplaces, visits to other projects, seminars, conferences, job swaps, secondments around the organisation, job shadowing).
4. Capture and record the knowledge in ways that can be used: eg the internet and intranets, newsletters, e-mail updates).
5. Do not rely on the written version to tell the story – make sure that someone brings it to life (you or a designated person).
6. Actively reward knowledge sharing and learning – too often the rhetoric is matched by little or no action.

One way to start with this is to identify an organisation or department that is really good at capturing and sharing its knowledge. Visit it, find out how it is done and make an action plan of what you could apply to your own organisation.

Assuring quality and reporting on it requires managers to have reliable, regular information about how different aspects of the service or organisation are performing. The youth service does not have a good record for specifying the information it needs, establishing systems for collecting it, interpreting it and then using it so that plans can be made and actions taken in the light of it. The National Youth Agency's recently developed Youth Base system for gathering information on youth work activities in local authority youth services, has the potential to link to The Agency's annual census of local authority youth service providers.

However, there are wide-ranging and complex reasons for the lack of impact that such knowledge should deliver but they can usually be traced back to the fact that local authorities and voluntary organisations have discretion in determining the level, nature and range of youth work and how it is organised. Because of the variations, it is hard to agree about such items as:

● **Demography** – who is included for youth work: age range, universal or targeted provision?
● **Participation** – what counts, types of contact, levels of attendance, intensive use of service.
● **Achievement** – what counts and how is it measured?
● **Staffing** – calculation of numbers and ratios to cover full-time workers, part-time

Reflection

What steps do you take to ensure that the implicit knowledge in the heads of your staff is shared, captured and learned from in your organisation? What more could you do?

workers, volunteers, administrative support, secondments.

● **Finance** – what is to be included in working out income and expenditure, what is gross and net.

● **Partners** – which organisations and groups are to be included; what status should they be given – voluntary, assisted, independent, community-based.

Overriding all these variations is the key question, 'what counts as youth work?' This covers both the types of activity undertaken and the organisations and departments responsible for them, which sometimes extend beyond what is usually referred to as the local (authority) youth service.

The National Youth Agency and the Association of Principal Youth and Community Officers have established a Management Information Steering Group to examine data, definitions, performance indicators, data protection, how information is managed and how ICT systems might help, bearing in mind the different policies, interpretations and services' and organisations' capacities. Without valid data and the ability to compare like with like, benchmarking is going to remain elusive. It has already become apparent from work done by a team of consultants to compare youth services' and organisations' financial returns that there are significant differences in the ways in which returns are made. This is due to variable factors such as the treatment of overheads, grants given and received, and assistance in kind given and received.

Unless and until some agreement can be reached about:

● an irreducible core of provision to be offered by services and organisations;
● the kind of management information that can reliably indicate how a service or organisation is performing in making such provision;
● how that information can best be collected, including use of ICT; and
● how to build the capacity of services and organisations to collect, interpret and use such management information.

then it is going to be difficult to make any firm judgments about the sufficiency and adequacy of youth provision.

Managing risk

The need for effective risk management

Any attempt to deliver continuous improvement within resource constraints demands innovative approaches to service delivery. All innovation involves an element of risk and effective risk management is needed to enable the service to deliver its objectives. Services working with young people must be able to demonstrate that they have taken reasonable steps to identify and protect against risks to young people and staff.

The Audit Commission states that 'risk is the threat that an event or action will adversely affect an organisation's ability to achieve its objectives and to successfully execute its strategies. Risk management is the process by which risks are identified, evaluated and controlled.'[23]

---

23 Audit Commission (2001), *Worth the Risk: Improving Risk Management in Local Government*, London: Audit Commission.

The media has drawn attention to incidents, scandals and accidents in all sectors (eg the Maxwell affair, the Enron scandal, accidents occurring on adventure holidays, child abuse, drug dealing on a charity's premises). Organisations are expected to have policies and approaches which minimise these risks. This runs from frameworks for good practice, robust and effective systems and good procedures, to plans to respond to emergencies, dealing with the media in the event of a major incident and so on.

Work with young people, particularly those who face disadvantage and discrimination, cannot be carried out without risk. Organisations that work with young people to create new opportunities are expected to innovate and to find better ways to involve young people. For example, staff working with young men to address violence need to operate within a framework of practices that keep risk to acceptable levels without stifling initiative. Trustees of voluntary organisations working with young homeless people will have been concerned about the two workers who were imprisoned after police found drug dealing was taking place on their organisation's premises. The defence that working with some groups of young people inevitably meant close contact with drugs culture was not successful. What case should managers make to Trustees to enable risky work to continue? What safeguards need to be in place?

Managers need to be able to take informed risks and to manage them effectively. They need to strike a balance between risk and control. Managers are also responsible for actively managing an **appropriate culture** with respect to risk. For example:

● making sure all staff are aware of good practice (induction and training);
● ensuring that there is an effective system of staff supervision;
● ensuring effective reporting (reporting on risk might be part of the balanced scorecard (see page 142);
● demanding rigorous application of key processes and procedures – such as accident reporting, reporting incidents, child protection, health and safety, recording of evidence of progress and learning; and
● encouraging innovation, allowing reasonable mistakes to be made, enabling people to grow and learn from their mistakes.

Risks fall into two broad categories – strategic and operational.

Strategic risks

● **Political** – failure to deliver local or central government policy or local manifesto commitments.
● **Economic** – failure to meet financial commitments, budgetary pressures, inadequate insurance cover, consequences of investment decisions.
● **Social** – impact of changes in demographic, residential, socio-economic trends on council's ability to meet its objectives.
● **Technological** – capacity to deal with pace/scale of technological change or to use technology effectively.
● **Legislative** – current or proposed changes in national or EU law eg TUPE (Transfer of Undertakings (Protection of Employment) Regulations), pensions rights, Disability Discrimination Act.
● **Environmental** – energy efficiency, pollution, landfill requirements, emissions etc.
● **Competitive** – affecting the competitiveness of the service (in terms of cost or quality)

and/or its ability to deliver Best Value

- **Customer/citizen** – associated with the failure to meet customers' and citizens' current and changing needs and expectations.
- **Reputation** – damage to the reputation of the service or organisation from poor publicity leading to loss of public confidence and possible loss of resources.
- **Criminal** – risk of criminal prosecution for failing to manage risk, or risk from criminal activity.

Operational risks

- **Services** – risks associated with the purpose, objectives and nature of the services provided.
- **Process** – the way the services are provided (eg detached youth work may carry greater risk than centre based work).
- **Professional** – associated with the particular nature of each profession.
- **The staff** – processes of recruitment, selection, performance management etc.
- **Financial** – financial planning and control and the adequacy of insurance cover.
- **Legal** – possible breaches of legislation such as employment law, Child Protection and Duty of Care.
- **Physical** – buildings, vehicles, equipment, health and safety issues.
- **Contractual** – failure of contractors to deliver services/products to the agreed cost and specification; failure to honour contracts of employment.
- **Technological** – degree of reliance on technology.
- **Environmental** – e.g. pollution, noise, energy efficiency.
- **Reactions** – of the public, local community or relevant service users.
- Theft, fraud and other **criminal activity**.
- **Management practice**.
- **Governance practice**.

Effective risk management involves three stages:

1. Identifying risks – the audit of risks.
2. Prioritising risks – identifying those that need attention most urgently and over time.
3. Assessing exposure and establishing appropriate control strategies.

Identifying risks

Risks are associated with all aspects of the organisation. The list of categories, above, could be used as the basis for an initial audit of risk. Every organisation should review its exposure to risk and develop a clear risk management strategy in response.

Managers should identify and assess the risk in relation to each of the critical success factors identified for their organisation. This means establishing what could go wrong and why that might happen. For example, risks are likely to be associated with:

- the voluntary nature of young people's involvement, which may mean that targets are not met;
- the methodologies employed may not achieve the desired outcomes;
- some methodologies may carry an inherent risk eg outdoor pursuits, sporting activities;

- individuals may not follow established codes of practice; and
- funding bids may be unsuccessful.

The increase in partnership and collaborative working means that many of the risks will be outside the control of the senior manager. Good risk management is essential in these circumstances with a clear allocation of responsibility for the control of specified risks.

Prioritising risks

A large number of risks will be identified during the audit stage. This needs to be prioritised so as to put effort where it is most needed. Clearly, risks which put the very existence of the service at risk are highest priority, followed by those which have a significant adverse impact on the service's ability to achieve its objectives. The matrix shown in figure 7.11 can assist this process.

Figure 7.11: Prioritising risks

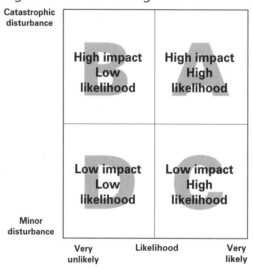

Catastrophic disturbance

High impact Low likelihood

High impact High likelihood

Low impact Low likelihood

Low impact High likelihood

Minor disturbance

Very unlikely — Likelihood — Very likely

Key:

A: **Immediate action needed**

B: **Consider action and have a contingency plan**

C: **Consider action**

D: **Keep under periodic review**

From: Worth the risk: improving risk management in local government,
Audit Commission 2001

Risk management involves deciding, in the first instance, whether the desired outcomes are worth the risks involved and then putting in place controls which minimise the risks. Proportionality is crucial here, and the cost of controls versus the impact of an incident needs to be considered.

Assessing exposure and establishing appropriate control strategies

For each significant risk it is important to establish:

- whether the risk is acceptable at all (if not, action must be taken to eliminate it);
- the measures needed to avoid or mitigate the risk;
- who is accountable for managing the risk and maintaining and monitoring the controls;
- the residual risk which remains after control measures are applied; and
- what early warning mechanisms can be put in place.

If a decision is made to accept a risk, then an appropriate control strategy must be adopted. Possible strategies include:

Reflection

How do you manage risk in your organisation?

Have you considered the categories of risk listed?

Are there any risks which you consider to be a high priority that need urgent attention?

- accepting or tolerating the risk;
- transferring the risk eg by changing contract terms;
- planning to deal with service interruption without disturbing business continuity to a material extent;
- controlling the risk through the performance management system;
- sharing the risk with another party;
- insuring against some or all of it; and
- avoiding the risk in other ways.

Stakeholders will need to be involved in parts of the risk management process both to get their views and to win their support for action that may result. The aim of risk management is not to eliminate all risk. It is unlikely that objectives could be achieved without some degree of risk but it is important that all reasonable steps have been taken to reduce significant risks to manageable proportions.

Chapter Eight:
Managing for high performance

Introduction

One of the main drivers of change in services provided by all three sectors has been the development of new approaches to managing performance. Organisations have been encouraged to refocus their attention towards the customer or service user. Staff are expected to find ways to improve services continually, and managers need to develop a culture in which this is encouraged and rewarded. Public services are under greater scrutiny from inspection bodies than ever before. UK Government, both central and local, is insistent on raising performance standards so that users of public services get a better deal.

In this chapter we will explore what needs to be in place to **create a culture of high performance.** We explain some of the key concepts and tools that can be used to drive up quality and explore the process of external scrutiny by inspection regimes.

The second part looks at **quality assurance and its management**. The Excellence Model is introduced as a framework particularly well suited to local government services, including youth work. We then touch on some of the key aspects of **self-assessment**. We end by highlighting some of the challenges involved in trying to measure **adequacy, sufficiency and quality** across the youth work sector. This chapter covers:

- Creating a culture of high performance
- Connecting the strategy to the action
- Performance indicators
- Standards
- Building high-performing staff
- Quality assurance and management
- Service quality
- Existing quality frameworks relevant to youth work organisations
- A quality assurance framework relevant to youth work organisations
- Quality self-assessment
- Continuous improvement

Figure 8.1: The experiential cycle

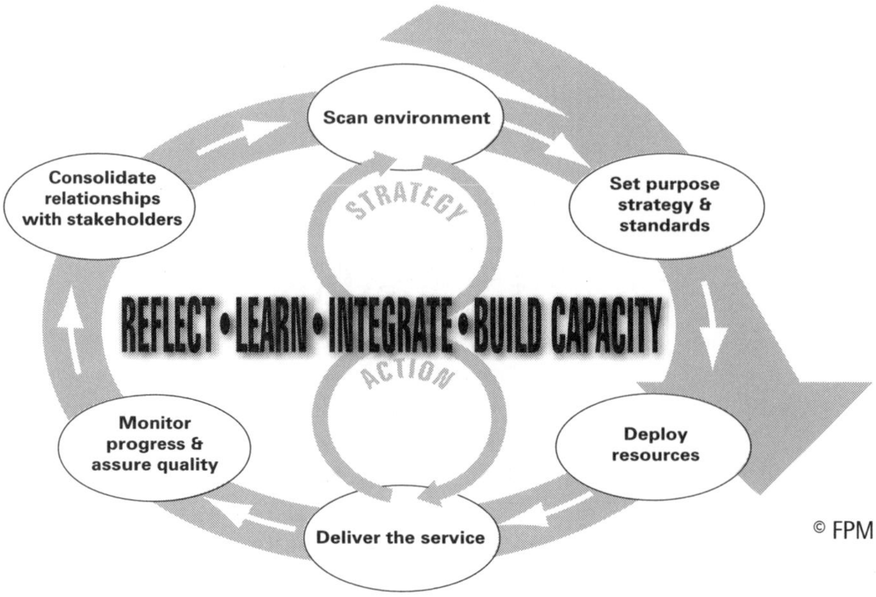

© FPM

This chapter is located in the lower left hand quadrant of the management model – monitoring progress and assuring quality. It also refers to the centre of the model and looks across to the importance of setting clear objectives and standards (top right quadrant).

Creating a culture of high performance

We have explored the manager's role in influencing organisational culture in earlier chapters. We now focus on the role of the manager in securing a culture of high performance in the organisation.

What do we mean by performance management and high performance?

> ### Example
>
> The captain, and star player, of a national football team was sent home from the World Cup before kicking a ball because he believed that the standard of facilities and travel arrangements set up for the team prior to the tournament were not good enough. He felt they would prevent the team from achieving high performance. This led to a steaming row with the team manager in which the captain's behaviour fell far short of the standard of interpersonal conduct expected of any team member. The behaviour was felt to be disruptive of group cohesion and would thus impair the team's high performance. No one player, no matter how good, could be more important than the team. The governing body backed the manager – to do otherwise would have made the manager's job untenable.

Performance denotes what an organisation does and its consequences. How we look at performance is affected by the way we see organisations (see the metaphors on page 43). We might see the organisation as a machine. Machines perform 'like clockwork' but do not learn as a result of their performance. They inevitably suffer wear and tear but rely on their controllers to learn and change them in order to perform better.

If we see the organisation as an organic system, culture or brain, then we expect it to be able to learn from its performance, judge its quality and consider ways of improving it. Far from wearing it out, performing better leads to better performance. Think about learning to play a guitar. The more you practise the better you get. The better you get the more new and interesting challenges you can take on, so motivating you to practise more. It is a virtuous circle.

Managing performance requires:

● **Clarity about the work to be done** – purpose, aims and targets – and agreed standards by which the work is judged.

  Non-profit organisations find it very hard to answer the question of what 'results are. Results can be quantified ... The Salvation Army is fundamentally a religious organisation. But it knows the percentage of alcoholics it restores to mental and physical health and the percentage of criminals it rehabilitates. It is highly quantitative because it realises that work is only done by people with a deadline. By people who are monitored and evaluated. By people who hold themselves responsible for results.[1]

● **The capacity to do it** – roles and responsibilities clearly determined, understood and agreed – and with sufficient resources and sensible procedures to ensure people can do these jobs to the required standard.

● **Information about actual performance** – so that actual performance can be compared with plans and expectations.

Jackson and Palmer[2] describe the manager's role in relation to performance as' ... to create an organisation culture in which individuals and groups take on the responsibility of searching for continuous improvements in performance through improvements in their own skills and contributions'.

The pressure for higher performance comes from a variety of places, including:

public accountability: to demonstrate to stakeholders that the service is good

pressure on public spending: UK Government (and other purchasers of public services) want to see value for money (or Best Value). They want more performance for the same money, or less. Service providers rely on people to deliver services. They represent the biggest cost. Improving the 'productivity' of people in public services is therefore a priority

competition: what matters is not who provides the service but that the service is of high quality

customer care: we want young people to keep using our services. We have pride in what we do. In youth work organisations this is linked to values that promote young people's learning and development. We want our 'customers' (those who pay for the services) to keep paying us to provide the services

consumerism: users of services (the consumers) expect quality, variety and choice

1 Drucker, Peter (1990), *Managing the Non-Profit Organization*, USA: Butterworth-Heinemann.
2 Jackson, Peter, M. and Palmer, Bob (1992), *Developing Performance Monitoring in Public Sector Organisations – a Management Guide*, Leicester: University of Leicester Management Centre, p4.

professionalism: to do our best as a professional, to meet or exceed the standards expected of a professional, to push back the boundaries of practice and performance.

This echoes many of the points in the list of features of modern public services from Osbourne and Gaebler (see page 55).

The sharp growth of interest in performance management can be traced back to the rise in economic power of Japanese industry. Western companies, which were being outperformed, looked to Japan to find out why: 'If Japan can, why can't we?'. The quality movement has its origins here.[3]

Example: The sad case of British motorbikes

Does anyone remember the days when Britain made motorbikes? The industry produced loud, unreliable and dirty machines that were hard to start and hard to control. They sold to a smallish clientele that turned these vices into virtues – this was what motorcycling was about. The British motorbike industry was the envy of the world ... Enter Japanese motorbikes in the 1960s to much derision from the British industry. At first the bikes were flimsy and unattractive, but with Japanese performance management it took less than two decades for the entire British motorbike industry to be wiped out. The Japanese talked to customers and potential customers. They introduced novelties such as electric starters, indicators and brakes that worked. Even more revolutionary, they made bikes reliable and clean. Not only that, they made them faster and sportier. All of this was greeted with the disinterest of dinosaurs faced with predictions of catastrophe 'don't be ridiculous – we've been here for millions of years without changing ...'

The same opportunity and threat faces most public service providers. They must perform at least as well as competitors, or risk losing out to someone who does.

Any good organisation should be managing for high performance, regardless of external pressures. It is simply bad management to allow performance to decline, to lose contact with users of the service. The function of external drivers is to add an incentive to a natural management priority.

UK Government has created a demanding regime of external accountability for performance as part of its drive to improve public services. It is rewarding high performance (for example with Public Service Agreements) and punishing poor performance.

Providers of public services face increasing pressure to show clearly how they are performing. There are external (Ofsted and Comprehensive Performance Assessment) and internal (Best Value) regimes that require us to provide information about our performance and account for the way we use resources so that informed judgments can be made about how well we are doing.

In order to improve continuously and achieve high performance, providers of services have to show that they are:

● responsive to government (and other funders') policy, to the changing needs, aspirations and circumstances of the service users, and to the ideas and creativity of those who

---

3   Deming, W. E. (1982), *Out of the Crisis*, Cambridge Massachusetts: Massachusetts Institute of Technology.

service providers
- innovative in approach and seeking new solutions to enduring problems, introducing and managing change tempered with consistency and continuity (we look at innovation in Chapter 9). Too much change can generate instability and anxiety, which can impair performance.

A high performing organisation is one that learns, adapts and improves. It is one where people take time to pause, consider and reflect on their activities; identify strengths and weaknesses; seek to build on the one and remedy the other. It is one where there is continuous discussion among staff about measuring and improving performance.

Whether we are paying for a service or being paid to provide one, we are conscious all the time of whether we are getting or giving good value for the money being spent. We continually make judgments about how things are being done and think about whether and how it might be possible to do them better.

Managers (and commissioners) of services therefore need to be able to compare:

- the expected level of performance – usually described in terms of objectives, targets and standards (which need to be explored in terms of the different stakeholders, for example young people, funders, local politicians, trustees)
  with:
- the actual level of performance being achieved.

Your organisation therefore needs to build a culture of planning, evidence gathering, review and reflection. This takes resources – it is a real cost. For many hard-pressed service providers, the enemy of high performance can be the demand to keep on performing. The show must go on regardless; you can never stop to think, and so risk wearing out the staff and compromising the level of performance.

Connecting the strategy to the action

As discussed in previous chapters, to create an effective organisation there must be a clear strategic direction. It is the first step to a high performance culture. Strategy should inform operations and, in turn, should be influenced by them. The relationship between the two may be illustrated in the form of the fallen figure of 8, which we introduced in Chapter 4 (page 68).

Figure 8.2: The double loop process

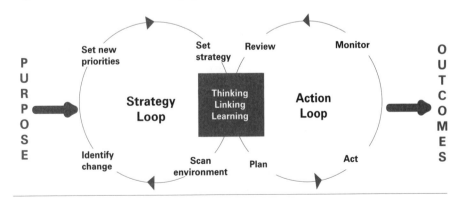

Reflection

Reflect on the drivers for high performance.

Why is it that so many professionals see this as an imposition from outside, rather than something to be welcomed?

Did some organisations working with young people fall into the British motorbike industry trap of assuming their high performance and not really listening to either their users or their paying customers (funders)?

Sustained high performance is only possible if the strategy is linked to action and the action linked back to the strategy.

The failure to make this link was identified by Henry Mintzberg as one of the three reasons why strategic planning tends to fail: 'it is this disassociation of thinking from acting that lies close to the root of strategic planning's problems'.[4] (The other two were the impossibility of forecasting future events and problems caused by making the planning process rigid and over-formal.)

Plans into action: objectives, goals and targets

Converting the strategy into action requires the organisation to establish strategic priorities and more specific objectives (sometimes called goals) for each priority. This process may be second nature to you, but we rehearse it briefly here as a reminder and because it is fundamental to managing performance.

Your organisation's objectives should conform to the SMART test: specific, measurable, achievable, relevant to the purpose of the organisation and have a timetable for achievement.

Planning terminology is confusing as different UK Government agencies, local authorities and organisations use the same terms in different ways. What is consistent is the hierarchy of planning illustrated in figure 8.3. It shows the relationship between the overall purpose, broad strategic priorities and specific, measurable objectives. You may use the terms differently, but it is essential that your organisation uses its own terms consistently. It would be helpful if all youth work agencies did the same!

Reflection

What are you doing in a direct and measurable way, that is helping to create and sustain a culture of high performance in you organisation?

Are all your staff aware of what high performance would look like?

Refer back to Chapter 4 for discussion of converting your strategy into action.

Figure 8.3: Planning hierarchy

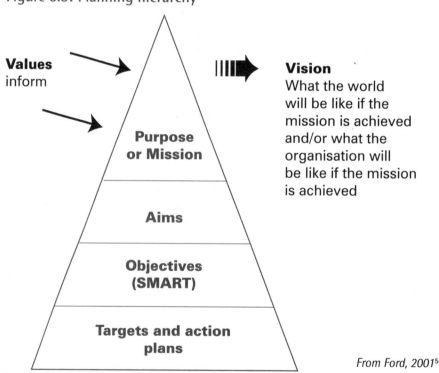

Values inform

Vision
What the world will be like if the mission is achieved and/or what the organisation will be like if the mission is achieved

Purpose or Mission

Aims

Objectives (SMART)

Targets and action plans

From Ford, 2001[5]

4   Mintzberg, H. (1994), *The Rise and Fall of Strategic Planning*, Hemel Hempstead: Prentice Hall International.
5   Ford, K. (2001), *Improving Youth Work Management*, Leicester: FPM.

- The values of the organisation inform its purpose (sometimes also called its mission). The achievement of the mission will lead to realisation of the organisation's vision.
- The high level (and consequently rather general) statement of mission translates down into the operations through increasingly specific statements of intent. The first level down are the broad strategic priorities – usually no more than five – which set out where the main efforts of the organisation will go, over the next several years, to achieve the purpose.
- Below the strategic priorities lie the specific (and SMART) objectives (or goals), for each priority.
- Targets are measures of progress towards achieving the objectives or goals. They usually have some numerical value attached because it helps the organisation to measure with some degree of precision whether it has achieved them.

For example, a youth service may be currently in contact with young people ranging in age from 11 to 25. Under *Transforming Youth Work*, local youth services are being directed to focus at least 80 per cent of their resources on young people aged 13 to 19.

Reflection

- What strategic priorities do you have for your service?
- What objectives have you set to achieve them? Are these really SMART?
- What targets have you established to help you achieve the objectives? Are these clear?
- What performance standards have you agreed?
- Do your staff understand the planning terms and use them appropriately?
- Do staff know what evidence they need to gather to demonstrate their performance?
- Have sufficient resources been allocated to encouraging higher performance?

A **new objective** is set to redirect resources towards the priority age range. This has a target for the proportion of young people in that age range with whom the service plans to be in some kind of contact. For example, a perfectly reasonable target might be for the local authority youth service and its partners in the voluntary sector together to be in contact with 20 per cent of the 13 to 19-year-olds in the area (on whom 80 per cent of the resources will be spent).

The right hand (action) loop of the Double Loop Process (page 159) shows how a manager might adjust targets in the light of experience.

Example

The UK Government has for a long time set itself the strategic priority of keeping as many young people in learning as possible. One of the objectives for achieving this has been to reduce the number of permanent exclusions, at the same time as increasing the provision made for alternative learning arrangements for disaffected pupils.

The target was to reduce the number of excluded pupils by one third between 1997 and 2002.

This has led to unintended results. By not excluding disruptive pupils, the performance of other pupils in the school and their teachers has been adversely affected. There has been unacceptable behaviour, which has damaged the learning environment. This in turn has negatively impacted on attendance and achievement.

The UK Government adjusted its strategy and the targets derived from it accordingly. Head teachers and governors are no longer being so strongly discouraged from permanently excluding pupils and, from September 2002, all excluded pupils will be found alternative education provision amounting to 25 hours a week.

Performance indicators

In order to compare actual with expected performance, the manager needs to have information, which will involve measurement. Measurement entails looking at both quantity and quality. To tackle the task of measuring performance, we must make use of performance indicators and performance measures. These terms are used inconsistently throughout the public and voluntary sectors – sometimes they are used interchangeably; sometimes they are given different meanings.

Performance indicators (PI) are observable changes or criteria that suggest certain types of performance are taking place. PIs are likened to signals that require further contextual information before a satisfactory explanation can be offered. Examination results are taken as an indicator of a school's overall performance, but will require more information to tell you whether a school is doing as well as it should.

Performance measures (PM) are a type of performance indicator, which show an unambiguous causal link between an activity and a change in performance. You can draw an analogy with dials on a machine that give a clear reading about what is happening, such as your speed when driving or the amount of electricity consumed over a given period. It is the undeniable output of a particular input and process – in this case the conversion of fuel to energy.

> ### Example: Ofsted's use of numeric performance indicators
>
> Ofsted reports on local authority youth services list the performance indicators used. These are items of statistical information, such as the proportion of the LEA's expenditure that goes on the youth service, the unit cost of each young person aged 13 to 19 reached, the percentage of the net budget spent on in-service training and so on. These figures provide a clue about the priority the authority has given youth work. There is also a common assumption that more spending suggests higher quality work. This is not necessarily the case. The figures also allow comparisons to be made between members of 'statistical families' of local authorities (those of similar size, composition and character). The data only offers proxies to quality, it does not provide a complete picture. That will only emerge after further investigation of more qualitative data is undertaken and the findings processed and interpreted.

Every organisation that wants to perform well needs to have a clear set of performance indicators used consistently by all staff. One method is the Balanced Scorecard (see Chapter 7). This begins with converting the strategic priorities into success criteria (broad performance indicators) which are in turn converted into specific and measurable indicators.

It is essential to be strategic when deciding your organisation's performance indicators. If you are funded by UK Government you must be able to show that your organisation is meeting UK Government targets and priorities – that is what they are paying you to do!

So what makes a good performance indicator? It must be fit for its purpose. Blundell and Murdoch have suggested 15 questions to test your PIs.[6] These are described below, with one or two additions related to organisations that work with young people.

---

6   Blundell, Brian and Murdoch, Alex (1997), *Managing in the Public Sector*, London: Butterworth Heinemann, pp235–236.

Questions to test your PIs

1. Are the definitions of performance consistent over time, between units and organisations? How reliable are the methods used for collecting the data?
2. Do the PIs compare like with like? How well do your performance indicators allow you to compare your performance with others' and against UK Government priorities? (Use the list of PIs associated with the *Resourcing Excellent Youth Services* document on page 64 as a starting point.) Do your PIs match up with those of Ofsted, other inspection or review PIs, for example Best Value, internal review systems, internal quality indicators, so that your data can be used for inspection purposes?
3. Are the PIs clear: well-defined, easily understood and easy to use? Does everyone know about them and understand how to use them?
4. Do the PIs help managers to control those things under their control (ie they do not relate to things outside the manager's or organisation's control)?
5. What other contingencies might affect the PI? (change in the PI might be a result of something completely unrelated).
6. Do the PIs give a full and comprehensive picture of progress and provide enough information for good decision making? How useful are they in telling you how well the service is doing?
7. Have you identified which PIs provide the most important information (proportionality)? These become the most critical to pay attention to.
8. Do the PIs give you relevant information on changing needs and circumstances?
9. Do the PIs relate to feasible goals and targets?
10. Do the PIs give information on the three Es – economy, efficiency and effectiveness?
11. Is each PI associated with a clear target?
12. Is the information about the PIs gathered quickly enough to be timely ie of use in making management decisions?
13. Are staff who will use PIs involved in setting them? Are young people involved in setting the PIs?
14. Is the information about the PIs communicated to all who need to know about them?
15. Are the PIs fully integrated into the culture and processes for planning and delivering the service?

What do we measure?

Most organisations use an open systems model to understand and monitor their performance (see figure 8.4). This involves identifying inputs, the process of transforming input into output, and the outcomes these can lead to.

Figure 8.4: A performance model

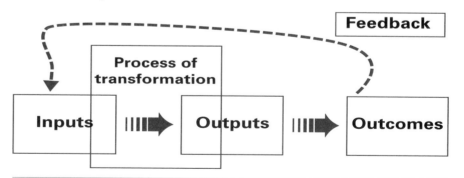

Inputs are what goes into providing the service, usually the people, plant and pounds, including staff's knowledge and skills and the resources invested in them. The cost of the inputs gives you a measure of the **Economy** of the activity.

The process is the variety of ways we work with young people (the heart of most youth work).

The **outputs** are a measure of the activity that has taken place, such as the volume of service, range of activities and levels of achievement. The volume of the outputs divided by the cost of the inputs gives you a measure of the **Efficiency** of the activity.

The **outcomes** are the results our services have on the lives of the young people who use them. This might include progression to training or employment; better health, better and safer relationships. The outcomes also include the results of our services for the wider community. Examples include raising standards of educational attainment or declining incidents of youth crime. The number and quality of the outcomes achieved tell you the **Effectiveness** of your organisation.

It is hard to prove that an outcome is the direct result of a youth work intervention (see Chapter 2 for discussion of reasoning and argument). For example, is the reduction in teenage pregnancies and sexually transmitted infections in a neighbourhood due to high levels of youth work activity targeting informal sexual health programmes at those young people judged to be at risk? This is particularly hard to establish when we are seeking elusive, 'soft' outcomes such as changes in attitude and behaviour, which can themselves be multi-causal, and which tend to take place over extended periods of time.

One way to define outcomes in youth work is to seek to measure social and emotional competences, which derive from the purpose of youth work and are highly relevant to the kind of learning, which young people gain in youth work settings. The report called *Step it Up – Charting Young People's Progress*[7] is a useful resource for youth work managers to explore with regard to measuring 'soft' outcomes. *Managing for better outcomes in youth work*, also provides further guidance on this matter[8]. We discuss the challenge facing youth work managers if they are to find effective methods to demonstrate the impact of the development of young people's relationships in the final chapter of this book.

The three Es

The three Es – Economy, Efficiency and Effectiveness – are described above. All organisations are asked to provide data on all three. The most important is effectiveness, as it tells you whether you are achieving your strategic priorities, whether you are having a real impact. Efficiency matters because it shows you are using resources well. Economy matters because resources are limited.

Economy: when resources are finite, minimising costs is an important consideration. So key questions prompted by this are:

● How much do different inputs cost?
● Could other resources be purchased for the same cost in order to deliver the service in different ways?
● Are resources properly controlled?

7   *Step it Up*, (2003), Community Education Department of the University of the University of Strathclyde and the Prince's Trust Scotland. Available from www.youthlink.co.uk
8   *Managing for better outcomes in youth work*, (2004), Leicester, The National Youth Agency.

● Will quality standards be compromised if costs are reduced?

Efficiency is the relationship between the inputs and outputs of a process.

● Are we making the best use of the resources we have?
● Has maximum output been secured from a given input?
● Is minimum input used to produce given output?
● Can service throughput be improved without sacrificing quality or changing costs?

Effectiveness is the relationship between intended and actual outcomes.

● Have we achieved the desired results?
● What benefits have been gained?
● Has the service been consistently good?
● What feedback have we had from users, providers and stakeholders to inform our judgments?

The Best Value regime has added two further Es:

● Excellence: with a focus on achieving ever-higher standards of service.
● Equity: which seeks to ensure fairness in the allocation of resources and the quality of service.

Standards

High performing services achieve their goals and perform the tasks necessary to achieve high standards. What do we mean by a standard?

Standards describe the level of performance expected if targets are to be achieved. They can also be used as criteria for assessing the quality of performance of those engaged in particular activities or tasks. They can be used for comparative judgments. Standards are therefore very closely related to performance indicators – indeed in some cases they are the same.

Standards have been established and are still emerging for youth work. The National Youth Agency has produced a helpful reference pack[9] which acts as a guide to the different standards currently in use. Some are concerned with the quality of youth work and some deal with professional practice and training. The pack includes:

● Draft standards of youth work provision (produced by The National Youth Agency).
● An extract from Ofsted's revised framework for inspecting youth work which details the quality criteria under seven headings:
  1. access and participation
  2. achievement and standards
  3. effectiveness of youth work practice
  4. responsiveness of provision to young people's needs and interests
  5. availability and quality of resources
  6. effectiveness of partnerships and inter-agency liaison
  7. effectiveness of leadership and management

---

9   The National Youth Agency (2002), *Reference Pack of Youth Work Standards*, Leicester: The National Youth Agency.

- A youth pledge of entitlement, specifying the minimum that young people can expect from a local youth service.
- A summary of the statement of principles of ethical conduct for youth work.
- A summary of the definition of key aspects and units in the national occupational standards for youth work.
- A set of standards for local councils to aim for in involving and engaging young people in local democracy.

Finally, youth work managers will be well versed in the four benchmarks that have been set for the Youth Service nationally for 2004–05 and onwards as discussed earlier.

For a service to provide value for money, it must ensure that good quality outputs and outcomes are being secured at a reasonable cost. This is a matter of balance. It is questionable how cheaply a truly effective service can be provided. As a former Senior Chief Inspector of Schools once said of education 'there are no cheap routes to quality'. Or to quote the much-repeated refrain of business analysts, 'you only get what you are prepared to pay for'.

Best Value required a thorough review of every aspect of each service provided by a local authority every five years. Best Value regimes required a local authority to have authority-wide objectives and ways of measuring them (linked to community planning).

Best Value entails **performance review** which:

- challenges the purpose of the service
- compares performance with best practice
- consults with users and stakeholders
- shows how the service competes with others.

In the White Paper *Strong Local Leadership – Quality Public Services*[10] the UK Government announced that Best Value is to be streamlined by, for example, reducing the number of Best Value performance indicators to 95, almost half of what they were two years previously. Best Value reviews are becoming more strategic and fewer. The UK Government intends to make reviews more challenging and will encourage more cross-cutting and joint reviews. More effective councils will have greater flexibility in determining these reviews. Summary information on how a council has performed will be targeted at local taxpayers and service users and will be published with council tax bills at the start of each financial year.

The same White Paper introduced **Comprehensive Performance Assessments (CPAs).** Through these, each council will be identified as one of the following:

- **High-performing** – to receive targeted support and extra freedoms to lead the way to further service improvements; they will enjoy reduced ring-fencing of revenue and more freedom in how they use their income.
- **Striving** – also to receive further freedoms and access to a package approaching that available to high-performers; lighter touch inspections and more discretion over best value review programmes.
- **Coasting** – will receive support for capacity building, concentrating on areas of weakness and have their performance monitored against their action plan.

10 Office of the Deputy Prime minister (2002), *Strong Local Leadership – Quality Public Services*, London: ODPM.

● **Poor-performing** – will also have their performance monitored against their action plan and will receive directed support for capacity building; government will intervene where necessary to tackle failure.

The CPA programme includes:

● a self-assessment carried out by each local authority
● a corporate assessment carried out by a team including peer representatives
● assessments of performance in key service areas.

The Audit Commission's approach to performance assessment enables inspection teams to assess community focus, structures and processes, risk management and internal control, service delivery arrangements, standards of conduct and common indicators.

Inspections last around four weeks, with two of these spent on site. The Audit Commission will follow the approach used in Best Value service inspections: assessing documentation, interviewing key personnel, holding group discussions with staff, the public and stakeholders, and briefing the council throughout.

At the end of the process judgments will be made about how well the council is doing and to what extent it has the capacity to improve. Corporate and service performance information will then be summarised in a 'balanced scorecard'. This will identify each council as being in one of the four categories mentioned above.

Whilst the CPA does not directly affect youth services and organisations funded by local government, your performance has an effect on it. Therefore, if services for young people are high performers they will help to drive up the results of the authority. This is an opportunity to promote the quality of your organisation or service.

Building a high-performing staff team

So what action should you take to build a culture of high performance in your staff? The following provides a start to your thinking and action.

Seek and demand good performance
● Encourage self-management, with staff being clear about individual and team goals and with individual work programmes to achieve the goals.
● Ensure there is regular, consistent, good quality supervision, with opportunities for staff to give and receive feedback and reflect on the development of professional skills, knowledge and insight.
● Ensure that supervision is driven by the objectives of the service, translated into relevant targets for staff's own work, so that they are able to focus on their contribution to achieving high performance.
● Ensure that staff are given and make use of relevant development and training opportunities.
● Provide an appropriate form of personal appraisal, linked to both work and personal development objectives that serve to focus on the improvement of individual skills, knowledge and experience whilst, at the same time, rewarding and recognising the contribution of the individual concerned to the overall performance of the organisation.

- Lead by example – make sure you do for your own work all that you expect of others.

Confront and challenge poor performance

- Intervene early: the longer you leave a problem the more likely it is to become embedded and the harder it is to shift.
- Review the performance of any worker who is thought to be under-performing against the expectations agreed for her or him – targets, standards, etc. If the expectations are unclear it is almost impossible to manage poor performance.
- Insist that records are kept of supervision sessions; these should include decisions taken and actions agreed. These are reviewed each session. If there is no change, then introduce coaching and mentoring to enable changes to be made. If there is still no progress you have a choice: change the workload or change the worker.
- Invoke reporting and disciplinary procedures if there is still no change and the worker has not taken action promised to remedy weaknesses.
- It is essential that you carry out the above processes with rigour and discipline and strictly according to agreed procedures in your organisation. The process can be gruelling, arduous and deeply unpleasant.

Secure support for yourself as the manager

- Accept that you will have to tackle poor performance. If you do not, other staff will take their lead from the reality of the poor performers – you will lose authority and standards will fall.
- Accept that the process can be ghastly – build appropriate support for yourself to tackle these issues. This includes personal (somewhere to go to scream!), professional (including legal advice where necessary) and organisational (making sure that your bosses will back you) in respect of both the organisation's interests and your own.

Reflection

Consider what you do as a leader to inspire and direct high performance in your staff. What approach do you take to poor performance? Are there any ways you might improve?

Quality assurance and management

Policy context

The global movement of goods, services, labour, capital and information across international boundaries has created a climate of greater competition.

Many governments have sought to provide incentives for service providers to compete effectively, so as to create a more flexible, plural market of public services. The emphasis on education by New Labour is, at least in part, a response to the threat to the economy of competition from elsewhere, from organisations with a better educated workforce. If our services are to be competitive they must be of high quality. (The alternative is to make them cheap and develop a low skills, low wage economy.) This political imperative is one of the drivers of the quality agenda. It runs hand in hand with the rise of consumerism and increased expectations from service users that they will get quality services. Put another way, is there an argument in favour of providing poor quality services?

To respond to the quality agenda we need to have effective management processes that help to maintain and drive up standards of our services. It can be helpful if the processes themselves are considered to be good ones – for example carrying a seal of approval nationally or internationally (such as the EFQM Business Excellence Model (see page 175), Investors in People or International Standards Organisation (ISO) 9001

The drive for **continuous improvement** in public services is an expression of this preoccupation with quality. There is recognition in some quarters that it will take a long time, not merely to improve public services, but to **transform** them. At the same time people are impatient for change. There is acknowledgement, for example, that elimination of child poverty and the renewal of the most disadvantaged neighbourhoods could take 20 to 30 years. At the same time there is political pressure to make a difference that can be easily measured within the lifetime of a parliament. As a result we see the introduction of such things as Governmental floor targets for neighbourhood renewal; national targets for increasing basic skills and school attainment; and, the four benchmarks for youth services in England.

Public service providers are required (or expected, in the case of voluntary organisations) to introduce **quality assurance frameworks** so they have in place various procedures, processes and techniques for determining the quality of the services they provide.

Quality management is full of jargon and includes terms that appear to mean one thing but actually mean another. Before exploring quality management frameworks we provide some definitions and explore some key concepts.

Quality terms

There are three common uses of the term quality when describing goods or services:

1. **Quality as excellence**, where the term is used to determine how far a product or service achieves a level of absolute excellence; it is about striving to raise good standards even higher and get to a point recognised by those in the field as top of the range. Certain luxury cars would be an example and are on occasions used as a metaphor. People sometimes refer colloquially to a particular service or product being a 'Rolls Royce model'. Most people would typically use the word quality in this way.
2. **Quality as fitness for purpose** is used to determine whether a product or service is satisfactorily performing its intended function. Here quality is 'good enough' because it adequately meets the needs of users in particular circumstances. The Ford Fiesta is an example of a car that is supremely fit for its purpose. Most people would not describe a Ford Fiesta as a 'quality car'.
3. **Quality as freedom from faults** is used to determine whether the product or service actually works and can be relied upon to do what is expected. For most people this is a basic requirement – you are not likely to describe your pen as a quality pen just because it actually writes! However, our railway providers might claim to be providing a quality service if the trains ran on time (or at all) and did not crash.

All three usages are often found in the same organisation about the same service. People talk about 'world-class services' (excellence) in services that are struggling to be free of faults. It is, in our view, helpful to be consistent about the meaning attached to quality in respect of particular activities or services.

To manage the quality of a service, a manager must be clear about:

- its precise purpose
- how it will achieve this purpose
- how to gain commitment of all involved to delivering the service

- the standards of quality by which the service should be judged (see page 172)
- the methods that will be used to gather information about the quality of the service
- the methods for reporting back from staff, service users, volunteers etc. about the quality of the service
- how the feedback will be incorporated into planning and developing improvements.

To provide a quality service the staff, volunteers and service users should:

- agree the standards (for the service and its delivery)
- assess standards (for the service and its delivery)
- identify and set targets
- measure performance against targets
- judge the quality of the performance
- continually work together and individually to identify and implement ways in which the service could be improved.

Quality management

The process for bringing all these requirements together is that of quality management. This has a number of levels:

Quality control

This is the most basic approach to checking out the quality of a service. It is taken from the manufacturing sector and is concerned principally with the quality of goods. It is now regarded as very limited when dealing with the service sector, although it has its place.

Quality control tends to be undertaken internally by workers within the organisation. It 'requires the setting of standards and is essentially a process of inspection, rejection and correction. Quality control is a widely used method for ensuring quality'.[11]

It is defined in standards as 'the operational techniques and activities that are used to fulfil requirements for quality' (ISO 8402).

For this to happen it is important that those who supply the service have sound working procedures that everybody understands and observes. This entails a common set of generic standards that can be applied to specific services. This is the purpose of international standards such as ISO 9000, which:

> ... will not of themselves solve the problems associated with poor management. They are best seen as tools to make good management even better – ISO 9000 is more likely to highlight problems of poor management than resolve them.[12]

As far as youth services and organisations are concerned, quality control means that front-line workers take responsibility for ensuring work is planned, reviewed and evaluated. It involves securing feedback from service users, attending to weaknesses and building on strengths.

---

11 Bone, C. (1991), *Modern Quality Management*, Harlow: Longman.
12 Ibid.

Total Quality Management (TQM)

TQM lies at the other end of the spectrum. It is a more holistic and comprehensive approach to securing continuous improvement. It has been described as a blend of 'passion and system'.[13] People at all levels are expected to listen and engage with each other continually to review performance and find ways to improve.[14]

Somewhere in between the limitations of quality control and the ambitions of TQM resides the more manageable but still challenging task of establishing **quality assurance (QA).** Quality assurance entails creating systems, procedures and processes which make it more likely that the service will be provided at a suitable quality, first time and every time. To be any use, the system needs to be easy to understand and implement. It must be explained to and understood by those who provide the service as well as by any interested external parties. It must generate evidence so that all concerned can know whether the service is living up to the standards set. Evidence of achievement has to be provided.

QA is based on the idea that prevention is better than cure. Rather than do it wrong, be told what was wrong and try to put it right (the Quality Control/Inspection approach), QA seeks to engage all concerned in getting it right in the first place. It also builds in systems to identify and rectify problems quickly (rather than waiting for quality controllers or inspectors to intervene).

Quality assurance involves developing a framework to ensure that there is:

- agreement by everyone about standards
- action to embed and achieve the standards (this works best if everyone has a say in the process of agreeing them, rather than imposing them from above. This does not mean negotiating the standards; it means people being able to discuss, understand and gain ownership of them)
- leadership to ensure action is taken
- a system, procedures and processes for monitoring standards and recording and analysing the outcomes – involving reflection, review and evaluation
- action **planning** to improve the service, set new challenges and so on

The framework is likely to be a number of documents that describe and explain the procedures and processes, with tools and techniques to help in their implementation. Working through the quality framework should be a standard part of induction. It also informs supervision and reporting. It should be:

- user-friendly – those who apply the framework should see it as integral to effective youth work and not as an obstacle or a diversion
- rigorous (not rigid) – combining internal and external assessment
- reliable – the procedures and those who operate them should enjoy the confidence of those who fund, provide and use the service
- responsive – open to change and development so that it too improves

Processes and tools should be simple to operate and manage. They should also be timely, fitting in with the annual cycle of planning and review. The language and techniques used should be straightforward.

---

13 Burnham, John West (1997), *Managing Quality for Schools*, London: Longman.
14 Morgan, Colin and Murgatroyd, Stephen, *Total Quality Management in the Public Sector: An International Perspective*, Milton Keynes: Open University Press. ch.3.

The real test of such a framework is whether it is visible in the practice of the youth work staff. If it is not then it is a waste of time and effort. Managing quality is a process – it involves winning the commitment of all staff to providing services to an agreed set of standards or better, within a clear set of values and principles. It also involves winning their commitment to systems and procedures that provide evidence of the quality of their practice. Above all, the quality system should be proportionate and should not predominate; the tail of assessment should not wag the dog of front-line service provision.

Example

A national voluntary youth organisation invested in a comprehensive pack of materials that provided a quality framework for the wide variety of youth work that was delivered in dispersed locations all over the UK. The pack was written by experts in the field and was excellent.

Many of the youth workers had never seen the pack, had not had a chance to discuss it and were therefore unaware of its contents or the standards of practice promoted. They went about their work, some of which was good, some less so, but most unaffected by the quality framework.

To change this situation the youth workers' line managers (most of whom were not youth work professionals) needed to prioritise induction and use of the quality framework. In their view, delivery of projects was the overriding issue and quality came a distant second. To change this required culture change among the mangers as much as producing the quality framework.

Reflection

Does your organisation have a clear quality framework? How well does it match the description given?

The quality framework should involve all interested parties – elected members, officers and managers, full-time, part-time and volunteer staff, young people, staff from other services and organisations with a stake in youth work, and the wider community. It should be discussed and tested to see that it conforms to the four requirements mentioned above.

Any framework introduced by a youth service or youth work organisation must be compatible and consistent with existing quality assessment arrangements. These include *Resourcing Excellent Youth Services*, Ofsted inspections and Best Value requirements. Rather than start from scratch, it should draw on these relevant, existing standards.

Service quality

All organisations that provide services face the challenge raised in Chapter 3, that the service is provided through an interaction between staff and the user which can be affected by many variables. Therefore service quality is harder to achieve than, say, manufacturing quality. The most widely known general service quality model, SERVQUAL, suggests ten features of service quality, which relate to a greater or lesser extent to all service provision:

1. Reliability – providing the same service every time
2. Responsiveness – providing prompt, willing and flexible service
3. Competence – the skills and knowledge of the providers of services
4. Accessible – contact is as easy as possible
5. Courtesy – the service is polite and respectful

6. **Communication** – the service is well explained
7. **Credibility** – trustworthy and believable (both the provider and the organisation)
8. **Security** – free from danger, confidential
9. **Understanding** – the provider takes care to learn the customer's specific needs
10. **Tangibles** – the facilities, materials equipment are appropriate.

The list was adapted for use with health care organisations.[15]

- Access to services
- Relevance to need for the whole community
- Effectiveness for individual patients
- Equity
- Social acceptability
- Efficiency
- Economy

Reflection

How relevant are these generic service quality indicators to an organisation working with young people?

Identify one or two that you might adapt or use.

The second list takes account of a range of stakeholders, including funders (economy and efficiency), the whole community (relevance) and society at large (social acceptability and equity), in addition to the service user (the patient) while the essentially private sector SERVQUAL views quality purely from the perspective of the customer. This highlights a further complexity in managing quality in a public sector organisation; stakeholders may have differing views of the relative importance of the various dimensions of quality.

Existing quality frameworks relevant to youth work organisations

To some extent, every organisation is unique and needs to have a quality framework of its own. However, all organisations share things with others, so it makes sense to borrow from those that come closest to meeting the requirements and circumstances of your particular service or organisation. Each of the following is a variant from quality assurance systems designed for different forms of organisation.

The Ofsted self-assessment schedule for youth work (June 2001) derives from a framework for inspecting schools. A school is a more 'closed' institution than a youth service. Many voluntary youth organisations have a clearly defined purpose, without the captive audience who have no choice about whether they attend, and must attend for an extended period. The framework was originally for inspection undertaken by a group of external inspectors. It has also been adapted for the purpose of self-assessment, particularly.

The *Connexions Partnerships inspection framework* (June 2001) contains elements that deal directly with the quality of these new Partnerships. How well do they meet the needs that young people aged 13 to 19 have for good quality information, advice, guidance and support in navigating their way through opportunities for learning and development? The main activities of the Connexions service are assessment, support guidance and programmes of teaching and learning. They have similarities to opportunities for association and informal personal and social education provided by the youth work organisations.

The *EFQM Excellence Model* is a process approach to managing quality that comes from

---

15 Maxwell, R. J. (1984), 'Quality Assessment in Health', *British Medical Journal*, vol. 288, 12 May, pp1470–1472.

the commercial world. It is divided into nine elements each of which is defined in more detail in figure 8.5. Note the division between 'enablers' – activities the organisation undertakes to deliver its work – and 'results'. This echoes the division between 'means' and 'ends', or inputs and outputs.

The model is based on self-assessment and so fits in with the current direction of Ofsted inspection and Comprehensive Performance Assessment, which emphasise self-assessment. It can apply to the work of any organisation, company or managed unit.

This model has been adopted by the British Quality Foundation for its UK Quality Award. It provides a 'framework for all organisations to assess themselves, identify areas for improvement and bring themselves up to the same level as the best'. The Quality Standards Task Group of the National Council for Voluntary Organisations has recommended its use by the voluntary sector. The Audit Commission and the Local Government Association have also supported it.

Figure 8.5: The EFQM Excellence Model

Enablers	
Leadership	How the behaviour and actions of the executive team and all other leaders inspire, support and promote excellence as the best way to achieve the organisation's objectives.
Policy and strategy	How the organisation formulates, deploys, reviews and turns policy and strategy into plans and actions.
People management	How the organisation releases the full potential of its people.
Partnerships and resources	How the organisation manages resources effectively and efficiently.
Processes	The management of all value-adding activities within the organisation. How the organisation identifies, manages, reviews and improves its processes.
Results	
Customer results	What the organisation is achieving in relation to the satisfaction of its external customers.
People results	What the organisation is achieving in relation to the satisfaction of its people – staff, board members, volunteers, etc.
Society results	What the organisation is achieving in satisfying the needs and expectations of the community at large.
Key performance results	What the organisation is achieving in relation to its planned objectives and in satisfying the needs and expectations of everyone with an interest or other stake in the organisation.

Finally, the PQASSO (Practical Quality Assurance System for Small Organisations) is worth considering, particularly if you manage a small or medium sized voluntary organisation. The framework provides you with standards for three levels of performance, is simple to understand, and fits well with the Excellence Model.

A quality assurance framework for youth work organisations

Any framework for a youth service or organisation should set out the standards expected if the service is to be of good quality. This applies to all levels of the organisation: at the strategic level so that managers can take a clear lead on quality and at the operational level so that staff know what is expected, can deliver it, provide relevant information back up the line and, most importantly, take action to improve it.

Ten elements of quality assurance for a youth service have been outlined in a National Youth Agency discussion paper.[16] These are:

Reflection

Review your service or organisation against the Marken list, identifying what action is being taken on each criterion at whole service or organisation level, and at unit or project level.

Does this list apply equally to voluntary organisations? If not what are the specific elements that are different?

1. Curriculum statement which is understood and valued by staff and which clarifies service expectations about the nature and quality of youth work. NB 'curriculum' is a much favoured term in education which can be exasperating to those outside; strictly it means a course (eg of study). It describes the process or course that young people will be taken through. An alternative description would be a statement of youth work activities (that lead to the achievement of the organisation's purpose).
2. Staff development strategy and programme exists, which takes account of service values, priorities and goals, assesses organisational strengths and weaknesses and enables staff to acquire the attitudes, knowledge and skills to work effectively;
3. Regular opportunities to update staff on major policy developments at national, local and corporate level.
4. A system of professional supervision and peer review and support enables staff to perform effectively.
5. The organisation provides regular opportunities for initial training of part-time staff.
6. Performance at unit and service level is regularly monitored in time-efficient ways and in a manner that allows individual staff and managers to make sense of the data in assessing and improving performance.
7. Appropriate benchmarks are identified and used.
8. Management regularly assesses internal and external perceptions of performance.
9. The change implications of performance review are translated into targets within service planning.
10. Complaints are handled efficiently and effectively and are used as an indicator of performance.

These ten elements have to a large extent been superseded by the 14 standards for a youth service set out in *Resourcing Excellent Youth Services*.

Quality self-assessment

All the above frameworks make use of self-assessment. Done well, self-assessment of quality, by the organisation, is a cornerstone of continuous quality improvement.

Table 8.6 sets out a sequence for self-assessment.

---

16 Marken, Mary (2000), *Higher Performing Local Authority Youth Services*, Leicester: The National Youth Agency.

Table 8.6: A sequence for self-assessment

Plan the process	Decide what activities, programmes and processes you are going to assess; the methods you will use; who is to be involved; the timetable for doing it.
Assemble the evidence	Agree your standards and performance indicators; decide what kinds of evidence you need; collect it from different sources, checking that it meets the requirements of sufficiency, validity, accuracy, reliability and currency; interpret and process it.
Make the judgments	Judge the quality against the standards; grade it; identify strengths and weaknesses.
Create a plan	Create an action-plan derived from a balanced scorecard of strengths and weaknesses; identify action to be taken so as to build on the one and remedy the other.
Act on the plan	Set in place the processes needed to implement the plan; monitor the implementation process; evaluate the effectiveness of the plan.

There are three key activities for those involved in self-assessment: look, listen and learn.

1. **Looking:** observing the youth work first-hand, the arrangements for supporting young people, the social as well as educational aspects of the experience.
2. **Listening:** finding out from people what they think of the provision – from the young people, the youth workers, support staff and volunteers – this entails interviews, meetings, and less formal conversations.
3. **Learning:** scrutinising documents and data that will yield important facts and figures. This is the kind of evidence that might confirm or challenge a judgment or point of view you may be forming on the basis of what you have seen and heard. Or you can use the data to form hypotheses, which you can then test against the evidence gathered from what you see and hear.

You may need to get all your staff up to speed on the process of self-assessment.

Continuous improvement

There is a danger that managers will get lost in the detail of quality and lose sight of what really matters. We finish this chapter with a reminder that the purpose of quality management is to deliver better services to young people. How will you know they are better? You will have systems that provide evidence to prove it. You will ask young people, staff and other stakeholders, show what impact your service has made and demonstrate progress towards your strategic priorities.

As a leader you will build and sustain a culture that is constantly striving to do better, to improve and to make more of an impact. This is a culture of continuous improvement.

Continuous improvement cannot be achieved through periodic monitoring and annual self-assessment. It must be embedded in the culture of the organisation so that it becomes ' the way we do things around here'. It involves commitment from every member of staff, whatever their role, to improve their own performance continuously and to support others in doing the same.

The quality management and planning processes should satisfy the needs of external agencies but this must not be their sole purpose. The primary aim must always be to enhance the experience of the learners for whom the service exists.

Chapter Nine: Managing innovation

Introduction

We live in times of turbulence and change. There are great opportunities to find new ways to provide services and meet young people's needs more effectively. All our stakeholders are looking for more innovation. They want us to learn from what we have done and to be creative and innovative in our services in the future.

This section explores **innovation**, which is a hallmark of any high performing organisation. Innovation is also one of the features that voluntary organisations promote about themselves. We define innovation in the context of youth work, offer a typology, and specify the drivers and the factors that can support and obstruct it. Finally, we set out how managers can help to ensure innovation takes place, is sustained, and provides the spur to professional knowledge and development.

- Innovation
- Drivers of innovation
- Factors influencing innovation
- Managing innovation and its consequences

Innovation

A high-performing service or organisation has a culture of creativity and innovation. The drive for this is both political and professional. Improving public services means not only investing additional resources, but also finding new and creative solutions to long-standing problems. The commercial sector invests in research and development; so too should the public service sector to enhance its capability and capacity.

> ### Example
>
> The Neighbourhood Renewal Unit, established in the Department of Transport, Local Government and the Regions, as part of the Government's National Strategy Action Plan for Neighbourhood Renewal, is developing a learning and development strategy which includes a knowledge management strand to ensure that what is learned is not lost. It is also determined to ensure that new responses are made to some of the more stubbornly persistent issues that characterise attempts to regenerate some of our most disadvantaged communities.

What is innovation?

Innovation in youth work can be defined as activity that:

- breaks new ground and pushes back the boundaries of professional knowledge and practice;
- develops the capacity of young people and youth workers for original ideas and action; and
- fosters creative achievement that adds value to the quality and range of work.[1]

Innovation involves professional risk-taking, combining the freedom to experiment with the use of proven skills, knowledge and understanding. It may draw on others' ideas and achievement in order to adapt and apply them in new ways.

Innovation is the hallmark of a responsive service. It evokes responses to emerging needs in the marketplace and the development of new products. It is sometimes taken to mean using an existing product with a different market in a new location, eg youth provision in a mental health institution. This new setting can alter or perhaps transform the product.

In other cases, a service or organisation might highlight the existing product to meet new policy demands or equip young people with new skills. Examples include parenting skills (YMCA's 'lads and dads'), reading (YouthBoox), financial literacy (YouthBank) ,and study support, where youth work underpins the goals of formal education.

Innovation can also mean youth workers operating in new arenas or supporting other professionals in theirs, for example as members of Youth Offending Teams trying to reduce the risk of youth crime or as personal advisers providing support to young people as part of the emerging Connexions services.

Innovation does not necessarily mean any short-term initiative. Such work might well be innovative if it either breaks new ground or involves the successful exploitation of new ideas. Innovation can be longer-term and still have the dedicated purpose of finding new ways of doing things.

Innovation could and should be sustainable. It often attracts special funding because Government or some other sponsor wants to back youth work that can be shown to 'make a difference' and provide solutions to problems that other services cannot. If it is successful it should be replicated and absorbed within the main bloodstream of the service. At this point, its claim to be innovative might be forfeited. Yet that does not mean the work ceases to be dynamic or effective. A learning organisation will absorb the lessons of innovation, disseminate them, and apply them within its networks.

Some people believe that innovation is no different from effective youth work (which may be regarded as neither new nor experimental). But equating innovation with effectiveness is mistaken. Certainly innovative work can be effective but this is not always the case. Moreover, there are many examples of effective youth work which are by no means innovative. For example, providing alternative learning programmes based on youth work principles for disaffected school pupils has been taking place for 30 years; what is different now is the high policy profile given to inclusion and the consequent legitimisation of such youth work interventions. Innovation must denote 'new' or it means nothing.

---

1   Merton, Bryan (2001), *So What's New? Innovation in Youth Work*, Leicester: The National Youth Agency.

There is some degree of scepticism, indeed envy, in the field towards innovation, perhaps because it commands a great deal of attention and consequently resources. This is understandable if it does so at the expense of effective mainstream provision but if innovation can demonstrate new ways of making a difference to the lives of young people and their communities then it should be justifiably recognised, rewarded and replicated.

A typology of innovation

A typology can be derived from the following ten dimensions of youth work:

1. **Opportunities** provided for young people
2. **Roles, rights and responsibilities** taken up by young people
3. **Issues or problems** faced by young people
4. **Groups** of young people taking part
5. **Settings or contexts** in which youth work takes place
6. **Methods, approaches and skills** used by youth workers
7. **Values** which inform and underpin youth work
8. Ways of **managing** or organising youth work
9. Ways of **recording** or measuring participation, achievement and progress
10. Ways of **learning and disseminating** lessons from practice

Drivers of innovation

A recurrent theme of much innovative practice is that it is **young people-led** This means that the young people themselves identify the need for action and have a considerable say in how the project, programme or activity should be designed and run.

Innovative youth work seems to be driven by different factors. Commonly there is some **national initiative or policy** that requires the service or organisation to respond in new ways. Examples include the Government's unveiling of the Connexions strategy, requiring whole youth services to develop partnerships with other agencies, particularly the Careers Service, and consider how it can contribute to the supply, training, development and support of personal advisers. Another example of government policy influencing youth work is the Department of Health's drive to reduce teenage pregnancies, or if young people are going to defy such a policy and become parents, the Home Office's determination that they should develop better parenting skills. Similarly, the emergence of the Children Bill and the document, *Every Child Matters: Next Steps* will further stretch the capacity of managers to respond to that agenda, whilst at the same time, providing a clear opportunity for services to position themselves and influence the direction of change.

A further driver of innovation has been the recent attempt by local authorities to develop more **corporate and joined up youth strategies** This places demands on youth organisations and projects to look beyond their boundaries and form partnerships to improve the range and quality of services for young people. This is intended to result in more holistic and comprehensive needs assessment and consequently more innovative approaches to planning, providing and managing programmes. An example is the cooperation between the police, Barnardo's and the local authority youth service in Bradford to provide support for young women in Keighley at risk of being sexually exploited.

Most frequently innovation is internally generated by **practitioners and managers** coming together to discuss issues or problems emerging with young people that demand a fresh approach since the existing ones are clearly not working. This often results in inter-agency initiatives since it is recognised that youth work, on its own, cannot provide the answer.

One of the most frequently cited external drivers of innovation is the incentive of **additional funding**. But there are sometimes less pecuniary prompts; for example, community groups and organisations such as the black-led churches, have been the spur to innovation in cases where they think their young people need new responses to their needs.

Innovative practice can therefore be driven by internal forces, external forces or sometimes a combination.

Factors influencing innovation

Innovation is the means of change. Organisations that need to change what they do sometimes find it difficult because much is invested in their existing culture. There is often resistance to taking the risks which inevitably are part of change. In local authorities, elected members as much as officers find it hard to sanction and support new ways of undertaking the work, even when they can see that existing methods are not proving effective. No doubt similar conservative forces exist within some voluntary organisations.

Some of the factors that seem to be key in determining whether innovation is likely to occur are set out below.

Factors supporting innovation	Factors obstructing innovation
Accepting uncertainty	Empasis on short-term results and gains
Strongly committed individuals prepared to challenge the status quo, take risks and have a go at something different	Highly controlling management; excessive rules and regulations.
Accepting controversy and contest	Conforming behaviour; expecting people to do as they are told
Lateral thinking; working 'outside the box' and across professional boundaries	Excessive rationalism; expecting things to happen in a logical, pre-determined pattern
Knowledge, responsiveness, openness, shared values, creative staff recognising each others' skills	Cautious, competitive and mistrustful staff unwilling to share knowledge and skills
Willing to trust partners in other agencies and contribute to broader policy agenda	Reluctance to engage in multi-agency initiative or make resources available for broader policy purposes
Acceptance of initial costs	Over-emphasis on early accurate costs

Need and determination to (a) find a new focus and interest in the work; (b) find radical responses to issues	Contentment with status quo
Achievement of 'soft' outcomes recognised as valid for funding purposes	'Hard', measurable outputs being sought as a condition of funding
Being prepared to work from young people's perspectives and concerns	Adults setting the agenda

Managing innovation and its consequences

The challenge for managers is to ensure that innovative work is sustainable, replicated and capable of transforming existing practice. It requires managers to give intensive support to those who practise it; to ensure that people learn from what transpires; and that the policy context and bending of main programmes are managed as a consequence.

Managers should apply the same standards of quality assurance and the same rigour and consistency in monitoring and evaluating innovative work, as they do to more 'mainstream' practice. Procedures have to be in place to assess its impact and potential. This means having a clear plan for communicating the outcomes of innovation, convincing the service of the benefits of investing in this work and overcoming professional or lay cynicism. It requires managers to give innovation their full support, rather than demand unreasonably quick results; also to ensure that outcomes are timely enough to secure further funding. Resources need to be deployed to make the best use of opportunities, and this means ensuring that sufficient supervision is available to workers. Risk-taking is as important a facet of managing innovation as doing it because there are unlikely to be policy guidelines when new ground is being broken. In fact the guidelines are usually derived from the practice itself.

The essence of innovation is experiment. It is concerned with establishing and then testing hypotheses. Successful outcomes cannot be guaranteed; indeed there is a strong possibility of failure, in the sense that objectives may not be achieved. In all experimentation there is a degree of trial and error. The point is that managers should support experiment and not condemn error, as long as the failure is explored and explained and lessons are learned from what transpires.

Example

The Edge is a project managed by the Derby City Council Youth Service. It is targeting young people involved in the sex industry who have fallen through the net of provision and protection. Social services and the police acknowledged they could not effectively engage with these young adults and turned to the youth service for help, as part of a multi-agency initiative.

The features of the response are not rocket science. The key is to listen carefully to what the young people are saying and start to build trust. Help can be very

> practical – feeding them when they are hungry, providing them with decent clothes if necessary. Flexibility is essential and this might mean bending the rules. The local Child Protection Committee has re-written procedures to include The Edge as a referral agency. Multi-agency support has moved beyond rhetoric to provide practical help, such as using the police phone system to provide safety cover for youth workers when they are on the streets.
>
> The project works because individuals with vision and commitment have been encouraged to develop their ideas. The youth service was prepared to come forward and take a risk. The project has been supported by senior staff in all the key agencies. Business support has been used to try to secure external funding. There have been risks – no outcomes guaranteed, no blueprint to work from, putting reputations on the line, having to cope with difficult information, differences and misunderstandings between agencies. But the rewards have been immense – seeing young people use the project responsibly, being able to get alongside deeply troubled and mistrustful young people to contain their anxieties, help them move on and begin to realise their ambitions.

It is important for innovation to lead to learning, not only for the young people directly involved but for all those in the service or organisation. This learning concerns both the intended and unintended outcomes of innovation. There should be four sets of beneficiaries from the learning:

- the young people
- youth workers and other practitioners
- the communities to which they belong
- the organisations and services to which they are attached.

Reflection

How do you encourage and manage innovation in your organisation?

Do you successfully translate the learning from innovative projects and activities into the mainstream of the organisation? What evidence have you to support this?

Does your organisation have a culture of creativity and innovation? How do you know? How do you reward creativity and innovation?

What therefore needs to happen if learning is to take place? The work should:

- be linked to supervision and appraisal
- become the focus of team meetings
- yield models that can be tested out across different projects and centres
- be built into planning and resourcing
- establish baseline measures against which to assess impact
- be continuously interrogated by posing questions such as 'so what?' ... 'what else can we do with this information?' ... 'where does this take us now?'

Making the learning available to others is an important strand of innovation and those responsible for it should have a strategy for communicating the outcomes. What is learned should not be confined to those directly involved in a particular piece of work but managers should exploit the scope for replication and build the fruits of the innovation into their procedures. This should make the innovation sustainable and lead to more systemic change.

It is often much easier to crush innovation than to nurture it. The box below identifies ten ways in which innovation can be held back. The task is to make sure that these blocks do not develop or are swiftly removed.

Ten ways to crush creativity and innovation

1. Encourage people to take risks, then blame them if things go wrong.
2. Reward people for doing things right and by the book, not for trying to do things differently (and perhaps better).
3. If given a paper full of ideas comment on the grammar, punctuation and detail.
4. Use phrases like 'That's interesting ... but' or 'it will never work' or 'we've already tried that ... [in 1902] and it didn't work' or 'get to the point', as often as possible.
5. Suppress all humour. Never smile. Look bored.
6. Make people work so hard they are too tired to be creative and have no time to play with ideas.
7. Create fear of real expression – encourage people to avoid conflict at all costs.
8. Build a strict and tall hierarchy.
9. Expect things to stay the same, resist change.
10. Build as much order and rigid routine as possible.

Chapter Ten:
Managing your stakeholders

Introduction

Managers in voluntary organisations and public sector service providers have to build relationships with a wide variety of internal and external stakeholders (those with an interest in the services). These include those that pay for services (government departments, local authorities, sponsors, charities, donors), those who use or might use the services (young people), those whose opinions affect the services (trustees, senior managers, politicians, the general public) and so on.

The external stakeholders are analogous to the market within which a commercial organisation operates, so consideration of managing your external stakeholders draws from the discipline of marketing.

This chapter looks at the management task of building and sustaining effective relationships with the key stakeholders and provides concepts and tools to help you with marketing and promoting your organisation's work with young people.

Managers of youth work organisations increasingly work in a wide variety of partnerships – with public agencies, voluntary and private sector organisations. The latter part of the chapter explores the concepts that lie behind partnership working and provides tools for working more effectively in and with partnerships.

Figure 10.1: The experiential cycle

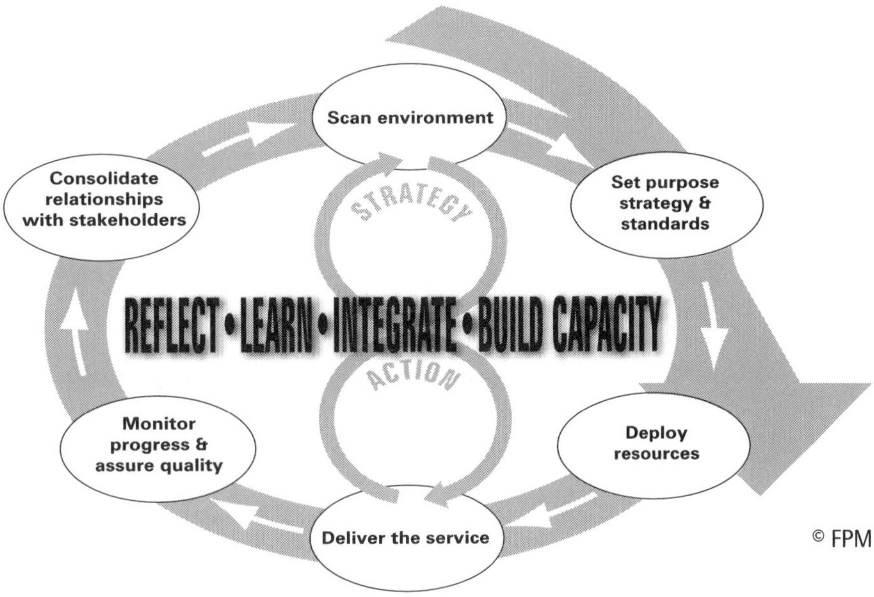

Scan environment

Consolidate relationships with stakeholders

Set purpose strategy & standards

STRATEGY

REFLECT • LEARN • INTEGRATE • BUILD CAPACITY

ACTION

Monitor progress & assure quality

Deploy resources

Deliver the service

© FPM

This chapter refers to the top left hand quadrant of the management model – consolidating relationships with stakeholders. We use consolidate to mean 'reinforce or strengthen' and it therefore includes both using existing relationships and building new ones. This chapter covers:

- The concept of stakeholder management
- Marketing
- The rise of partnership working
- A strategic approach to partnerships

The concept of stakeholder management

The term 'stakeholder' is used widely in discussion of the work of voluntary organisations and public sector agencies. A stakeholder is anyone with an interest in the activities of the organisation. It includes those within and those outside the organisation.

The term is much wider than 'customer' and is increasingly used in the private sector. It allows managers to look carefully at a range of perspectives and interests that affect the organisation (many of which will conflict) and to weigh them against each other.

The stakeholders include:

- The users: young people.
- The beneficiaries: young people, their families and communities.
- The customers: those who pay for the service. This includes the authorities who fund the service, taxpayers (indirectly), politicians who make budget decisions, donors, sponsors and so on. In some organisations it may also include young people and their families who pay fees for services they receive.
- The members of the organisation (if it has a membership).
- The staff and volunteers.
- The organisation's supporters.
- Your partner organisations and agencies.
- The organisation's competitors.
- The organisation's suppliers (including, for example, equipment suppliers, but also, more distantly, colleges that train youth workers and so on).
- Local and national politicians.
- The general public.
- The media.

Each stakeholder has a view of the organisation, and has a degree of power or say in what it does. For many this connection is very weak and distant, but for some it is both close and strong.

To manage the stakeholders you need to do five things:

1. Know who the stakeholders are.
2. Gather information on their views; understand their wants and needs.
3. Reflect on their power and importance to the organisation.
4. Scan the wider environment for opportunities and threats and be aware how these affect the stakeholders (see Chapters 4 and 6).

5. Develop appropriate relationships to influence their opinions and actions so as to achieve the purpose of the organisation (promoting your work with young people and how it benefits them) and to satisfy their wants and needs.

This is a large part of marketing your organisation and its work.

Marketing

Marketing has been defined by the Chartered Institute of Marketing (CIM) as: 'the management process responsible for identifying, anticipating and satisfying customer requirements profitably'.

In the voluntary and public sectors 'profitably' is usually replaced with 'effectively' – which might include generating a surplus to reinvest in future work – and 'customer' with 'stakeholder'.

Marketing means finding out: what your stakeholders want and whether you can meet their expectations and demands; what your partners are hoping to achieve and how you can help them do so; and what your competitors provide. It means being absolutely clear about what your service is offering – what is distinctive and special – your unique selling point.

The external stakeholders for an organisation working with young people could be categorised as shown in table 10.2.

Table 10.2: External stakeholders

Consumer or Service user	Customer (pays for service)	Indirect beneficiary	Supporter Ally	Competitor Opponent
Young people using services	UK Government funders, local government funders, grant makers, donors, sponsors, etc.	Local community parents, schools, colleges, partner organisations, etc.	Politicians Members of the organisation	Politicians Press and other media
Young people not using services			Press and other media	Other agencies and organisations
	Taxpayers (indirectly)		Most of the indirect beneficiaries?	
	Parents (sometimes)			
	Young people (sometimes)			

It is important to note that the customer is usually separated from the user/consumer of a public service. Some public service providers and voluntary organisations have developed good relationships with their customers without really being focused on their users (the young people).

Young people may not see themselves as service users. If young people actually get practical help and emotional support from some of the youth workers, they may see themselves as 'clients'. If they have a high level of involvement in shaping the service they might see themselves as 'members'.

Assessing young people's needs and wants is commonly agreed to be a characteristic of an effective youth service or organisation. Many claim to do this but few have developed effective means of doing so, as Ofsted reports frequently testify. How do you do this?

The main problem seems to be the scale of the task. Where do you start and where do you finish? How do you find out? The box below gives an example.

Example: Assessing young people's needs and wants

Approach: Every three to five years the organisation needs to refresh its picture of:

- the population of young people served (size, breakdown into years, gender, race, disability, etc.)
- the characteristics of the area served (broad demographics, social and economic data, school and college performance data, deprivation indices, etc.)
- service users' views (this should be an annual process)
- views of those young people not using the services
- views of a sample of young people about the wider services they receive and how they could be improved
- other stakeholders' views about what young people need

Methods: A mix of methods can be used:

1. Filleting existing reports and information (such as census, UK Government data, local government data)
2. Surveys and questionnaires
3. Group discussions and one-to-one interviews

With proper planning, sufficient time and support, young people can themselves carry out substantial parts – or all – of this process.

This sort of data is an integral part of the Transforming Youth Work Plan 2003 – 2006 required for all youth services in England, as subsequently revised by the planning guidance issued in December 2003 by the Secretary of State.

Mapping your stakeholders

Once you have identified your key stakeholders, you need to develop a regular process for mapping your relationships with them, so that you can plan action to sustain or develop the relationships.

Your stakeholders have different wants. A training provider may want you to provide an alternative life skills programme for those young people at risk of dropping out of learning. The drugs action team may want you to provide a safe environment where they can carry out informal education with potential users. The educational welfare service may want you to use the good relationships you have built up with local families to encourage parents and carers to get their children to attend school. Local politicians may want to see young people off the streets and away from the shops where they alarm older shoppers, and so on.

Stakeholder mapping helps you to get a picture of the players in the arena in which the organisation/service operates. It can help you understand what various people, groups and organisations may want of you, what they can offer you, how they can and may influence you. It can help partners to understand their similarities and differences, as they come together and continue to work together.

It is helpful to use a matrix to analyse each stakeholder's interests (see below). For example:

- What do they care about?
- Their power and influence in relation to your organisation.
- What do they want from your organisation?
- Judge how the organisation/service is currently performing in relation to these wants. (a very useful discussion can be prompted by very simple categorisations such as poorly, okay, well).
- What you need from the stakeholder.
- What they think about your organisation.

Stakeholder	What do they care about	Their power in relation to your organisation	What they want from your organisation	How you think you are doing in satisfying these wants (rating)	What you want and need from them	What they think about your organisation
A.						
B.						
C.						

This sort of matrix allows you to rate the relationship with each of your important stakeholders. You could use a rating scale as simple as:

- Green: good ongoing relationship. They know us, trust us and want to use (or support) our services.
- Amber: some contact, and the beginnings of a useful relationship. They do not fully understand us, nor we them. More work is needed.
- Red: no relationship to speak of. Priority for information gathering and relationship building.

A simple list of stakeholders, followed by the appropriate colour code, provides the basis for an action plan and will contribute to your long-term marketing strategy.

Scanning the wider environment

All your marketing activity takes place in the context of the wider world in which your services operate – the macro environment. Effective marketing means identifying, anticipating and, as far as possible, satisfying the demands and opportunities they present you with; keeping out your antennae, sitting in the crow's nest and observing what is within the short and middle distance and scanning the horizon for what may be coming next. Marketing means being alive to opportunities and alert to threats. This is environmental scanning. It requires managers to be well informed and networked; to be able to 'read the signs' of change and be just in front of the crest of any wave.

Reflection

How well do you know your organisation's stakeholders?

Can you describe their wants and needs accurately, based on reliable information?

Do you have a way to analyse and describe the state of your relationship with each important set of stakeholders?

The marketing function is therefore highly strategic and must be linked to the organisation's overall strategy. It is not the same as selling your services to your customers.

Targeting

Reflection

How do you go about scanning the environment?

Why do so many organisations have no formal system or procedures for doing this? What would be the benefits, barriers and costs to your organisation improving this?

A market can be described as the place where the core business of the organisation is carried out. It is where you provide your services.

Targeting is the process of focusing services to fit the requirements of the users and customers. Refer to the model for focusing a service on page 54. Your marketing follows whatever strategy you have agreed regarding the focus of the service. The great danger in work with young people is to have little or no focus. The whole concept of universality pushes youth services away from focus. It is possible to have universal access to a targeted service. Some very successful voluntary organisations are tightly focused (the Prince's Youth Business Trust for example); others are less so.

Without a focus it is very difficult to define a clear purpose. Without a clear purpose it is well nigh impossible to manage effectively.

Targeting provision means ensuring that you are able to 'customise' your offer to be responsive to particular sets of requirements.

Segmenting

You may find it helpful to break down the wider market into sub-groups according to some logic or rationale. This is called segmenting the market. The segments that emerge must be meaningful. For commercial organisations market segments should have:

● a characteristic or characteristics that distinguish it from the overall market
● a significant potential, (ie enough customers to be viable).

The market potential of the segment should be measurable, and the people in it accessible.

Things to think about

● Note what constraints, if any, would affect your service's ability and willingness to use these criteria.
● Identify, if you can, a small segment of the market which your service has not yet reached.
● Decide, using the criteria, whether that segment is meaningful as far as bringing benefits to justify the investment of effort and costs.
● List the benefits, if any, of market segmentation to your organisation and its users and customers.

Positioning

Positioning means seeking to position your product or service in the mind of the user, customer or other stakeholders. It is based on your understanding of stakeholders' wants and needs, plus your organisation's purpose and strategy.

Crucial to your positioning is the 'offering' your service makes. This includes the 'x' factor that makes your service special, the unique selling point that makes it distinctive. Once it is found and proved to be successful, then it can be 'branded' as yours and used to promote the service.

Reflection

Think of a public or voluntary sector service that has achieved a really effective position in the minds of key stakeholders.

How has this been done? What lessons can you draw from this for your own organisation?

Positioning is about placing your organisation and its services in the mind of key stakeholders, in the way that you want. Consider two major retail cosmetic companies you will find on most high streets: Boots and the Body Shop. Outline how you see their position in the market and how you think their positions differ. Think then of your own organisation's services; how do they differ from those of an organisation which most closely compares or competes with yours?

Promoting the service

Managers of organisations that work with young people must be able to promote the benefits and impact of the work to their stakeholders.

To do this well you need to understand the stakeholders' interests (see above) and use appropriate styles of leadership and influencing to build support. You will need to be able to back up your arguments with evidence, which requires good management information (see Chapter 7).

Promotion takes time and is intimately linked with your overall strategy and your marketing strategy. The time is needed to:

- identify which stakeholders you are promoting to. Focus on those that will contribute most to achieving the purpose of the organisation. Very little effective promotion can be done to a vague blanket audience; the sharper you are about who you want to influence, the greater your chance of having an impact
- build your case: what does your organisation have to offer (the service offering)? why is it of interest to the particular stakeholder?
- set out the data to support your case
- decide on the most influential way to approach the stakeholder. People take far more notice of a third party[1] – are there third parties who could promote your organisation's services? (An obvious and powerful group is the young people who use the service. they are sometimes your strongest promoters – are you engaging and involving them in this?)
- make contacts with the stakeholders: choose a method that is fit for purpose.

Example

A youth centre was concerned that it was not in contact with young people from minority ethnic communities in its area. The centre had previously been promoted through general information sent to schools and word of mouth.

The manager gathered population data and found that there was a substantial Sikh community with which it had virtually no connection. Further research found there were three Sikh community projects and a Sikh temple.

---

1 van Looy, Bart, Van Dierdonck, Roland and Gemmel, Paul (1998), *Services Management – an Integrated Approach*. London: Pitman Publishing, p80.

The manager made inquiries and was able to identify three community leaders. She arranged to meet them. In preparation for the meeting she produced a short factsheet about the centre. Her purpose in meeting the leaders was to find out what they wanted from the centre and to discuss their perception of the needs of the Sikh young people.

The meetings led to a better understanding of the Sikh community and an invitation to talk to several young people. This led to offers to promote the centre to the target audience. A small number of Sikh young people started to attend the centre as a result.

Example

The Draft Standards of Youth Work Provision offer an opportunity for organisations to demonstrate their effectiveness and to promote themselves.

Authorities must specify their key target groups, and identify and plan the range of interventions designed to promote their personal and social development.

Stemming from this objective are three standards:

- YS1: clear definition of target group, by age and any other relevant characteristics, including ethnic diversity.
- YS2: clear specification, in a planning framework, of the needs and of the range of opportunities for personal development to which young people in the target group have access (to include cultural activities, counselling, international and residential experiences, sport and outdoor adventure and voluntary action).
- YS3: a defined curriculum framework which links YS1 and YS2 in 90 per cent of the provision secured by the local authority.

Evidence of achievement on these three standards will help promotion.

The slogan of one of the public advertising campaigns of the Youth Training Scheme (YTS) of the 1980s and 1990s was 'The best advertisement for YTS is the young people themselves'. This was meant to encourage employers, in particular, to take on young people who had been through one of the programmes.

Although the scheme was heavily flawed and provided poor quality training for many young people who needed the best, the slogan has some merit. It could helpfully be applied to youth work. If the youth service can demonstrate that young people have achieved and moved forward through their experience of youth work, then all stand to benefit.

One way to do this is to identify, record and accredit the learning and achievement of the young people through informal education. While most youth officers sign up to this, some may not know what schemes are in place and how to choose the one that will best fit the needs, capabilities and interests of the young people they work with.

To help in this respect in April 2002 The National Youth Agency (NYA) published a national framework of informal education awards.[2] This is very timely in view of the Green Paper

---

2   The National Youth Agency (2002), *Network for Accrediting Young People's Achievement, National Framework of Informal Education Awards*, Leicester: The National Youth Agency.

on 14-19 education (*Extending Opportunities, Raising Standards*), which proposes to recognise the wider achievements of young people beyond those secured in school and college through an overarching award for young people when they reach the age of 19. The NYA's guide lists the most commonly used award schemes, gives detailed information on each, groups them by type and level, identifies the skills and attributes they seek to develop in the young, and maps them against the national qualifications framework. It also gives level descriptors for the awards included.

Reflection

How do you promote your service?

Is there an agreed strategy?

Does your greatest effort go into promoting the service to the highest priority stakeholders?

Senior officers and managers of youth services and organisations could usefully examine the information provided in this publication to assess which particular suite of awards might be most fitting for the young people they work with.

We move on next to look in detail at a particular kind of stakeholder relationship – working with partners and in partnerships.

The rise of partnership working

Partnerships are regarded as key in driving forward social policies, including those directed towards young people. The concept is in danger of being seriously over-worked as public sector services are seeking to 'join up' their policies and programmes, recognising that so many of the challenges they face are inter-connected and can only be seriously tackled through inter-agency work. Young people do not recognise departmental boundaries. If they are to be seen as whole people, rather than as fragments, then the challenge to youth services and organisations is to ensure coordination and coherence in whatever they provide.

This means forging alliances (strategic and operational) with other services and organisations both inside and outside the local authority. In the same way that 'education cannot compensate for society' so youth services and organisations on their own cannot deal with the problems of young people and provide them with a sufficient range of opportunities for personal development. To sustain a high-performing service means building and developing partnerships.

Partnerships offer benefits with regard to three major objectives:

● Coordination and integration of service delivery, for example, community safety or crime and disorder partnerships and Connexions.
● Development of new approaches to service provision, for example Education Action Zones.
● Increasing financial and other resources available for local services, especially where partnership is a pre-condition of grant aid, for example, Single Regeneration Budget, Sure Start and Early Years Development Plans.

The New Labour UK Government has made partnerships and implementation agendas to modernise the governance and delivery of public services a central plank of its policy. MP Philip Hope suggests 'partnership' is emerging as the big idea of the second term Labour government. Like 'stakeholding' and the 'third way', Labour is attempting to give an identity to its pragmatic 'what works' approach to governance.[3]

Partnership has been emphasised as a critical element in the relationship between central

---

3 Philip Hope MP, in a paper to Leicester University ESRC Seminar, October 2001.

and local government.[4] It is seen as key to joining up services and thereby delivering Best Value.[5] By working as partners, organisations can bring a rich variety of resources to bear on shared issues and problems. Specialist (and expensive) resources can be harnessed together, rather than single agencies seeking to produce their own pale shadows of other agencies' products or services. Increasingly the cost of going it alone is prohibitive. Partnership is fundamental to the design and delivery of the entire neighbourhood renewal programme, where Local Strategic Partnerships (LSPs) are a requirement for funding.[6]

Despite its apparent importance as both mechanism and philosophy, the meaning of partnership is seldom defined. Different people use it to mean a wide variety of different things at different times: from agencies loosely working together (as in learning partnerships) to forming a separate legal joint entity (regeneration companies or Connexions Service partnerships); from improving contractual relationships ('partnering' in the housing sector, or in public private partnerships) to building a better relationship with service users (partnership between helping services and families in child protection[7]).

What sort of 'organisation' is a partnership?

We can apply Gareth Morgan's ideas[8] about the impact of how we see organisations (explored in Chapter 3) to partnerships. The five metaphors of machine, organic system, political system, a culture and a brain (network) can all be used. How does this help us to understand partnerships? The players involved are likely to perceive the partnership using different metaphors. As a consequence, different players have completely different analyses of what is happening and how to take things forward, and so are frequently unable to think and plan effectively together.

There appears to be a schism in the UK Government's perception. On one hand most partnerships seem to be seen as a culture – a way of working together towards shared values and vision. At times the UK Government seems to adopt the 'organisation as brain' metaphor. However, when it comes to implementation, the civil service kicks in and we hurtle back to the machine.

A variety of partnership arrangements

Partnership has been defined as 'Three or more organisations – representing the public, private and voluntary sectors – acting together by contributing their diverse resources in the furtherance of a common vision that has clearly defined goals and objectives.'[9]

Many partnerships consist of only two organisations – for example the statutory Youth Service and Connexions (although Connexions itself fits under the above definition).

The Audit Commission defines partnership as 'a joint working arrangement where the partners:
- are otherwise independent bodies
- agree to cooperate to achieve a common goal
- create *a new organisational structure* [our italics] or process to achieve this goal, separate from their own organisations
- plan and implement a jointly agreed programme, often with joint staff or resources
- share relevant information
- pool risks and rewards.'[10]

4 *Strong Local Leadership – Quality Public Services*, Government White Paper, December 2001.
5 *Modern Local Government in Touch with the People*, Government White Paper, 1998.
6 Neighbourhood Renewal Unit (2001), *Accreditation Guidance for Local Strategic Partnerships*, London: DTLR.
7 Social Services Inspectorate/Department of Health (1995) *The Challenge of Partnership in Child Protection: Practice Guide*, London: HMSO.
8 see Chapter 3, footnote 7.
9 From Wilson, Andrew and Charlton, Kate (1997) *Making Partnerships Work – A Practical Guide for the Public, Private Voluntary And Community Sectors*, York: Joseph Rowntree Foundation.
10 Audit Commission (1988), *A Fruitful Partnership – Effective Partnership Working*, London: Audit Commission, para 13.

More cynically, partnerships have been described as two organisations 'temporarily suppressing mutual loathing in the joint pursuit of scarce resources.'

Our work on partnerships, federations and decentralised organisations[11] suggests multi-agency arrangements ('partnerships') can be typified using a spectrum ranging from the loose network at one end to the new legal entity at the other. This approach is echoed by Taket and White[12] who identified nine types of multi-agency arrangement. Lowndes and Skelcher[13] have explored modes of governance in multi-agency arrangements, identifying three main modes: market, hierarchy and network.

Jackson also adopts this approach.[14] He suggests 'This is the age of the networked society. Lying between the governance structures of markets and hierarchies, networks have emerged as an organisational form which seeks to confront many of the 'wicked problems' faced by public and private organisations.' Networks lie somewhere between markets and hierarchy because 'it is not reasonable to stand back and leave everything to anonymous market forces to deliver enhanced value for money. Nor is it feasible to intervene and manage purely by administrative fiat.'

Jackson cites four possible ways that organisations might inter-relate, depending on whether the external environment is predictable or unpredictable when set against whether the goals are individual or collective. These are:

- cooperation (individual goals; low predictability)
- competition (individual goals; high predictability)
- coordination (shared goals; high predictability)
- coevolution (shared goals; low predictability).

In table 10.3 (page 198) we have attempted an integration of the views on multi-agency arrangements.

Taket and White also discuss the 'rhizomatic network' – a complex, decentralised structure, heavily reliant upon modern communications and information technology. They give as an example the series of protests organised at international summits from Seattle to Genoa. Spontaneous and organic in their appearance and growth, these networks rely on the ability of their members to communicate effectively and a sense of some commonality – in this case 'anti' feelings towards symbols of global power and commerce.

The level of fit between partners has an impact on the success of the partnership. This is borne out by research from the commercial sector.[15] We have identified four more possible positions for the partners in a venture to occupy, based on the degree of difference (or distinctiveness) of their offering to the partnership set against the degree of shared purpose. It is our experience that partners with distinctive offerings but who share a common purpose are likely to form value added collaborations (high potential for 'synergy').

11 See for example Ford, Kevin and Smith, Douglas (2001), *balancingacts@Vol.Org.Uk: Responding To Devolution and Regionalisation*, London, ACEVO, pp30–32.
12 Taket, Ann and White, Leroy, (2000), *Partnership and Participation: Decision Making in the Multi-Agency Setting*, Chichester: Wiley.
13 Lowndes, Vivien and Skelcher, Chris (1998), 'The Dynamics of Multi-Organisational Partnerships: an analysis of Changing Modes of Governance', *Public Administration*, vol. 76, summer, pp313.
14 Jackson, P. M. (1999), *Managing Between Markets and Hierarchies*, Leicester University Management Centre Discussion Paper.
15 Moss-Kanter, Rosabeth (1994), Collaborative Advantage: The Art of Alliances, *Harvard Business Review*, July-August

Table 10.3: Types of joint working arrangement found in 'partnerships'

	Market	Network			Jointly owned organisation
		Information sharing or consultation	Joint planning	Joint planning and delivery	
Level of shared commitment	None needed	Low	Low to medium	Medium to high	High (to set up) then medium/low
Nature of interactions	Prices and deals	Trust and relationships	Trust and relationship with formal agreement (loose)	Formal agreement (tight)	Administrative, governance for founding partners
Leadership	None obvious	Shifting: dominant partner may set the agenda	Key partners take lead	Increasingly shared between the main partners	Shared between the main partners; delegated to the governing board of company
Style	Competitive	Loose: mutual benefit or dominant partner(s) may dictate plans and action (token networks)	Tighter: mutual benefit Shared involvement in setting the agenda and agreeing action Delivery is by each of the partners acting separately but with coordination and close liaison	Formal mutual benefit Shared involvement in setting the agenda and agreeing joint action Delivery is throughout joint working in multi-agency teams	Formal, bureaucratic Each party clear about its legal responsibilities in the partnership
Flexibility	Very high	High	Medium	Low	Low
Dependency on other agencies	None	Minimal	Medium	High	High (setting up); medium to low once going
Problems	Uncoordinated	Unstable especially if token involvement	Requires resource to coordinator; may be unclear who has control and ownership; eats into agency sovereignty	Must overcome differences in organisational and professional culture and philosophy from top to bottom	Becomes a separate entity – may need to forge new partnerships to join things up again!

Adapted from Lowndes and Skelcher, 1988, Taket and White, 2000 and Jackson, 1999

Figure 10.4: Levels of 'fit' between partners

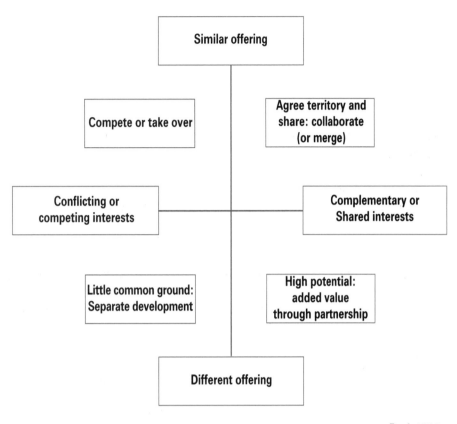

Ford, 2002[16]

If we apply this model to a typical multi-agency partnership we find a scattering of different positions depending on which of the partners is examined. The big public agencies (health, local authority, police) appear to have a great deal in common, and are drawn towards collaboration. Smaller service providers within the partnership are likely to be competing with each other. Many of the community groups and voluntary organisations would appear to be likely to pursue separate development, whilst some may have different offerings which could lead to high value joint work.

Organisations working with young people have very particular skills and experience to offer partnerships. They can often add great value to the others' present, but need to be wary of the costs of participation.

A dynamic process

It is also important to recognise that a partnership is not static. Its development follows a similar pattern to that of any group, and some commentators have offered an analogy with Tuckman's sequence of forming, storming, norming, and performing.[17]

Lowndes and Skelcher[18] offer another, and in many ways more useful analysis of the dynamics of partnership development, suggesting that the partnership operates in different modes as it develops:

Reflection

Look at one or two of the partnerships within which your organisation is operating and analyse them using the models described.

Do the models help to cast light on why some things have happened in the way they have?

---

16 Ford, K. J. (2002), *Doing the Hokey Cokey*, paper to Leicester University ESRC seminar on partnership.
17 Tuckman, B. and Jensen, M. (1977), 'Stages of Small Group Development Revisited', *Group and Organisational Studies*, vol. 419, p27.
18 See footnote 13.

- Pre-partnership collaboration (network mode)
- Creation and consolidation (hierarchical mode)
- Programme delivery (market – commissioning and contracting)
- Termination and succession (back to **network**)

Lessons from the private sector

Over the last two decades or so alliances and partnerships have attracted considerable attention in the private sector, where the dynamics of global competition and business complexity have driven many companies to ally themselves in search of stability and profitability. Little of what has been learned appears to have been translated to help with the development of public and third sector partnerships.

Benjamin Gomes-Casseres[19] draws strategic lessons from the experiences of IT companies which flocked together into alliances in order to pool resources to develop pioneering new computer processes:

Alliances stand and fall by the strength of the relationships within them: these must be managed carefully.

Effective alliances are worth more than the sum of individual contributions; leading and managing the overall partnership is the most important priority.

The governance of alliances requires a great deal of effort. Leading alliance members must be willing to accept ambiguity and some loss of control or risk stifling the freedom of peripheral members.

More is not necessarily better in an alliance – increasing the number of members may often be costly, increasing the complexity of relationships and the administrative workload. Only add new partners when there is a clear and demonstrable benefit to doing so.

He notes that networks of companies working towards joint ends must be constructed carefully, and that the size, composition and speed of growth of these networks (amongst other things) must be determined by the environment within which they work and the competencies of the companies involved.

Rosabeth Moss Kanter[20] suggests a series of factors that contribute to positive partnerships. These are shown below in table 10.5. The kind of factors that tend to obstruct are listed in the right column.

Table 10.5: Factors that contribute to and obstruct positive partnerships

Contribute	Obstruct
Individual excellence, with all partners being strong and having something of value to contribute.	Some partners have more clout than others and tend to dominate; the less influential feel they are being dragged along in their wake.

19 Gomes-Casseres, Benjamin (1994), 'Group Versus Group: How Alliance Networks Compete', *Harvard Business Review*, July–August.
20 See footnote 15.

Contribute	Obstruct
Importance, meaning that the relationship fits the major strategic objectives of each partner, so there is a strong commitment to making it work	It is not clear that the objectives of each organisation in the partnership are going to be advanced equally so there are diifferent levels of engagement
Interdependence, which leads the partners to provide complementary assets and skills	Some partners have clearly more to give while others have more to gain
Investment in the relationship provides tangible signs of commitment to make the partnership work	There are differentials in the amount of cash and kind invested according to the extent to which the partnership contributes to the strategic objectives of each partner
Information is freely shared between partners	There is wariness in the disclosure of information for fear of losing competitive advantage
Integration, which results in building connections between people at all levels and sharing ways of working	There are worries about the loss of professional and cultural identity as differences are submerged in the interests of the partnership
Institutionalisation, which means giving formal status to the relationship with clear responsibilities and procedures for making decisions; this is sometimes encapsulated in a memorandum of understanding.	Expectations and responsibilities are not clearly specified; there is no written agreement about the sharing of risks and rewards. This leads to confusion and mistaken assumptions and can be a recipe for breakdown
Integrity, people behaving well and building trust between the partners	People do not trust each other and withhold information. Cooperation gives way to 'competition'

Kanter also argues that the most important factor in creating valuable and enduring partnerships is the management of relationships between partners. She asserts that many of the most serious management difficulties in partnerships arise from conflicts between 'front-line' workers, after top-level managers have worked out their differences and agreed joint guidelines. Most of the staff in individual organisations will not have been involved in the decision to undertake joint initiatives, and may be less used than senior managers to making the compromises necessary for different cultures to work together successfully. Kanter notes 'they may lack knowledge of the strategic context in which the relationship makes sense, and only see the operational ways in which it does not'. The result can be mutual suspicion, hostility and administrative conflict.

Reflection

Do the lessons from the private sector strike you as having relevance to your partnership working? Which, if any, struck the loudest chord with you?

How might you apply the lessons to your side of work in partnerships?

Kanter suggests that this can be overcome by focusing staff efforts on projects with achievable goals, and then building upon success. Staff must be given the freedom to develop new, common, working methods, which means top management surrendering a degree of control. These two factors of autonomy and success are vital to the viability of the partnership as a whole; without them workers will be unable to develop new collaborative working methods, and will not build trusting relationships with their opposite numbers.

The resistance may not be most marked among front-line staff. Our work in partnerships suggests that it is often middle managers who resist most stoutly. They have been described as forming a layer of 'perma-frost' between the strategic management and the front-line staff. Winning over the middle managers to new ways of working collaboratively can use Kanter's two key factors. You might also draw on the material about change management from Chapter 5.

The partnership dance

Many partnership arrangements work very well and add value to what the partners could each do on their own. At their best, the benefits of joining things up far exceed the costs. However, partnership should not be approached uncritically as a good thing.

We have observed many partnerships in which the players appear to be working in a fog. They keep hoping the fog will clear, but just in case it doesn't, each agency sends representatives who are less and less senior, with little background to the partnership, and no clear authority to make decisions. There are no clear rules of engagement, and leadership is hazy to say the least. The resources to support the partnership are minimal (although the in-kind cost of the partnership is often very significant but not so often audited).

What emerges is a complex, if not chaotic, system, in which players appear to be working in contradictory ways towards vaguely agreed, abstract goals. All the players have such a wide range of choice about the positions they can take up at any time that the partnership is in a state of continuous instability. This often appears to induce a response of mild panic in the lead organisation, and may lead to a desire to re-establish machine-like control.

Reflection

Do you take part in the partnership hokey cokey? Are you guilty of moving in to agree and moving out and ignoring the agreements?

How could you secure stronger commitment to the partnership ideal?

Should you devote time and effort to this?

We have observed regular versions of the partnership hokey cokey. It starts with a small number of dancers moving into a circle for a short period and agreeing to wave their arms and legs about in some sort of unison. In the next phase all the players move out of the circle and do their own thing (getting on with business as usual). With each repetition of the music more or different players join the dance, the tempo increases and the sense of any real order begins to fade. It becomes impossible to tell who is in the circle, who is moving in, who is moving out and who is out. It is still possible to perceive the tune, but it is not quite clear where the tune is coming from.

Time is limited. Youth work organisations cannot afford to dance in too many chaotic hokey cokeys. They must and should work in partnerships but only where there is a real chance to secure added value. The added value should be measurable benefits to the young people served.

Some lessons for practitioners

Practitioners in partnerships need above all else to stand back from just responding and to think through very carefully what they are seeking to achieve. UK Government timetables allow little space for this. There is no doubt that partnership working offers potential benefits, but it is not a universal panacea.

We offer a series of nine short reminders to aid practitioners in thinking through their partnerships. After that we suggest practitioners may need to develop a surfing mentality: do not seek to control the wave – learn to surf it!

The following principles provide practitioners with a starting point for looking at partnerships.

1. Is the context out of which the partnership has developed clear to all and is there a shared understanding of it? If not what can be done to build this?
2. Do the partners know and understand each others' interests, agendas, strengths and weaknesses? If not, what can be done to build this understanding?
3. Are the purpose and values of the partnership clear and shared by all? If not who is responsible for developing this clarity and how will it be done?
4. Is the level of participation required of partners clear and realistic?
5. Is the nature and structure of the partnership, appropriate and effective and understood by all?
6. Does the partnership have clear and appropriate leadership? Are the processes for working together clear and effective?
7. Have the partners agreed a suitable level of resources to support the working of the partnership?
8. Is accountability clearly defined and are there effective processes for the partnership to account to all its stakeholders?
9. How do young people fit in to the partnership and make their voices heard?

A strategic approach to partnerships

Youth work organisations are usually small. The youth service is often one of the smallest local authority services. Effective strategic managers must have a clear purpose in mind when they decide to allocate resources to particular areas of work. There is simply no slack in the system – if a youth worker or manager does one extra task, there is something else that he or she will not be able to do.

Working in partnership potentially brings significant benefits for young people as service providers develop new and better ways to provide services. It can benefit youth work organisations by giving a platform to promote youth work approaches. This requires clarity and evidence, not mere rhetoric. It also helps if youth workers realise that they do not have a monopoly of skills in working with young people and are willing to listen to staff in partner organisations who may have similar skills and attitudes but whose practice may differ. For example, a great deal could be learned from the rigour of supervision in some social work departments, the assessment experience of some careers advisers and evidence-based practice in some health promotion teams.

Reflection

Spend a few minutes thinking about a partnership with which you are working. Identify what sort of organisation it is. Apply the nine principles to it and use the analysis to consider your strategy towards developing the partnership.

Improved services

UK Government is keen to see young people's views represented in most partnership working arrangements. As a direct consequence, organisations working with young people are in demand to participate in partnerships – and none more so than the local youth service. These agencies are often seen as the gateways to young people.

As the pressure on all public service providers to consult (ie increase the service user's voice) has risen, so have the demands on youth work professionals to help others to consult young people.

In market terms the agencies now have a commodity which is in demand. In a market this would make the commodity more valuable. In traditional public sector terms there is a limited resource and the agency must decide how it is to be rationed.

The advent of the Children Bill in England and the accompanying paper *Every Child Matters: The Next Steps* will increase the pressure on youth services and youth work organisations to work in partnership with a very wide variety of organisations that work with children and young people. This provides an immense opportunity for those that are clear about what they offer and on what terms. It also represents a huge threat to those youth work organisations that are not able to remain true to their purpose and values and run the risk of being pulled in a variety of directions by larger and more powerful partners.

In local authorities there are two levels of planning, both of which may involve the youth service and possibly local voluntary youth organisations. The first is the list of plans the authority and its partnerships must produce, by statute:

1. Annual Library Plan
2. Best Value Performance Plan
3. Behaviour Support Plan
4. Cabinet Statement
5. Children's Services Plan (Children and Young People's Local Strategic Partnership)
6. Community Care Plan
7. Community Strategy (through the Local Strategic Partnership)
8. Crime and Disorder Reduction Strategy (normally including or referring to the Drugs Action Team Young People's Substance Misuse Plan) – involving the Community Safety Partnership, Crime and Disorder Reduction Partnership and Drugs Action Team
9. Cultural Strategy
10. Early Years Development Plan
11. Education Development/Strategic Plan
12. Food Law Enforcement Service Plan
13. Health Improvement Plan
14. Housing Improvement Plan
15. Lifelong Learning Development Plan
16. Local Agenda 21
17. Local Transport Plan
18. Quality Protects Management Action Plan
19. Unitary Development Plan
20. Youth Justice Plan

The Transforming Youth Work Plan became a requirement from Autumn 2002 and, in its initial format, was required to secure detailed youth work objectives covering the financial year 2003–04, and longer-term objectives for the following two years. These have since been revised by the Planning Guidance for 2004–05 to include the four key benchmarks on reach, participation and recorded and accredited outcomes.

The second level of joint working concerns the wide range of other partnership and collaborative arrangements with which a youth work organisation might be asked to get involved.

1. County Council/Borough Council Plan
2. District Plan
3. Neighbourhood Management Plan
4. Single Regeneration Budget (SRB)
5. Social Inclusion Strategy
6. Community Cohesion Strategy
7. Social Inclusion Partnership Fund
8. Urban Initiative (EU)
9. Neighbourhood Renewal Strategy
10. Community Empowerment Fund
11. Estate Action
12. Education Action Zone
13. Employment Zone
14. Health Action Zone
15. Sports Action Zone
16. Sure Start
17. New Start
18. Excellence in Cities
19. New Deal for Communities
20. New Commitment to Regeneration Pathfinders
21. Basic Skills – Pathfinder
22. Special Education Needs and Disability Action Plan
23. Multi-Agency Mental Health Strategy
24. Carers' Joint Investment Plan
25. Care Leavers' Behaviour Support Plan
26. School Organisation Plan
27. Drugs Treatment and Testing Order Pilots
28. Drugs Action Teams
29. Substance Misuse Plan
30. Early Excellence Centres
31. Healthy Schools Initiative
32. New Deal for Disabled People
33. Early Education Places Plan
34. Basic Skills Strategy
35. Literacy Strategy
36. Numeracy Strategy
37. Business/Education Partnerships
38. Specialist Colleges' Community Strategy
39. Early Years Development and Childcare Partnerships
40. Children's Fund
41. Youth Offending Teams
42. Youth Justice Board
43. Connexions
44. Adult and Community Learning Plan
45. Adult Learning Plan
46. Health Improvement Programme (HimP)
47. Healthy Cities Programme
48. Community Care Plan
49. Mental Health Services Users' Plan
50. Community Legal Services Partnerships
51. Sport Strategy
52. Tenants' Compact
53. Statutory/Voluntary Compact
54. Careers Joint Access and Development Plan
55. University for Industry
56. FE College Development Plans
57. Disability Action Plan
58. Race Equality Plan
59. Modern Apprenticeships
60. Regional Development Plan
61. Local Initiative Fund (LSC – Learning and Skills Council)
62. Rural Strategies Plan
63. ICT strategy
64. E-Government strategy
65. Public Service Agreements
66. New Opportunities Fund
67. European Social Fund
68. LMS (Local Management of Schools) Fair Funding
69. Primary Care Trust Plans
70. Economic Development Plan
71. Refugee and Asylum Seekers Plan
72. Travellers Strategy
73. Employee Training & Development Plan
74. Community Transport Plan
75. 14-19 Transition Plan

You can apply the same principles as discussed in Chapter 2, under focusing service management (page 53), to your engagement with partnerships. Will you focus on a small number of partnerships into which you offer a small contribution? Or will you be spread far and wide offering everything to everybody?

The term 'initiativitis' describes the condition of managers faced by an avalanche of initiatives: a heightened sense of gloom; a bag stuffed with papers; listlessness; confusion and powerlessness.

If youth work managers, who have some of the fewest resources at their disposal, are to seize the opportunity the changing landscape presents, they must tackle involvement in partnerships strategically.

This means managers need to:

- be absolutely clear about the purpose of their service/organisation
- have absolute clarity about what the service/organisation is offering to partnerships (core competencies)
- develop a strategy for partnership working, identifying those partnerships most likely to add value to their work with young people
- understand and apply the principle of proportionality in allocating resources to these partnerships. This means devoting their time and resources in proportion to the likely benefit the work will give to achieving the purpose of the youth service. It also means managers will have a clear sense of focus and priority
- work effectively in those partnerships with which they do engage so as to maximise the benefit of involvement to the youth service and therefore young people. This means a clear process for delegating authority to the staff involved to act on behalf of the service.

Applying proportionality

To make sure that effort goes in the right places, managers need to:

1. **Map the partnerships** – Develop a full list of all partnerships/collaborative arrangements in which youth work organisations and/or the involvement of young people is required

2. **Analyse the most important partnership** – For each partnership:
   a) What is the driver for our involvement:
      - Have to – statutory requirement
      - Have to – management instruction from above
      - Must be – expected to be involved, cannot afford to be missing etc.
      - Want to – can see clear or probable strategic advantages
      - Might be – unsure about benefits – need more information/ time
   b) Is the purpose and nature of the partnership clear? (This does not mean that the partnership has set outcome targets. A partnership might start by simply exploring the grounds for developing the partnership. This is still a clear purpose.) Avoid partnerships that meet because they have to (because of UK Government instruction) and have no real end in mind.

c) Is the nature of the partnership – the relationship between the partners – clear? If not is there a reasonable chance that it will become clear?

d) Is the purpose for which the youth work organisations might get involved clear? (How would involvement contribute to achieving the youth work organisation's purpose? Map the youth work organisation's goals against those of the partnership and check how one relates to the other.)

e) What level of involvement is required from the youth work organisation? This ranges from a loose information sharing network, through joint planning with separate delivery, to joint commissioning, right up to the creation of a new partnership company. The amount of resources required is progressively greater as you move through this range.

f) What level of people would be best involved in the partnership (partnerships tend to work best when people are working at similar levels)?

g) How much will it cost for the youth work organisation to be involved?

h) How will you manage the expectations of your boss, the politicians or the trustees for the organisation's involvement in partnerships? How will you win their support to be strategic?

Reflection

Use the applying proportionality list to reflect on your organisation's approach to partnerships.

Do you have a strategic approach?

How will you go forward in the most cost effective way for the service and the young people you serve?

3. **Be clear what the youth work organisation is offering**

a) Identify precisely what it is offering to the partnership. Do you have evidence to back up your claims?

b) Is anybody else offering it?

c) Is the youth work organisation the best agency to offer it?

d) Is the youth work organisation offering something that the partnership should be paying the organisation for? Is it a contribution made by the organisation to the partnership? Can the organisation afford this contribution?

From this analysis, the youth work manager can decide whether the organisation should be involved in a partnership, why and in what way. Will the benefit to the youth work organisation and young people be sufficient to justify the cost of involvement? If involvement appears to be a low priority what is the minimum acceptable level?

Our experience suggests that for many partnerships the answer to the questions will be 'currently not clear, but greater clarity is expected soon'. But when and how much time will be spent in fruitless meetings before the clarity emerges?

Partnerships are only worth having if they add to the total of what the partners can do on their own. Devote the greatest proportion of your partnership time to those most likely to achieve this.

Chapter Eleven:
Managing youth work: a look to the future

For the loser now

Will be later to win

For the times they are a changin'

Bob Dylan 'The times they are a changin' 1963

Introduction

The provision of youth work is taking place in an environment of considerable change in the UK. The Government has announced far reaching modernisation of services for children and young people (set out in the Children Bill which followed the *Every Child Matters* consultation paper[1] and *Every Child matters – the next steps*[2]).

This modernisation needs to be seen against the backdrop of wider change in the public services. The role of the civil service is changing with pressure to cut red tape, improve efficiency, reduce the level of micro-management and take a more strategic role, as outlined in the review of efficiency by Sir Peter Gershon[3]. Local government has been changing following the Local Government Act 2000, with local authorities developing their roles as leaders and enablers rather than large scale service delivery organisations. Many public services have already moved from under their direct control and more are set to follow. Government has established its compact with the voluntary sector and is pressing ahead with efforts to involve the sector more directly in the delivery of public services. New resources have been allocated to build the capacity of 'frontline' voluntary and community organisations to deliver public services[4].

A large number of the New Labour government's initiatives are set to deliver their results by 2010, so the next five years are likely to bring new challenges, new opportunities and much change to managers of services and organisations which deliver youth work. The environment will offer a stern test of the leadership of the services – how to seize new opportunities without being diverted from the primary purpose of delivering good youth work. How to preserve what is good and right in youth work whilst developing new ways of working which fit the new environment.

Youth services have often seen themselves as Cinderellas – forever losing resources to other more powerful services. Will the next decade mark a change? Will more resources be released to support youth work? Will the losers come to win?

1   *Every Child Matters* (2003), Department for Education and Skills.
2   *Every Child Matters – the next steps* (2004), Department for Education and Skills.
3   Cabinet Office and HM Treasury (2003), *Efficiency Review – releasing resources to the frontline.*
4   The Voluntary Sector Infrastructure Review.

This chapter explores some of the main opportunities and potential hazards that will face youth work managers. We look at how youth work might be delivered in the future and how youth services and organisations might operate in the new arena of Children's Trusts, extended schools, children's centres and the like. We finish by exploring how managers might meet the challenge of demonstrating the impact and value of youth work to young people. The overall aim of the chapter is to provoke thought and provide some ideas and tools to aid that reflection.

Living in interesting times

It is a mantra in organisations across all sectors as we move into the 21st century that change is the only constant. We have discussed much of this in preceding chapters. Public service organisations face unprecedented change which affects not only their way of working but the whole way in which the role, purpose and value of public service is understood.

The relationship between the individual, organisations and the state is in a state of flux. For example, the rapid growth of participative politics, in which citizens (or service users) are involved directly in helping to make decisions about the nature of public services, priorities for spending money and so on, has a direct impact on the role and power of elected politicians. When there is disagreement who has the power to decide? There may be tensions when the course of action in, for example, a neighbourhood, is decided by a process of wide ranging consultation and agreement as opposed to decisions made by locally elected politicians. It represents a shift towards pragmatism, compromise and dialogue rather than the pursuit of ideology. With an ever more strident media, the politics of compromise and complexity seems increasingly difficult to sell. There are similar tensions when the shape of a service is no longer decided by professionals (because they have unique knowledge) but through a dialogue with service users.

The way in which modern local democracy works is under scrutiny. What is the proper role of local government? How will it attract good people when so much of the decision making power about what can and cannot be done locally rests elsewhere – in Whitehall, with regional agencies, in Europe, etc.? Are local authorities capable of playing an enabling and leadership role as envisaged by Osbourne and Gaebler[5] and discussed in Chapter Seven? How will local authorities connect and lead the increasingly complex array of independent and semi-independent public service providers?

The creation of Local Strategic Partnerships has led to new possibilities for the public, private, voluntary, community and faith sectors to work together. In so doing they have softened the boundaries between the roles of elected local politicians, (often un-elected) board members of public agencies (such as health trusts); officers and staff in all sectors; service users; activists, lobbyists and so on. It is no longer entirely clear who has the mandate to make what decisions about publicly funded services. That said, decisions about the allocation of resources from the public purse still rest nationally with the Government and more particularly, with the Treasury, and locally with elected councillors.

The drive to modernise

The UK Government has pledged to improve the quality and efficiency of public services. This has become a major political issue and appears to be the main battleground for the next general election, probably in 2005. The Government talks of making our public

---

5   Osbourne, David and Gaebler, Ted (1993), *Reinventing Government – How the entreprenurial spirit is transforming the public sector*, Middlesex: Penguin.

services 'world class'. It has highlighted the need for improved leadership and management as an essential part of this modernisation programme, and invested heavily in training for leadership in public services[6]. Four principles for public service modernisation were set out by the Prime Minister in 2001[7]:

- Government should set national standards within a framework of clear accountability, to ensure that citizens have the right to high quality services wherever they live.
- The standards should be delivered by devolution and delegation to the front-line, giving local leaders responsibility and accountability for delivery, and the opportunity to design and develop services around the needs of local people.
- More flexibility is required for public service organisations and their staff to achieve the diversity of service provision needed to respond to the wide range of customer aspirations. This means challenging restrictive practices and reducing red tape; greater and more flexible incentives and rewards for good performance; strong leadership and management; and high quality training and development.
- Public services need to offer expanding choice for the customer. Giving people a choice about the service they can have and who provides it helps ensure that services are designed around their customers. An element of contestability between alternative suppliers can also drive up standards and empower customers locked into a poor service from their traditional supplier.

In this pursuit of modernisation the UK Government has pursued a 'stick and carrot' approach – naming and shaming those that under perform (using league tables, inspection reports etc) and rewarding those that do well (with more resources, freedom from regulation and further inspection, greater independence of decision making).

So how does this backdrop of modernisation and change affect managers and leaders of services providing youth work? We explore this next.

Every young person matters

Since 1997 the New Labour Government has pursued a raft of policies and initiatives aimed at securing a fairer and more inclusive society for young people. These emphasise action to improve educational attainment and employability, reduce anti-social and criminal behaviour and to give young people a stronger voice in matters that affect them.

Typically the policies focus on building the 'human capital' of each young person – their skills, knowledge and experience – so that they can become useful and productive members of their communities. They can be characterised as 'instrumental' – seeking to deliver predicted and tangible outcomes. Four initiatives have been of particular importance in England: *Transforming Youth Work, Resourcing Excellent Youth Services*[8], the Connexions Strategy and Service[9] and *Every Child Matters*. The outcomes sought from these policies have been discussed earlier, but focus on young people being safe, healthy, happy, achieving, able to get work, and able to participate in society. They identify particular targets such as reducing teenage pregnancy, improving performance at school, reducing harm from drug and alcohol abuse, reducing crime and disorder and so on.

Youth work, as discussed in Chapter One, is a developmental process. It works through the relationship between youth worker and young person on a negotiated agenda of activities, towards a broad overall curriculum. There is a tension between this developmental

---

6 For example the National Centre for School Leadership, the Centre for Excellence in Leadership for post-16 education, the NHS University and leadership initiative, the Local Government Leadership Centre.
7 Tony Blair, Prime Minister speech on public service reform, 16 October 2001.
8 *Transforming Youth Work: Developing Youth Work for Young People* (2001), Department for Education and Skills; *Resourcing Excellent Youth Services*, ibid.
9 Various documents available from: www.connexions.gov.uk

Reflection

approach and culture and the instrumental policy framework within which youth work is required to deliver pre-set results. This is not a new tension, but there has been a marked shift towards the instrumental in public policy which youth work must come to terms with or risk losing its support.

If youth work managers are able to demonstrate the impact of youth work in instrumental terms will they secure more support from government? If they do so, do they run the risk of losing the very things that make youth work special? Will they be pushed away from offering a process of development and learning which starts where young people are, and is negotiated with them, to one which starts with the adult and state agenda and seeks to process young people towards predetermined goals? How will Every Child Matters with its emphasis on reducing the risk of harm to children and young people affect work which has always encouraged young people to take reasonable risks?

There is no question that the way youth work is resourced and provided will change over the coming years. We explore below some of the possible changes in a little more detail.

Youth work or youth services?

Much of the economy in the developed world has changed from manufacturing to the delivery of services. This is a profound change and represents an acceptance that services create every bit as much wealth as manufacturing or primary industries do. It overturns years of economic dogma going back to Adam Smith who classified services as 'unproductive of any value' over 200 years ago. Public service providers at times still seem caught in the Smith dogma and associate themselves too closely with the tangible aspects of services rather than the service itself. So health is dominated by discussion of hospitals, education by schools, punishment and rehabilitation by discussion of prisons. The service comes to be seen as delivering a tangible product rather than looking at what the recipients of the service need and want and the best way to satisfy those needs and wants. The debate on the future of youth work has already been confused with concerns over the future of the youth service.

The UK Government flagged a small but significant change in perception of local authority youth services by defining them as 'complex networks of providers, community groups, voluntary organisations and local authorities'[10]. Every Child Matters emphasises joining up services, probably under one umbrella – the Children's Trust. This looser definition suggests that its leaders will need to think much more about how youth work is provided than about protecting a set of delivery mechanisms that happen to be located under local authority control.

Youth work appears to be in greater demand than ever before, with youth workers employed in a wide variety of organisational settings. Whilst the demand for youth work has increased, the position of youth work provided directly by the local authority is less clear. The youth service delivered directly by local authorities has occupied a very particular position since the services began, and has sometimes been seen as the home of 'true' youth work. Indeed, the status of professional youth worker is still demonstrated by the salary being paid on a local authority pay scale (JNC scale). Winning support from youth workers for changes to the nature of the local authority youth service will not be easy as it still has strong symbolic status for many youth workers.

---

10 *Resourcing Excellent Youth Services*, p1, ibid.

The symbolic importance of the means of providing the service, as opposed to the provision of youth work, is further strengthened by often powerful interest from local elected councillors. Councillors still have considerable discretion over the money spent on the youth service and many are very strong supporters of youth centres as a demonstration that the authority is doing something for young people.

The question will be, what balance between supporting youth work (wherever it occurs) and supporting local authority youth services will best meet the needs of young people? Is this balance about to change?

Where will youth work take place?

The introduction of new umbrella structures to bring together all services for children and young people will follow the implementation of the Chlildren Act later in 2004. It is unclear from the Children's Trust Pathfinders which began in July 2003, exactly what form these new umbrella structures will take. In some places a new legal entity has been developed, in others there is an emphasis on forming a light touch, virtual organisation with a minimum of new structure, which will lead, commission and coordinate services. There are signals that commissioning may take place across whole authorities but may also be carried out at a very local level – through schools, children's centres or possibly Primary Health Trusts.

Local authority youth services may continue much as at present in some places, while in others they may face re-location into a new structure, or may disappear in their current form altogether, with youth work commissioned by a number of local commissioning bodies.

At present local authority youth services must meet the standards set out by their regulatory body – Ofsted (the Office for Standards in Education). Ofsted is developing a new framework of standards for children's services which are expected to include the standards for delivery of youth work. Again the door is open for experimentation about the most effective way to regulate youth work.

Reflection

Do you see a distinction between youth work and the youth service?

Does it matter where youth work takes place and if so, why?

Do leaders and managers in local authority youth services have a symbolic attachment to the service? If so, where does the attachment come from and does it serve any useful purpose today?

All services working with young people need to be able to show two things to satisfy policy demands:

● that they actively involve young people in their planning and delivery; and
● that they are reaching and engaging with the most disadvantaged and disaffected young people.

These two forces provide an opportunity for youth work to become much more central to the thinking of mainstream services which work with young people. As a result it seems likely that more and more youth work will be located outside the local authority youth service.

In the diagram from Chapter One reproduced below, it appears likely that the diagonal line may be pushed upwards, with a possible shrinking in the size of the local authority youth service square (or indeed a disappearance of the local authority direct provision altogether).

Figure 11.1 – Possible change in location of youth work

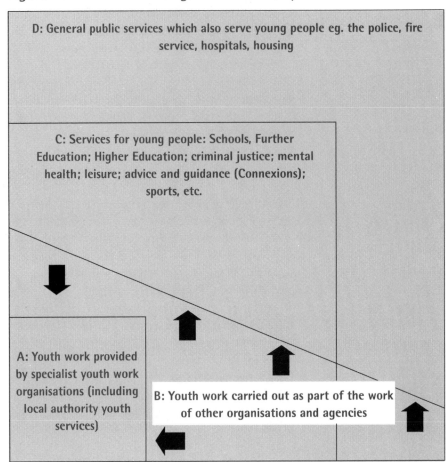

Resources for youth work

The local authority youth service in England is charged with leading the delivery of Transforming Youth Work and REYS, but does not have to provide the service itself. The bigger question for young people will be whether the new arrangements for children and young people's services will lead to more money being spent on youth work overall (from other budgets as well as DfES), or whether they will draw from the current, limited pot of money allocated through DfES as the youth and community sub block.

The Children Bill suggests that youth service budgets may be pooled into the budget for the Children's Trust, along with the much larger budgets from health, social services etc. It is not certain how far the pooling of budgets will create genuine flexibility of spending, as much of the money is already effectively 'hypothecated' for particular purposes and may not be available for other uses (eg money for schools is still likely to go to schools).

Pooling budgets could put pressure on any money that is not required to fulfil a statutory purpose, as the new Children's Trusts look for resources to develop new ways of working. This could have an adverse affect on resources available for youth work (which is not a statutory service) and will be a test of the government's commitment to resourcing youth work set out in *REYS*. Youth work managers will need to make a strong case for the contribution youth work makes towards the achievement of the goals of children's services.

There is a clear case to be made. There is powerful evidence from the testimony of young people, parents, professionals and so on, that youth work has a real and lasting impact on the lives of young people. The next few years gives youth work leaders and managers a unique opportunity to build on this evidence and win support for youth work.

If youth work becomes more mainstream and takes place in a wider range of settings outside the youth service, it will reach more young people and have more impact. However, the role of the youth service will change and control of the quality of youth work will become more complex.

At a macro level government has continued its commitment to education as part of its spending review for 2006-2009. However, within planned rises in spending on education the focus appears to be shifting to education in the first ten or eleven years, plus continued emphasis on schools. This situation will also test the capacity of the advocates of youth work nationally to sustain the political resolve that has led to the advances for youth work in both policy and resources since 2001.

Young people's wants and needs

The proportion of the population that is 13 to 19 is declining, as the population ages. Most young people have lives that meet the aspirations of Every Child Matters already. It seems certain that concern over the minority who remain disadvantaged will intensify. The pressure to secure better educational achievement for young people with the greatest level of disadvantage will be sustained. Targeting of resources to achieve this is likely to intensify.

The debate over generic versus targeted youth work is a well established one, but seems likely to be moved to a higher level of intensity over the coming years. It is possible to imagine generic youth work receiving less resources and being contracted out to the voluntary and private sectors, with the local authority commissioning targeted youth work, provided by a number of agencies and organisations.

Meanwhile, a great number of young people would still express the wish to have somewhere safe and warm to meet each other, to engage in interesting activities that are fun and over which they have a substantial say and to have the possibility of learning and developing. What many young people would argue for and would attend (their wants) may become increasingly different from the opportunities that are provided to particular young people, identified as in greatest need.

Generic provision through clubs and centres may be put under pressure and yet is an essential part of building contact between youth workers and young people so that more intensive youth work can take place.

Youth work managers will need to develop effective strategies if they are to keep and increase resources for generic work. In particular they will need to show what outcomes it produces and how these contribute to the achievement of key policy goals and targets. This is not a new dilemma but is likely to become much more intense. If advocates for youth work do not win the argument, we may be on the verge of a very significant change in the way youth work is provided.

Another way to tackle this may be to re-frame the outcomes and impact of youth work in terms of the development of social capital. This is discussed in more detail at the end of this chapter.

The government emphasis on accredited outcomes will continue, yet youth work must avoid becoming 'just like school or college' – the outcomes must flow from negotiated, voluntary engagement, starting where the young people are at. These tensions will provide a continuing challenge for youth work managers.

A youth involvement service?

The voice of young people is often weak or not heard at all in discussions on services that affect them, or about the shape of future society. There has been real progress to improve this through various initiatives but there is a long way still to go. Youth work organisations can and must engage young people to help them make the case for the kind of youth work that impacts on the majority of young people, as well as projects that target those in greatest need.

More widely, all public service providers are expected to demonstrate how they are engaging and involving young people in their plans and delivery of services. Youth workers are likely to continue to be in demand to provide advice, guidance and assist with the practice of achieving this. Managers must avoid the risk of this one facet of youth work becoming too dominant. Alternatively we may be seeing the start of a new service, dedicated to enabling young people's voices to be heard.

What will partners want?

Agencies which deliver youth work will operate under the umbrella of Children's Trusts once the Children Bill is implemented. The new legislation will require agencies to work together in the interests of children and young people. Youth work is likely to be in demand as a vital process for engaging with harder to reach young people. The way in which youth work has been described as part of the Connexions Service gives a foretaste of what is likely to happen.

This heightened interest offers youth work managers a tremendous opportunity to promote youth work and to increase the reach of their services to benefit more young people. It may, however, carry a price of further pushing youth work towards targeted work with young people most in need away from generic work with a wider range of young people.

It is possible to imagine a future in which the local authority youth service no longer provides youth work but is primarily a planning, commissioning and coordinating body that leads the provision of youth work in the area. The system diagram below can be used to explore some of the pulls that partner agencies are already exerting on the youth service. It seems likely that these pressures will increase.

Youth work occupies a particular territory concerned with informal learning and development and with relationship building. Formal education and training agencies are interested in how youth work can help them to meet their targets for improving the achievement of young people and ensuring they move on to employment. This pulls youth work away from the informal towards non-formal, accredited learning. This is very visible in government's policies which encourage an increasing proportion of young people participating in youth work to achieve an accredited outcome.

There has always been a close relationship (indeed, it is often seen as confusion) between generic youth work as delivered through youth clubs/centres and leisure facilities. Some youth services are still located as part of local authority leisure departments. It seems likely that some aspects of generic youth work will be pulled towards leisure activities, sports and the arts. This may lead to more outsourcing of provision to voluntary organisations and other providers as has already happened in some local authorities. The challenge for youth work managers will be whether and how to defend generic provision against this.

Figure 11.2 – Interaction of partners' interests in services for young people

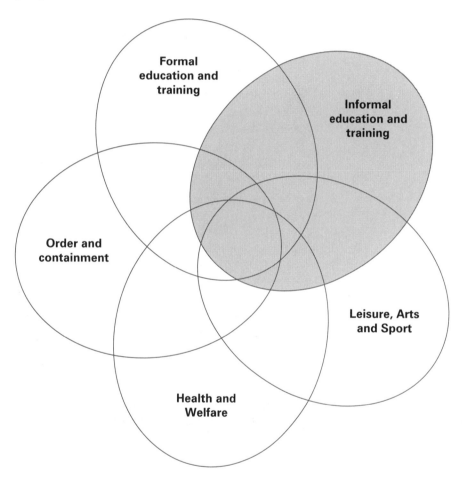

In a similar way, it is possible to plot the pulls on youth work towards order and containment (reducing crime and disorder), health and welfare (reducing teenage pregnancy, minimising harm from alcohol and drug misuse and improving teenage sexual health).

Overall, the diagram allows us to suggest that there will be a concerted pressure for youth work to take place on the boundary between the youth work zone for informal learning and development and the other main zones. There is a consequential risk that traditional generic youth work, as provided by the local authority may disappear. This would be a significant loss as it is in this arena that a great deal of preventative work takes place with young people who may otherwise appear to be presenting more serious needs. Indeed, as we have said before, youth work may be underselling its capacity to build relationships and build social capital which in itself is vital to the re-creation of active healthy, prosperous communities. This is discussed in more detail at the end of this chapter in relation to the challenge of demonstrating that youth work builds social capital.

Enhanced role for the regions?

If the role of the local authority youth service moves in the direction explored above, there may be a very significant role for the emerging Regional Youth Work Units to support the delivery of youth work to the highest professional standards. This would need to be linked to a professional body for youth work and to strategies for workforce development, sharing good practice and the like.

What do elected politicians want?

Resources for youth work are allocated on the basis of political decisions made at national level and local authority level. At the national level, there has been a significant advance towards a proper level of resourcing for youth work in England as a result of *Transforming Youth Work* and *Resourcing Excellent Youth Services*. Securing these resources has been achieved through the agency of supporting youth services and developing a specification for what an excellent youth service would be like. This is something that politicians nationally and locally can understand and be persuaded to support.

If the traditional youth service is dispersed into a number of targeted programmes located in a wide variety of different agencies, as discussed above, it becomes much more difficult to secure resources for youth work as a much larger number of agencies and organisations are involved. It runs the risk of being seen as important by everyone but not the most important by anyone.

Youth work leaders and managers may be able to counteract this by seizing the agenda and taking a lead role at the heart of the partnership delivering services to children and young people. In particular, youth work's history of effectively enabling the active involvement of young people gives it a lever to help it secure a unique position. Managers will have to think much more about delivering youth work to young people rather than provisioning youth services. They are likely to move to a strategic planning and commissioning role across authorities as part of Children and Young People's Partnerships.

What will the profession want and need?

If youth work is likely to take place in a wide variety of settings and agencies rather than through a single service, what will hold it together will be the strength and quality of its professional practice and the support given to professionals to deliver it. Youth work will need to have a very effective professional body ensuring that standards are high and met. This body does not exist at present. Rather the interests of professional youth work are caught between the Association of Principal Youth and Community Officers, the Community and Youth Workers' Union, PAULO (acting on behalf of the emerging Sector Skills Council for children's services), The National Youth Agency, higher education providers of professional training and government.

Support to ensure the highest level of professional practice may be best provided through Regional Youth Work Units which have emerged in each of the nine regions in England. Their role already includes coordination of youth work training, networking and support to youth workers and sharing of best practice.

The support of good professional practice will need to go hand in hand with the developments in the Sector Skills Council for children's services. These bodies (which the UK has been busy rationalising) set the standards for training and development in all sectors of UK employment. The model currently under discussion for the children's sector is for a core of common professional standards with a number of specific bodies relating to particular areas of professional practice.

How will youth work be delivered and assessed?

Reflection

Do you agree with the future trends identified above?

Are there any trends you would add to the list?

Draw a picture or diagram of the way you think youth work could be delivered in the context of 'joined up' services for children and young people?

How might youth work's leaders and advocates best secure more and better youth work in the environment described above? Would it matter if there was no local authority youth service, provided this led to more youth work reaching more young people?

The challenges faced by youth work managers in delivering youth work were looked at in Chapter One. Two stand out as crucial to securing future support and resources. Youth work organisations will need to be very effective at:

● demonstrating the impact of youth work on young people's lives and on the community around them; and
● working with other agencies to provide youth work in a wide range of settings without losing the particular purpose and characteristics of youth work.

Youth work as an engine of social capital

The definition of youth work is explored in Chapter One. The definition provides clues as to how we might measure the results of youth work.

Historically those evaluating youth work (particularly Ofsted) have emphasised the development or change in the individual young person. However, a vitally important part of youth work is its emphasis on developing relationships (between young people themselves and between young people and adults), enabling young people to have a voice and to participate in wider society. These elements appear to have been neglected in the efforts to measure the results of youth work, particularly the first – relationships.

The measurement of the impact of youth work is vitally important in enabling policy makers to defend the allocation of scarce resources to support it. In England, as a non-statutory service, it must compete with every other claim on local authorities' un-designated monies. If youth work managers cannot make a convincing case that money spent on youth work yields a tangible benefit they will not get consistent, reliable and adequate resources. Young people will experience patchy, inconsistent youth services and many will miss out on the opportunities that youth work has to offer.

Those seeking to demonstrate the impact of youth work have tended to focus on measuring increases in 'human capital' – the properties and capacities of individual young people and how they have changed as a result of youth work interventions. This is important, but tends to draw youth work into the same frame of reference as schools, further and higher education providers.

Youth work is also about the development of relationships. It appears to have the capacity to make a vital contribution to 'social capital' – the networks of relationships between individuals and the norms of reciprocity and trustworthiness that arise from them[11].

Social capital has been identified by a number of commentators and researchers as an essential ingredient of healthy democratic societies, as well as a means for enabling social action. It underpins people's sense of belonging and their sense of contentment. Putnam[12] describes two types of social capital: 'bonding' which brings people together on the basis of similarities (vital for a sense of belonging) and 'bridging' which brings different groups together (vital for creating inclusion, tolerance etc). A third form is sometimes described as linking and involves the connection of those with fewer resources at their disposal to those with access to more (creating greater influence, social mobility etc).

The impact of decline in social capital has been well documented[13] as shown in breakdown in social relations, particularly between generations, loss of trust between individuals, unwillingness of people to play wider roles in society outside their immediate family, handing over to others (particularly professionals) responsibility for increasingly large aspects of living (safety, health, education etc). Low levels of social capital have been correlated with high crime, low life expectancy, low levels of achievement and income, poor health etc. Writing on social capital appears to have been influential on the New Labour Government, particularly in its policies on social inclusion.

Putnam suggests a measurable correlation between high levels of social capital and success at school[14]. West-Burnham[15] argues that improving educational performance will not take place through a narrow schooling process but through increasing social capital. We make the proposition that youth work is fundamentally about just this – the development of the social capital of young people and their communities – but that this aspect of youth work lacks practicable methods for measurement and consequently does not secure the recognition it deserves.

Measuring youth work impact on social capital

Whilst interest in social capital has risen, it has remained a difficult phenomenon to measure. Its impact is indirect and is often perceptible only over a long time period. Government has relied on rather crude proxy measures for social capital – particularly indices of deprivation. Putnam made extensive use of the US General Social Survey set against voter turnout and other proxies for social capital.

Wendy Stone has suggested a theoretically informed approach to measuring social capital, based on her work for the Australian Institute of Family Studies[16]. She is highly critical of many existing approaches to measuring social capital as confusing the indicators with the outcomes. She puts forward a framework of core dimensions of social capital, which are open to measurement. These include:

- the structure of social relations – networks: informal – formal; limited – extensive; household – global; open – closed; dense – sparse; mixed – homogeneous; vertical – horizontal; and
- the quality of social relations – norms: social trust (family and more general); civic trust; institutional trust; reciprocity.

She also suggests making use of network analysis as a tool.

11 Putnam, Robert, D. (2000), *Bowling Alone – the Collapse and Revival of American Community*, New York, Simon and Schuster.
12 Putnam, Robert, D., ibid.
13 See Putnam (ibid) or Gelsthorpe, T. and West-Burnham, J. (2003), *Educational Leadership and the Community Strategies for School Improvement through Community Engagement*, London, Pearson Education, p4.
14 Putnam, Robert, D., ibid, pp296–297.
15 West-Burnham in Gelsthorpe and West-Burnham (ibid) pp4–5.
16 Stone, Wendy (2001), *Measuring Social Capital – towards a theoretically informed measurement framework for researching social capital in family and community life.* Melbourne, Australian Institute of Family Studies.

Roberts and Roche[17] argue for four domains from which can be developed accessible and serviceable indicators:

- Participation: voting; involvement in consultations; informal education
- Altruism: voluntary involvement in local activities
- Trust
- Sociability: numbers using clubs and associations

The Nottingham Social Action Research Project has developed indicators for evaluating social capital, through a process of participatory workshops.[18] The indicators are grouped as follows:

- Reciprocity
- Perception of Community
- Citizen power/Proactivity in a social context
- Celebration of Diversity
- Feelings of trust and safety
- Participation in the local community
- Value of life
- Networks and connections

The above examples show the marked similarity of the areas on which measurement of social capital might focus. They also show that it can be measured using simple, practicable methods.

Reflection

Do you consider that youth work is an engine of social capital?

What steps could you take in your work to provide evidence of building social capital?

Do you think that a social capital argument will be convincing to policy makers and lead to more stable resources to support youth work?

Were youth work managers to become effective in demonstrating the impact of youth work in increasing social capital, they would be in a stronger position to argue for resources on the basis that few other services that work with young people place an equivalent emphasis on the development of relationships. Showing an impact on social capital would also provide evidence of youth work's contribution to social inclusion goals, which are closely related.

An initiative to develop these methodologies is long overdue and would allow the advocates and leaders of youth work to demonstrate its true impact. This would enable youth work to be understood in a new way and give it the means to take up a new position as a critical mechanism to sustain active, vibrant communities.

In conclusion

It would be a tragedy if at the very moment when youth work is being feted and supported as of great value to a wide range of other public services, it were to lose sight of what might be its unique contribution to young people and their communities. Robert Putnam described how easy it was for a society not to notice that the glue which bound it together was weakening or breaking down altogether. He also maps out ways to reverse the decline. He provides evidence of the need to 'create new spaces for recognition, re-connection and debate' along with 'local leaders who choose to pursue their goals through the sometimes slow, frequently fractious, and profoundly transformative route of social capital building.'[19] Putnam could be describing youth work and in particular, generic youth work. Youth clubs and centres could be seen as providing exactly the kind of space he argues for.

17 Roberts, M. and Roche, M., Quantifying social capital: measuring the intangible in the local policy context, *Journal of Radical Statistics*, www.radstats.org.uk

18 Fleming, J. and Boeck, T. (undated), *Workshops to establish methods and indicators for evaluation of social capital*. Leicester, De Montfort University Centre for Social Action. www.dmu.ac.uk

19 Putnam, Robert, D., and Lewis, M. Feldstein (2003), *Better Together – Restoring the American Community*, New York, Simon and Schuster, p294.

Let us hope that youth work's leaders can make their case so that youth work is able to continue to build social capital, rather than becoming a rescue service for those most in need. As the singer Joni Mitchell put it in the song *Big Yellow Taxi*: 'Don't it always seem to go, That you don't know what you've got, Till its gone, They paved paradise, And put up a parking lot.'

Chapter Twelve:
Making it happen

To arrive where we started

And know the place for the first time

T S Eliot

Introduction

This chapter represents the end of your journey through the management of services that work with young people. In it we review what we see as some of the real and constant dilemmas that managers face, day in and day out. We will remind you about some of the concepts and tools we have covered previously, but which we think are particularly useful.

This book is underpinned by an experiential approach to learning. The lines from T S Eliot's poem capture the sense we hope you will have, of arriving back in the familiar territory of your job, but seeing, knowing or understanding it in new or different ways.

In this section we will use the 80:20 principle[1] (also known as the Pareto Law) – that 20 per cent of your actions as a manager will give you 80 per cent of the results you want. Put more generally, this is the principle of imbalance – that a small proportion of your actions and activities are responsible for a very high proportion of the best results. It is likely that a small number of the ideas and tools covered in this reader will yield a very high proportion of its value (but the actual ideas will be different for each individual).

We want to focus on a small number of things that we think will make the greatest difference to managers. In most of these we will make use of the Hampden Turner model of the strategic dilemma, explored in Chapter Five.

This final section brings us back to the critical role of the manager at the centre of the management model – thinking and leading processes to connect strategy with action.

Figure 12.1: The experiential cycle

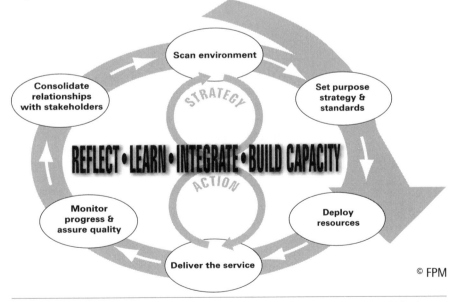

© FPM

---

1   See Koch, Richard (1997), *The 80/20 Principle: The Secret of Achieving More with Less*, London: Nicholas Brealey.

The chapter covers

- The courage to manage and lead
- Clarity of purpose
- Appropriate style of leadership
- Seize the time to manage
- Balance action with analysis and process
- Learning, adventure and respect, and good management
- The right tools for the job

The courage to manage and lead

Our courage breaks like an old tree in a black wind and dies

from Red Hanrahan's song about Ireland by W B Yeats

What makes a really good manager is the courage to manage and to lead. The courage to keep her or his mind on the purpose of the venture, to stick with priorities, to take the risk of standing by the plans. Most of all it is the courage to turn down the familiar, the safe and the well-trodden path in favour of the new way of doing things, of improvements and of the strategic priorities you have set.

It is easy to make and talk about plans. The real test is to have the courage to lead yourself and your people through the change that any plan requires. This means consistently setting and keeping to your agenda, not reacting to others' demands. It means saying no to things that you have always said yes to in the past.

It is not a case of either/or but of consciously fighting to steer a course back towards the strategy and priorities. It requires a style of 'insistent patience',[2] being supportive as well as demanding. The strategy will not be achieved overnight, but people need to believe it will be achieved. They must believe in their hearts and minds that you not only believe in the strategy, but will lead the organisation to achieving it.

Many managers fall at this hurdle. Your action will speak volumes, your words will not.

Courage to pursue the strategy; take the risk of doing things differently; stand by your plans and stop doing the same old things

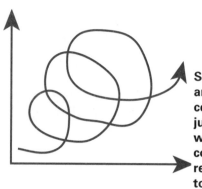

Safety of the known and of the old ways; ceaseless demands just to manage what is current; comfortable relationships; crises to sort, fires to fight

2   Maister, David, H. (2001), *Practice What You Preach: What Managers Must Do To Create a High Achievement Culture*, New York: The Free Press.

> ### Example
>
> The leader of an organisation working with young people was particularly good at 'pressing the flesh' – going out to meet key stakeholders, talk to them and inspire them with his vision, and as a result secure funding for all manner of projects. He freely admitted to having the attention span of a gnat, and was bored by day-to-day management. The result was an exciting and inspirational organisation that lacked even the most basic management procedures. Staff were always busy, but not always clear why. The projects were incoherent, and there was insufficient money at the core of the organisation to sustain the projects effectively.
>
> Every year the leader agreed the annual strategic priorities, new processes and systems for performance management, then proceeded to ignore them. 'It's just the way I am', he would say, and because most people admired his work or liked him personally, he was not challenged and felt no pressure to change. Eventually he left the organisation, as boredom had set in and he was not enjoying having to deal with the increasing number of difficult organisational issues he had helped to create. His leaving revealed an organisation in crisis, with a lack of core purpose, plunging staff morale and no money.
>
> The leader had never had the courage to change. If he didn't, why should anyone else?

Clarity of purpose

This is not a dilemma – your organisation will not succeed unless its purpose is clear – is it?

Can *everyone* involved describe in their own way, but clearly and consistently:

- the problems, needs or issues that concern us
- what we believe in (our values)
- what we are aiming to do about the problems issues or needs (our purpose)
- how we judge success (standards and performance indicators)
- who we work with (our users)
- who else we need to satisfy (our stakeholders)
- what we do to achieve our purpose (main activities).

What are you doing as a manager to keep this story alive and make sure everyone hears it? How are you actively sustaining the culture you want?

Appropriate style of leadership

This leads to another dilemma – how much of the iceberg to share with your staff. When should you share: a) your early thoughts and b) your final conclusions?

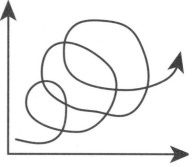

Provide clear thought-out ideas and plans for staff, for some comment, but mainly to give a clear lead. May be faster, but can lead to dependence and lack of commitment.

Engage staff in exploration of the ideas and a process to develop their own plans. Facilitating rather than directing. Takes more time but can secure greater commitment, and/or better plans.

This affects the culture of the organisation – when are you in charge and when are you empowering others to lead? Refer back to the range of leadership styles described in Chapter Five. The style you adopt will depend to a great extent on:

● **The quality of the decision required:** will any decision do? What requirements about quality must be met to make the decision acceptable (such as feasibility, suitability, acceptability to stakeholders, feasibility in the culture of the organisation)?

● **The information and skills required to make the decision:** does the decision require specialist knowledge or skills? Do you possess the knowledge and skills? If not, do your staff? Does the decision require particular information? Do you have the information?

● **The level of commitment to the decision:** do you need to win the commitment of staff (or others) to the decision? Will staff accept a decision they are simply informed about? Is there likely to be conflict between staff about the best solution?

● **The power and interests of other stakeholders:** who else will the decision affect? What is their power or influence in relation to the organisation?

● **The time taken to make the decision:** how much time is available? How much time will it take to make the decision? Is there time to take the route you would like (involving people invariably takes longer)?[3]

This can be applied to your the management team. In many cases having individuals or smaller groups making a decision will result in a better solution to problems than going for consensus.

Seize the time to manage

> *The great French Marshall Lyautey once asked his gardener to plant a tree. The gardener objected that the tree was slow growing and would not reach maturity for 100 years. The Marshall replied, 'In that case, there is no time to lose; plant it this afternoon!'*
> John F Kennedy, US President

How can we secure the time to manage the way we know we should? How do we cut back the amount of our lives spent reacting to short-term imperatives, fighting fires and being busy ('feeding the beast') so as to be more strategic, focused and able to lead effectively? We cannot afford to delay the moment when we make time to transform the way we manage. Our contacts and conversations with hundreds of managers over the last five years confirm this.

---

3   Developed from Vroom, Victor, H. and Yetton, Phillip, W. (1973), *Leadership and Decision Making*, Pittsburgh: University of Pittsburgh Press.

The demands on managers seem to rise inexorably. All your stakeholders want more of you. You are expected to know more, about more things than ever before. There is a tidal wave of information, regulation and procedure that shows no sign of abating. Most managers receive a daily bombardment of e-mails.

We are not talking about better time management. We assume you know how to mange time effectively. We are talking about the focus of your activity as a manager.

Secure time for thinking, planning, preparing and managing strategically. Keep time for managing your people properly. Say no to demands that distract from the priorities.

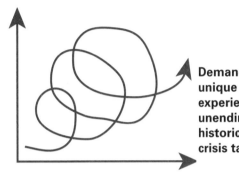

Demands for your unique skills and experience in an unending array of historic, routine or crisis tasks.

You cannot just switch off the past. You can press consistently to change what you do in the future. The strategy is to secure sufficient time overall for the really important things. This will achieve the 80:20 principle with your time – 80 per cent will be relatively low value but you will achieve huge impact with the other 20 per cent.

Balance action with analysis and process

An aspect of the first two dilemmas is the tension between taking action (from which you and the organisation may achieve change and learning) and stepping back to reflect, analyse and think things through in depth. Again there is no right or wrong – what matters is the balance you achieve, and that you do not get stuck in one position.

Stepping back, gathering data, reflecting, thinking.

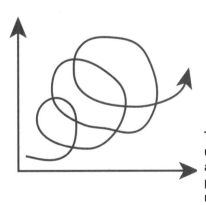

Taking swift and unconventional action from which progress can be made and a great deal learned.

You can apply the same tool to other dilemmas:

- The need to be strong, assertive and in control versus the need to be caring and supportive.
- The need to allow your management team to share and discuss issues versus the time it takes and the fact that you already have a solution in mind.

Learning, adventure, respect and good management

Youth work is about journeys made by young people, both alone and together. It starts with a belief in the value of learning, it seeks to empower and enable. It is based on respect for all young people. At its best it is a magical journey, which takes young people to a fuller realisation of themselves and their potential. It opens up new possibilities for young people to engage and grow in the society around them. It is possible to combine these values of respect, learning, development, adventure, risk, innovation with good management. It is not a choice – we must!

The challenge for senior managers is to manage youth work in ways that involve critical thinking about the concepts and tools being deployed. As leaders in the field you have the opportunity to transform the way youth work is understood by others, to demonstrate its value and to create more opportunity for more young people to benefit from it. That is good management. The tools can help, but only if they are understood and serve your purpose. Using a crowbar to polish a table will ruin the table ...

The right tools for the job

We have looked at a large number of ideas and models about management. You will only make direct use of a small number in your organisation, but to do so effectively means really understanding them yourself. The management tools you use will need to be explained to your staff and other stakeholders. You will need to make a judgment about the depth to go into. Good managers make things accessible to all their people. Generally you will provide people with the tip of a large iceberg. This should conform to the CSE test:

Clear	sharply described, unambiguous
Simple	easy to understand (this does not mean simplistic – it is often the opposite, the best and most complex ideas may be very simple)
Easy to use or do	can be put into practice without too much difficulty

This will test your management skills, as refining models, concepts and tools to fit this test can be a challenge.

We now draw your attention to some of the tools that we think do this well:

- For thinking: the PMI, CAF and TEC (page 29).
- For analysis of the environment: it's hard to beat the SWOT test provided it is used properly.
- For seeing and getting underneath your organisation (and partnerships): Gareth

Morgan's metaphors are profoundly valuable (page 42).

- For analysing the whole organisation: the 7S model (page 45).
- For creative strategy: the Seven Ways of Seeing (page 61).
- For checking your purpose: the service offering models (page 52).
- For managing the complex array of tasks and demands: Kotter's management agendas (page 80) and Stewart's demands, choices and constraints (page 79).
- For problem solving: Hampden Turner's strategic dilemmas (page 84).
- For leadership style: we think Tannenbaum and Schmidt is still relevant and useful, along with 'task versus people' (page 83).
- For managing resources: the difference between full and marginal costing (page 126).
- For managing information strategically: the balanced scorecard (page 143).
- For managing performance: look again at the transformation model and the excellence model (page 175).

Reflection

Think back over the wide variety of ideas and tools that have been covered both in this reader and during the coursework.

Identify:

- five concepts, ideas, models or tools that are new and interesting and that you might try out
- five concepts, ideas, models or tools that you have come across before and are worth revisiting and refreshing.

If good management is about courage, reflect on what you do and where you go to sustain your courage and resolve.

Courage to lead

If youth work is valuable and you as its leaders believe in it, then surely you must want more young people to have the opportunity to experience it. You must surely want youth work to be good, to improve and to get even better. Transforming Youth Work and Connexions provide enormous opportunities that can help this to happen. It is up to youth work's leaders to show the courage to make it happen.

What would life be if we had no courage to attempt anything?

Vincent Van Gogh

Any intelligent fool can make things bigger and more complex ... It takes a touch of genius and a lot of courage to move in the opposite direction.

Albert Einstein

229

Chapter Thirteen: Further reading

Public sector management

Audit Commission (1999) *Planning to Succeed: Service and Financial Planning in Local Government*, London: Audit Commission

Audit Commission (2001) *Worth the Risk: Improving Risk Management in Local Government*, London: Audit Commission

Battram, Arthur (1996) *Learning from Complexity*, Local Government Management Board, London: LGMB

Bean, Jennifer and Hussey, Lascellles (1997) Finance for the Non Financial Public Sector Manager, London: HB Publications

Blundell, Brian and Murdock, Alex (1997) *Managing in the Public Sector*, Oxford: Butterworth-Heinemann, in association with The Institute of Management

Chapman, David and Cowdell, Theo (1998) New Public Sector Marketing, Harlow, Essex: Pearson Education

Coombs, HM and Jenkins, DE (2002) *Public Sector Financial Management* (3rd edn.), London: Thomson Learning

Corrigan, Paul, Hayes, Mike and Joyce, Paul (1999) *Managing in the New Local Government*, London: Kogan Page

Employers' Organisation for Local Government (2001) *The Equality Standard for Local Government*, London: Employers' Organisation for Local Government

Exworthy, Mark and Halford, Susan (1999) *Professionals and the New Managerialism in the Public Sector*, Buckingham: Open University Press

Fenwick, John (1995) *Managing Local Government*, London: Chapman and Hall

Flynn, Norman (2001) *Public Sector Management* (4th edn), Hertfordshire: Prentice Hall/Harvester

Gelsthorpe, Tony and West-Burnham, John (2003) *Educational Leadership and the Community: Strategies for School Improvement through Community Engagement.* Harlow, Essex: Pearson Education

Johnson, Gerry and Scholes, Kevan (2001) *Exploring Public Sector Strategy*, Harlow, Essex: Pearson Education

Joyce, Paul (1999) *Strategic Management for the Public Services*, Bucks, UK: Open University Press

Kerley, Richard (1994) *Managing in Local Government*, Hampshire and London: The Macmillan Press Ltd

McKevitt, David and Lawton, Alan (1994) *Public Sector Management - Theory, Critique and Practice*, London: Sage Publications (in association with the Open University)

Morgan, Colin and Murgatroyd, Stephen (1994) *Total Quality Management in the Public Sector: an International Perspective*, Milton Keynes: Open University Press

Milner, Eileen M (2000) *Managing Information and Knowledge in the Public Sector*, London: Routledge

Osbourne, David and Gaebler, Ted (1993) *Reinventing Government - How the entrepreneurial spirit is transforming the public sector*, Middlesex: Penguin

Rose, Aidan and Lawton, Alan (1999) *Public Services Management*, Harlow, Essex: Pearson Education

Stewart, J (1995) *Innovation in Democratic Practice*, Birmingham: University of Birmingham, Institute of Local Government

Voluntary organisation management

Adirondack, S (1998) *Just About Managing* (3rd edn), London: London Voluntary Service Council

Batsleer, Julian, Cornforth, Chris and Paton, Rob (eds) (1992) *Issues in Voluntary and Non-Profit Management*, Wokingham: Addison Wesley

Botting, Nina and Norton, Michael (2001) *The Complete Fundraising Handbook* (4th edn.), London: Directory of Social Change (Published in association with ICFM)

Cook, Tim and Braithwaite, Guy (2000) *A Management Companion for Voluntary Organisations*, London: Directory of Social Change

Drucker, P (1990) *Managing the Non Profit Organisation*, London: Butterworth Heinemann

Handy, C (1988) *Understanding Voluntary Organisation*, London: Penguin

Hind, Andrew (1995) *The Governance and Management of Charities*, Maidenhead: Voluntary Sector Press

Hudson, Mike (1995) *Managing Without Profit - The Art of Managing Third Sector*

Organisations, London: Penguin

Kendall, Jeremy and Knapp, Martin (1996) *The Voluntary Sector in the UK*, Manchester: Manchester University Press

Lawrie, Alan (2001) *The Complete Guide to Business and Strategic Planning for Voluntary Organisations* (2nd edn.) London: Directory of Social Change

Service management

Johnston, Robert and Clark, Graham (2001) *Service Operations Management*, London: Prentice Hall

Normann, Richard (2000) *Service Management*, Chichester

Wiley van Looy, Bart, van Dierdonck, Roland and Gemmel, Paul (1998) *Services Management - an Integrated Approach*, London: Pitman Publishing

General management

Bartol, Kathryn and Martin, David C (1998) *Management*, New York: McGraw Hill

Shorter guides to management thinking

Crainer, Stuart (1996) *Key Management Ideas - Thinkers that Changed the Management World*, London: Pearson Professional

Kennedy, Carol (1996) *Managing with the Gurus: Top Level Guidance on 20 Management Techniques*, London: Century Ltd

ten Have, Steven; ten Have, Wouter; Steves, Frans; and van der Elst, Marcel (2003) *Key Management Models- the management tools and practices that will improve your business* London: FT Prentice Hall

Organisation

Chris Argyris (1999) *On Organisational Learning* (2nd edn), Oxford: Blackwell

Fons, Trompenaars and Hampden-Turner, Charles (1997) *Riding the Waves of Culture*, London: Nicholas Brealey Publishing Limited

Hampden-Turner, Charles (1994) *Corporate Culture*, Great Britain: Hutchinson Books Ltd

Handy, Charles B (1985) *Understanding Organisations*, Middlesex: Penguin Books

Morgan G, (1986) *Images of Organization*, London: Sage Publications

Morgan, Gareth (1989) *Creative Organisation Theory*, California: Sage Publications

Pedlar, Mike, Burgoyne, John and Boydell, Tom (1991) *The Learning Company - A*

Strategy for Sustainable Development, London: McGraw Hill

Pedler, Mike and Aspinwall, Kath. (1998) *A Concise Guide to the Learning Organisation*, Great Britain: Lemos & Crane

Pugh, DS (ed.) (1990) *Organization Theory - Selected Readings*, Middlesex: Penguin Books

Management self development

– General

Covey, Stephen (1992) *The Seven Habits of Highly Effective People*, London: Simon and Schuster

Goleman, Daniel (1995) *Emotional Intelligence*, New York: Bantam

Honey, P and Mumford, A (1992) *Manual of Learning Styles*, Maidenhead: Honey

Orbach S (1999) *Towards Emotional Literacy*, London: Virago

Pedlar, Mike, Burgoyne, John and Boydell, Tom (1994) A *Manager's Guide to Self Development* (3rd edn), London: McGraw Hill

Quinn, Robert E, Faerman, Sue R, Thompson, Michael P, McGrath, Michael R (1996) *Becoming a Master Manager - A Competency Framework* (2nd edn), New York: John Wiley

– Thinking

Buzan, Tony (1982) *Use your Head*, London: Ariel/BBC Books

Edward De Bono (1992) *Serious Creativity*, London: Harper Collins

Wycoff, J (1991) *Mindmapping*, Berkley Books: New York

– Leadership

Badaracco, Joseph (2002) *Leading Quietly*, Boston: HBR Press

Collins, James. C and Porras, Jerry I. (2000) *Built to Last - Successful Habits of Visionary Companies.* London: Random House Business Books

Collins, Jim (2001) *Good to Great.* London: Random House Business Books

DuBrin, Andrew J (1995) *Leadership - Research Findings, Practice and Skills*, Boston: Houghton Mifflin Company

Garratt, Bob (1997) *The Fish Rots from the Head*, London: Harper- Collins

Goffee, Robert and Jones, Gareth (2000) *'Why Should Anyone be Led by You?'*, Harvard Business Review, September-October

Goleman, Daniel (2002) *The New Leaders - transforming the art of leadership into the science of results.* London: Little, Brown

Goleman, Daniel; Boyatzis, Richard; McKee, Annie (2002) *Primal Leadership - realizing the Power of Emotional Intelligence.* Boston, Massachusetts, Harvard Business School Press

Hesselbein, Frances, Goldsmith, Marshall and Beckhard, Richard (eds) (1996) *The Leader of the Future*, San Francisco: Jossey Bass

Kotter, John P. (1999) *What Leaders Really Do.* Boston, Massachusetts: Harvard Business Review Books

Zeleznik, Abraham (1977) *'Managers and Leaders: Are They Different?'*, Harvard Business Review, March/April

– Leading teams

Belbin, M (1984) *Management Teams: Why They Succeed or Fail*, Oxford: Butterworth Heinemann

Katzenback, JR (1997) *'The Myth of the Top Management Team'*, Harvard Business Review, Nov/Dec

Margerison, CJ and McCann DJ (1995) *Team Management: Practical New Approaches*, Cirencester, Glos: Management Books 2000

– Social Capital

Anheier, Helmut K (2004) *Civil Society- Measurement, Evaluation, Policy*, London: Earthscan.

Putnam, Robert D (2000) *Bowling Alone. The Collapse and Revival of American Community*, New York: Simon and Schuster

Putnam, Robert D (2003) *Better Together: Restoring the American Community*, New York: Simon and Schuster

– Strategy

Bryson, John M (1995) *Strategic Planning for Public and Nonprofit Organisations: a Guide to Strengthening and Sustaining Organizational Achievement*, San Francisco: Jossey Bass

Garratt, Bob (ed) (1995) *Developing Strategic Thought*, London: Harper Collins

Johnson, G and Scholes, K (1993) *Exploring Corporate Strategy*, London: Prentice Hall

Mintzberg, H (1994) *The Rise and Fall of Strategic Planning*, New York: Free Press

Moore, JI (1992) *Writers on Strategy and Strategic Management - The Theory of Strategy and the Practice of Strategic Management at Enterprise, Corporate, Business and Functional Levels*, London: Penguin

– Managing change

Egan, G (1994) *Working the Shadow Side*, San Francisco: Jossey Bass

Fullan, M (1993) *Change Forces*, Lewes: Falmer

Kotter, J (1994) *'Why Transformation Efforts Fail'*, Harvard Business Review

Kotter, JP (1990) *A Force for Change: How Leadership Differs from Management*, New York: The Free Press

Saul Alinsky (1971) *Rules for Radicals*, New York: Vintage Books

– Managing people

Storey, J (ed.) (2000) *Human Resource Management - A Critical Text* (2nd edn), London: Thompson Learning

– Managing partnerships and stakeholders

Audit Commission (1998) *A Fruitful Partnership - Effective Partnership Working*, London: Audit Commission

Jackson, PM (1999) *Managing Between Markets and Hierarchies*, Leicester University Management Centre Discussion Paper

Kickert, WJ et al (1997) *Managing Complex Networks - Strategies for the Public Sector*, London: Sage

Kotler, P (1997) *Marketing Management: Analysis, Planning, Implementation And Control*, Englewood Cliffs, NJ: Prentice Hall

Lowndes, Vivien and Skelcher, Chris (1998) The Dynamics of Multi- Organisational Partnerships: an Analysis of Changing Modes of Governance, *Public Administration*, vol 76 summer, pp313-3

Moss-Kanter, Rosabeth (1994) Collaborative Advantage: the Art of Alliances, *Harvard Business Review*, Jul-Aug

Russell, Hilary (2001) *Local Strategic Partnerships - Lessons from New Commitment to Regeneration*, Bristol: The Policy Press

Taket, Ann and White, Leroy (2000) *Partnership and Participation: Decision Making in the Multi Agency Setting*, Chichester: Wiley

Wilson, Andrew and Charlton, Kate (1997) *Making Partnerships Work - A Practical Guide for the Public, Private, Voluntary and Community Sectors*, York: Joseph Rowntree Foundation

– Performance management

Armstrong, Michael and Baron, Angela (1998) *Performance Management - The New Realities*, London: Chartered Institute of Personnel and Development

Holloway, Jackie, Lewis Jenny, and Mallory, Geoff (eds) (1995) *Performance Measurement and Evaluation*, London: Sage Publications (with the Open University)

Jackson, PM and Palmer, B (1992) *Developing Performance Monitoring in Public Sector Organisations*, Leicester: Leicester University Management Centre

Kaplan, Robert S and Norton, David P (1996) *The Balanced Scorecard - Translating Strategy into Action*, Boston Mass: Harvard Business School Press

Lawrie, Alan (1995) *Managing Quality of Service* (revised edn), London: Directory of Social Change

Maister, David, H (2001) *Practice What You Preach: What Managers Must Do to Create a High Achievement Culture*, New York: The Free Press

– Work with young people

Merton, Bryan (2001) *So What's New: Innovation and Youth Work*, Leicester: The National Youth Agency

Davies, Bernard (1999) *A History of the Youth Service in England Volumes One and Two*. Leicester: Youth Work Press

Davies, Bernard (2001) *Connexions: Historical Roots and Critical Issues*, Leicester: FPM

Department for Education and Employment (2000) *Connexions: the Best Start in Life for Every Young Person*, from www.connexions.gov.uk

DfES (2001) *Transforming Youth Work: Developing Youth Work for Young People*, London: Department for Education and Skills

Huskins, John, *Quality Work with Young People - Developing Social Skills and Diversion from Risk*, Bristol: John Huskins
Available from: John Huskins, 3 Somerset Street, Kingsdown, Bristol BS2 8NB. Tel: 0117 924 3320

Marken, M (2000) *Higher Performing Local Authority Youth Services*, Leicester: National Youth Agency

National Youth Agency (2002), *Reference Pack of Youth Work Standards*, Leicester: National Youth Agency

PAT 12 Report (2000) *Young People*, London: Social Exclusion Unit

Smith, Mark (1988) *Developing Youth Work. Informal Education, Mutual Aid and Popular Practice*, Milton Keynes: Open University Press

Social Exclusion Unit (1999) *Bridging the Gap: New Opportunities for 16-18 Year Olds Not In Education, Training or Employment*, London: HMSO

Wade, Harry, Lawton, Anthony and Stevenson, Mark (2001) *Hear by Right - Setting Standards for the Active Involvement of Young People in Democracy*, Leicester: The National Youth Agency

The Active Involvement of Young People in Connexions: Guidance for Managers and *The Active Involvement of Young People in Connexions: A Guide for Practitioners* (2001) Sheffield, DfES

Ofsted inspection documents:

- *Inspecting Youth Work - A Revised Inspection Framework*
- *Self-assessment schedule*
- *Pre-inspection notebook*
- *The Common Framework for Inspecting Post-16 Education and Training*
  Available from Ofsted: www.ofsted.gov.uk

Index

7S Framework   45–8, 59, 102–3, 229
80:20 principle   223, 227

Activists   35, 74
Activity based budgeting   133–4
Activity based costing   127, 133
Adequacy of youth provision   129, 149
A–Ha Moment   28
Alimo–Metcalfe, Beverly   84
Alinsky, Saul   70
Allocation of resources see Resource
    management
Anticipatory public management   112
APC   29–30
Arendt, Hannah   82, 87, 89
Argyris, Chris   67
Aristotle   88
Ashworth, G.   133
Association of Principal Youth and
    Community Officers (APYCO)   63,
    149, 218
Audit Commission   111, 131, 132, 149,
    174, 196

Badaracco, Joseph   2
Balanced scorecard approach   142–4,
    146, 150, 162, 167, 176, 229
Bartol, K.   50
Beer, M. et al   138
Belbin, Meredith   91–3
Best Value   56, 112, 157, 163, 196
achieving   132
Code of Practice   124
excellence and equity   165
performance review   111, 131, 133, 166
service provision   56, 108
Blair, Tony   16, 211
Bleasedale, Alan   61
Blundell, Brian   162
Blunkett, David   8
Boeck, T.   221
Boisot, Max   59–60
Boundaries, public/private/
    voluntary   109, 113–14
Boydell, Tom   3, 67
Branding   116
Brighouse, Tim   58
British Airways   51
British Quality Foundation   174
Bryson, John   55, 109–10, 131

Buchanan, D.   38
Budgeting
    activity based   133–4
    budgets   130–2
    incremental   122, 131, 133
    priority based   134
    service leaders and   135–6
    zero based   133
    see also Resource management
Bureaucracy   39, 42, 55, 110
Burgoyne, John   3, 67
Burnham, John West   171
Buzan, Tony   31

Cadbury Report   116
Catalytic public management   111
Central Institute of Marketing (CIM)   189
Change, management of   69–74
Charging for shared resources   123–4
Charities   100–1, 114–16, 136
    see also Voluntary organisations
Children Bill   66–7, 181, 204, 209, 216
Children's Commissioner   67
Children's Trust   67, 210, 212, 214, 216
Children's Trust Pathfinders   213
Civil society   116–17
Climate change   118–19
Community-owned public
    management   111
Community Plans   111
Community and Youth Workers'
    Union   20–1, 120, 218
Competitive public management   111
Complexity   11, 12, 59, 81, 114, 117, 173,
    200, 210
Comprehensive Performance Assessments
    (CPAs)   166–7
Connelly, T.   133
Connexions   11, 12, 34, 66, 70, 196, 229
    Partnership Performance
    Indicators   64–5
    partnerships   40, 119
    Partnerships inspection
    framework   173
    strategy   60
    user-involvement   18, 56
Constraints, demands and choices
    model   79
Consumerism   117–18, 157–8, 168
Continuing professional development   36

Continuous improvement   111, 169, 176–7
Control systems   49
Convergent thinking   28
Core funding   128, 129
Costing of services   124–32
    activity based costing   127, 133
    core funding   128, 129
    direct costs   125
    doughnut costing   128, 136
    fixed costs   125
    full costing   126
    house of cards   128
    indirect costs   125
    marginal costing   126–7
    marginal costs   125
    opportunity costs   125
    overheads   123–4, 125
    strategies   126
    unit cost and price   129
    variable costs   125
    see also Resource management
Covey, Stephen   80–1
Creativity   28
    see also Thinking
Culture   23–5
    norms   42, 48, 49, 73
    organisation as   42–3, 59, 196
Customer-driven public management   111–12

Davies, Bernard   9
Davis, G.B.   142
Deakin, Nicholas   113
De Bono, Edward   27, 28, 29, 30
Decentralised public management   112
Deductive argument   33
Deming, W.E.   158
Democratic renewal   100, 210
Demographic changes   118, 119, 150
Director of Children's Services   66
Direct Payments scheme   18
Divergent thinking   28
Diversity   103–4, 118
Double loop process   3, 67–9, 161
Doughnut costing   128, 136
Drucker, Peter   81–2, 157
DuBrin, Andrew   81
Dylan, Bob   209

Earl, M.J.   145
EFQM Business Excellence Model   168, 173–5
Egan, G.   70, 71
Einstein, Albert   229
Eliot, T. S.   1, 223
Emergent strategy   59–60
Emotional intelligence   74, 87–90
Emotional literacy   74
Encams   143–4
Enterprising public management   112
Environmentalism   118–19
Equality and diversity   103–4, 118
Every Child Matters: the next steps   18–19, 66, 108, 119, 181, 204, 209, 211, 212, 215
Evidence-based practice   119
Experiential learning cycle   3, 35

Feedback   27, 87, 145, 163, 165, 167, 170
Feelings   31, 32, 74, 87
    emotional intelligence   74, 87–90
Financial plans   130–2
Fleming, J.   221
Fluid work agendas   79, 80
Ford, Kevin   19, 160, 199
Fowler, A.   137
Fullan, M.   70
Funding *see* Resource management
Fuzzy state thinking   30–1

Gaebler, Ted   55, 108, 158, 210
Garrett, Bob   3
Gershon, Sir Peter   209
Globalisation   108, 117
Goffee, Robert   87
Goleman, Daniel   3, 74, 87–9
Gomes–Casseres, Benjamin   200
Governance interests   21–2
Greiner, L.   40–1
Groundwork   11
Groupthink   95–6

Hampden Turner, Charles   24, 26, 60, 84, 229
Handy, Charles   49
Harvard Model of Human Resource Management   138–9
Hay Group   48
Hear by Right   18, 20, 47, 103

High performance   48, 69
   Best Value performance review   111,
   131, 133, 166
   Comprehensive Performance
   Assessments (CPAs)   166–7
   economy, efficiency and effectiveness
   164–5
   high-performing teams   167–8
   managing for   155–7
   standards   165–7
   strategy   159–60
   see also Quality
Hodge, Margaret   64
Honey, Peter   32, 33, 35
Hope, Philip   195
Horwood, A.G.   145
Huczynski, A.   38
Human Resource Management
   (HRM)   137
   Harvard Model   138–9
   see also People management

ideology   38, 39, 210
Incremental budgeting   122, 131, 133
Inductive argument   33–4
Information management   141–7
   balanced scorecard approach   142–4,
   146, 150, 162, 167, 176, 229
   information overload   146–7
   strategic development and   144–6
   systems   145, 148, 149
Innovation   179
   definition   180–1
   drivers of   181–2
   factors influencing   182–3
   typology   181
Inputs   64, 164, 165
   budgeting and   133, 134
   input measures   110, 111
   Inputs–Process–Outputs–Outcomes
   model   51, 163
   see also Performance management
Inspirational management   28
Internal Classification of Non–Profit
   Organisations (ICNPO)   113
International Standards Organisation (ISO)
   168, 170
Investors in People (IIP)   168

Jackson, Peter M.   157, 197, 198

Janis, I.   95
Johari Window   26–7, 30, 36
Johnson, G.   48, 130
Johnston, Robert   50, 51, 53–4
Jones, Gareth   87
Jung, Carl   32

Kaplan, Robert   142
Katzenback, J.R.   90, 95
Kennedy, John F.   226
Kilmann, Ralph   73
Kitemarking   65
Knight, Barry   116
Knowledge management   147–9
   definition   147
   explicit knowledge   147
   tacit knowledge   147
Koch, Richard   223
Kolb, David   3, 35
Kotler, P.   50
Kotter, John   70, 71, 79, 80, 84–5, 229
Kubler Ross, Elizabeth   73

Language   49, 72, 171
Lao Tzu   81
Leadership   15, 81–99, 224–5
   behaviour/style   83–4
   characteristics   86
   contingency theories of   83
   emotionally intelligent   74, 87–90
   strategic   60
   style of   83–4, 87–90, 95, 96, 97, 100,
   224, 225–6, 229
   of teams   90–9
   transformational   84–7
Learning   35–6
   activists   35, 74
   experiential learning cycle   3, 35
   informal   9
   non-formal   9
   pragmatists   36
   reflectors   35
   styles 32, 33, 35–6
   theorists   36
Lewis, David   147
Liebling, Mike   30
Local Government Act 1999   111
Local Government Act 2000   100
Local Safeguarding Children Boards   66
Local Strategic Partnerships   196, 210

Lowndes, Vivien   197, 198, 199–200

McGann, D.J.   93–4
Machiavelli, Nicollo   77–8
McKinsey 7S Framework   45–8, 59,
   102–3, 229
Maister, David   224
Management   5, 76–99, 224–5
   of change   69–74
   constraints, demands and choices   79
   definition 76
   of diversity, equality and
   equity   103–4
   fluid work agendas   79, 80
   for high performance   155–77
   of individual change   73–4
   of information   141–7
   of innovation   179–85
   inspirational   28
   of knowledge   147–9
   leadership see Leadership
   managing upwards   99–103
   modern management   75–104
   new public management   110–12
   of people   136–9
   of performance   140–1, 156–60
   principles   137–8
   process model of   3–5
   of public services   14, 15
   of resources   121–53
   of risk   149–53
   role of managers   76–9
   of stakeholders   5, 187–207
   strategic management   3, 58–9, 62–5,
   69, 202
   style of   39, 40, 42, 73, 74, 102
   of youth work   14–18, 209–22
Management development profile   36
Management information system (MIS)
   145, 148, 149
   see also Information management
Managing for better outcomes in youth
   work   65
Margerison, C.J.   93–4
Marken, Mary   62, 101–2, 175
Marketing   116
   definition   189
   positioning   192–3
   promoting the service   193–5
   segmenting   192

   stakeholder management
   and   189–95
   targeting   192
Market oriented public management   112
Marks and Spencer   50–1
Martin, D.   50
Mayo, Elton   43
Merton, Bryan   180
Mind mapping   31
Mintzberg, Henry   38, 39, 61, 77, 78–9,
   81, 106, 131, 160
Missionary organisations   39
Mission driven public management   111
Mitchell, Joni   222
Modernisation of public services   17, 75,
   209, 210–11
Morgan, Colin   171
Morgan, Gareth   42–4, 196, 228–9
Moss–Kanter, Rosabeth   197, 200–2
Mumford, A.   35
Murdoch, Alex   162
Murgatroyd, Stephen   171
Myers–Briggs, Isabel   32
Myers Briggs personality test   32–3, 94

National Youth Agency   7, 10, 63, 64, 65,
   145, 148, 149, 165, 194, 195
New Deal for Communities   111
Nias, J.   72–3
Nolan Report   116
Nonaka, I.   147
Normann, Richard   51, 52
Norms   23, 24–5
   cultural   42, 48, 49, 73
   standardisation of   39
Norton, David   142
Nottingham Social Action Research
   Project   221

Ofsted (Office for Standards in Education)
   12, 62, 70, 162, 213, 219
   inspections   17, 165
   self–assessment schedule for youth work
   173
Olsen, M.   142
Operational risks   151
Orbach, S.   74
Organisational culture   42, 47–50, 102,
   137
   changing   72–3

'culture bearers' 72–3
norms 42, 48, 49, 73
performance and 48–9
person culture 49
power culture 49
role culture 49
task culture 49
youth work organisations 49–50
Organisations 37–8
adhocracy 39
as brains 42, 43, 59, 196
configurations 38–40
coordinating mechanisms 38–9
as cultures 42–3, 59, 196
divisionalised structures 39
growth phases 40–1
ideology 38, 39
machine bureaucracy 39
as machines 42, 43, 59, 196
McKinsey 7S Framework 45–8
missionary organisations 39
as organisms 42, 43, 59, 196
as political systems 43, 196
power 49
professional bureaucracy 39
as psychic prisons 44
service-providing 50–2
simple structure 39
skills 47
staffing 46, 102
stage of development 40–1
strategy 46
structure 39–40, 46, 49
style 46–7, 102
supervision 38
systems approach 45–56
types of 39–40
values 42, 46, 47, 101, 102–3
Osbourne, David 55, 108, 158, 210
Outcomes 110, 111, 164, 183
budgeting and 134
Inputs-Process-Outputs-Outcomes
model 51, 163
Outputs 164, 165, 166
budgeting and 134
Inputs-Process-Outputs-Outcomes
model 51, 163
poor performance 141, 167, 168
specifying 39
standardisation of 38

Overheads 123–4, 125

Palmer, Bob 157
Pareto Law (80:20 principle) 223, 227
Partnerships 12, 147, 187, 195–207,
216–18
benefits 195
definitions 196–7
dynamic process 199–200
Local Strategic Partnerships 196, 210
partners' interests 22
practitioners in 203
private sector 200–1
proportionality 206–7
relationships between
partners 201–2
rise of partnership working 195–6
strategic approach 203
types of working arrangement 198
see also Stakeholder management
Part-time workers 20–1, 139
Paton, Rob 114
Pedlar, Mike 3, 67
People management 136–9
dispersed staff 4, 139
Harvard Model 138–9
meaning of 136–7
part-time workers 4, 20–1, 72, 139,
140, 175
poor performance 140–1, 168
principles 137–8
recruitment and retention 139
see also Performance management
Perceptions 31, 32, 175
Performance management 140–1, 156–9
Comprehensive Performance
Assessments (CPAs) 166–7
economy, efficiency and
effectiveness 164–5
performance indicators 162–3
performance measures 111, 162,
163–4
poor performance 141, 167, 168
Personality 31–2
Myers Briggs test 32–3, 94
types 32–3
Personal modelling 72
Personnel management 136–7
see also People management
PEST/PESTLE analysis 106

Peters, Tom   101
Pfeffer, J.   137
Plato   44
Platt, Lew   147
PMI   29, 228
Policy
   government policy   16
   quality and   168–9
   reasoning and   33
Policy Action Team (PAT)   106–8, 119, 131
Political system   43
Practical Quality Assurance System for
   Small Organisations (PQASSO)   175
Pragmatists   36
Prescriptive conclusions   34
Priority based budgeting   134
Privacy   118
Process model of management   3–5
Progress, monitoring   4
Project funding   136
Public Service Agreements   111, 158
Public services   54–5, 108–12
   funding   15–16
   governance interests   21–2
   management of   14, 15
   modernisation of   17, 75, 209, 210–11
   professional staff   20–1
   service provision   37
   see also Youth service
Putnam, Robert   220, 221

Quality   158
   assurance   4, 169, 171, 183
   Connexions Partnerships inspection
   framework   173
   continuous improvement   169, 176–7
   control   170
   EFQM Business Excellence
   Model   168, 173–5
   as excellence   169
   as fitness for purpose   169
   framework for youth work
   organisations   175
   as freedom from faults   169
   management   170–2
   monitoring and enforcement   72
   Ofsted self-assessment schedule for
   youth work   173
   policy context   168–9
   Practical Quality Assurance System for

Small Organisations   175
   self-assessment   175–6
   service quality   172–3
   SERVQUAL   172–3
   total quality management
   (TQM) 171–2
   see also High performance
Quality Develops – Towards Excellence in
   Youth Services   64
Quinn, Robert   33

Reasoning   33–4, 164
Recruitment   139
Reflectors   35
Regional Youth Work Units   218, 219
Relationships see Stakeholder
   management
Resource management   121–53
   allocation   122–3
   charging for shared resources   123–4
   deploying resources   4
   financial plans   130–2
   overheads   123–4, 125
   project funding   136
   public services funding   15–16, 17
   resource planning   129–30
   resourcing cycle   15
   service level agreements   124
   youth services funding   13, 14, 17
   see also Budgeting; Costing
Resourcing Excellent Youth Services
   (REYS)   8, 17, 25, 38, 56, 64, 119, 163,
   172, 175, 211, 214, 218
Results–oriented public management   111
Retention of staff   139
Risk management   149–53
   appropriate control strategies   153
   assessing exposure   152
   identifying risks   151–2
   operational risks   151
   prioritising risks   152
   strategic risks   150–1
Roberts, M.   221
Roche, M.   221
Routines and rituals   49
Russell, Hilary   47

Salamon, Lester   113
Salvation Army   157
Scanning the environment   4, 65, 68,

105–20, 188, 191–2
   PMI   29
Schmidt, W.   83, 84, 229
Scholes, K.   48, 130
Seeing   61
Service
   costing see Costing of services
   delivery of   4
   focusing   53–4
   provision   37, 50–2
   public see Public services
   quality   172–3
   service offering models   52–3
   service-providing organisations   50–2
   'service shop'   52–3
   volume–variety matrix   52–3
SERVQUAL   172–3
Seven ways of seeing   61, 229
Silvestro, R. et al   52–3
Skelcher, Chris   197, 198, 199–200
Skills   73
   7S Framework   47, 102
   creativity   28
   interpersonal   14
   organisations   47
   standardisation of   39
   of youth workers   14, 17
   see also Learning; Thinking
SMART objectives   160, 161
Smith, Adam   212
Smith, Mark   63
Social capital   7, 219–21
Social Exclusion Unit Policy Action Team
   (PAT) 12 report   106–8, 119, 131
Social institutions   118
Staff induction   72, 150, 171, 172
Staffing, 7S Framework   46, 102
Stakeholder management   5, 99,
   187–207
   assessment of needs and wants   189,
   190
   concept of   188–9
   external stakeholders   189
   funding of public services   15
   mapping of stakeholders   190–1
   marketing see Marketing
   partnerships see Partnerships
   promoting the service   193–5
   relationships   5, 15–16, 201–2
   risk management process   153

user-involvement in services   18–20
Standards   4, 25, 165–7
   national   16, 17
Standards Fund   112
Stewart, John   55, 117
Stewart, Rosemary   70, 79, 229
Stone, Wendy   220
Stories   49, 72, 141
Strategic development   144–6
Strategic leadership   60
Strategic management   3, 58–9, 69, 202
   youth work organisations   62–5
Strategic planning   51, 110, 131, 160–1,
   218
Strategic risks   150–1
Strategic thinking   60, 61–5
Strategy   4, 58–60
   7S Framework   46, 103
   communicating   68
   emergent strategy   59–60
   government strategy   65–9
   high performance   159–60
   levels of   61–2
   managing change   69–74
   organisations   46
   priorities   144–6
   putting into action   67–9
Structure   40, 110
   7S Framework   46, 102
   local council structure   100
   organisational structure   39–40, 46,
   49
   partnership structures   203
   social relations   220
   team structures   97–8
Style
   7S Framework   46, 102
   leadership style   83–4, 87–90, 95, 96,
   97, 100, 224, 225–6, 229
   learning styles   32, 33, 35–6
   management style   39, 40, 42, 73,
   74, 102
   organisational style see Organisational
   culture
Subsidiarity principle   112
Sufficiency of youth provision   129, 149
Symbols   42, 49, 197
Systems   110
   7S Framework   46, 102
   closed systems   42

complaints systems   67
control systems 49
information management
systems   145, 148, 149
open systems model   163
organisations   46
political systems   43
reward systems   73, 138
Team Management Systems   93
work systems   38, 138

Taket, Ann   197, 198
Takeuchi, H.   147
Tannenbaum, R.   83, 84, 229
Taylor, Frederick   43
Taylor, Marilyn   115
Teams   112
    accountability   98–9
    assessor–developers   93
    commitment   96–7
    composition   91
    concluder–producers   93–4
    controller–inspectors   94
    creator–innovators   93
    explorer–promoters   93
    groupthink   95–6
    high–performing teams   167–8
    leading   90–9
    motivation/energy matrix   96–7
    myths about   95
    operation of   94–6
    personality profiles   94
    purpose   90–1
    reporter–advisers   93
    roles   91–4
    structures   97–8
    thruster–organisers   93
    upholder–maintainers   94
Theorists   36
Thinking   27–8
    APC   29–30
    convergent   28
    divergent   28
    fuzzy state   30–1
    lateral   28
    mind mapping   31
    personality and   32
    PMI   29
    reasoning   33–4
    six thinking hats   30, 34

tools for   29–32, 228
Third sector   108–9, 112–17, 200
    see also Voluntary organisations
Thompson, Alan   9–10
Thurlbeck, John   99
Tilburg City Council   134–5
Total quality management (TQM)   171–2
Transformational leadership   84–7
Transforming Youth Work   8, 64, 66, 72,
    205, 211, 214, 218, 229
Transforming Youth Work Development
    Fund   112
Transforming Youth Work Management
    Programme   1, 15
Trompenaars, Fons   24
Tuckman, B.   94, 199

Values   23, 24–7, 31
    7S Framework   46, 102
    organisational   42, 46, 47, 101, 102–3
Van Gogh, Vincent   229
Voluntary organisations   10, 20, 113–16
    accountability and quality   116
    branding and marketing   116
    charities   100–1, 114–16, 136
    governance of   100–1
    Voluntary Sector Compact   113
Vroom, Victor   226

Waterman, Robert   101
Weber, Max   42
West–Burnham, John   220
White, Leroy   197, 198
Work systems   38, 138
Wycoff, Joyce   28
Wylie, Tom   11

Yeats, W.B.   224
Yetton, Phillip   226
Youth service   9–10, 12, 56, 196
    adequacy and sufficiency   129, 149
    delivery   18
    funding   13, 14, 16, 17
    governance interests   21–2
    user–involvement   18–20, 213, 216
    see also Public services
Youth work   7–9, 211–14
    future of   209–22
    location of   11–13, 213–14, 217
    management of   14–18

other services compared   13–14
part–time   20–1
as profession   20–1
purpose of   63
Regional Youth Work Units   218, 219
resources for   213, 214–15
skills   14
social capital and   219–21
Youth workers
shortage of   120
status of   212

Youth work organisations
funding   8, 16, 17
organisational culture   49–50
quality assurance framework for   175
strategic management   62–5
user–involvement   13, 18–20
values   25–6
voluntary   10, 20

Zaleznik, Abraham   85
Zero based budgeting (ZBB)   133